# HOW THE
# WORLD WORKED

From the Pharaohs to Christopher Columbus

OLD TREE BOOKS

# HOW THE WORLD WORKED

## From the Pharaohs to Christopher Columbus

### Sue Bessmer

OLD TREE BOOKS

First Edition

OLD TREE BOOKS

Published by
**Old Tree Books**
P.O. Box 1411
Pacifica, CA
94044
oldtreebooks.com
info@oldtreebooks.com

# Acknowledgements

First, I must thank my students at San Francisco State University. The best of them continually inspired me to see more complexity, nuance and depth in the subjects I was teaching, while others taught me to present difficult material in the clearest and most accessible terms. The combination was a lesson in simultaneous translation for which I am truly grateful.

After I retired in 2004, I formed a study group with two students, Lorilei Griffin and Chris Simmons, which read and discussed wonderful books too difficult to assign in a regular class. This experience, together with lecturing on cruise ships, gave birth to this book.

In the process, another former student, and long-time friend, Richard Price, read draft after draft, providing suggestions for improved clarity in the argument or a more felicitous phrase. Richard introduced me to an excellent copy editor, Barry Cleveland, whose assistance ranged from tightening my prose to guiding me through the many steps involved in transforming a manuscript into a book. Along the way, Barry also became a very good friend and mentor. Ultimately he introduced me to Paul Haggard, whose skills in formatting the text and designing the overall look of the book, including its elegant cover, deserve both my praise and my gratitude.

I was also fortunate to meet a fellow writer, Ruth Hoppin. She asked me to read and comment on her marvelous new book of poetry, *Spinning the Arrow of Time*. In return, she read my manuscript and made astute suggestions to give it a final polish.

My husband, Richard, also read the manuscript, oh so many times. That is only one of the many reasons this book is dedicated to him.

With love to my husband,
Richard Dean Klapp

In Memoriam
Elizabeth and Stewart Bessmer

# Table of Contents

# Prologue

For as far back as I remember, I have been interested in how the world worked, probably as a result of my vagabond childhood. My father was in the Army, so we moved frequently and encountered very different ways of life. In the small town in rural New Jersey where my mother's sister lived and where I was born, we had close friends and neighbors, the Bradshaws, an African-American family.

By contrast, when we lived in Virginia, segregation was strictly enforced. I will never forget the time I started to use a water fountain and a woman exclaimed in horror, "Don't drink that! It's colored water!" I turned it on anyway, expecting it to be pink or blue and was terribly disappointed. My mom had to explain what had happened. She did not put it in these terms, of course, but the gist was that the world worked differently in the old South.

When I was nine, we moved to France, where my father had a very unusual job. He was to coordinate American military police with French and Spanish civilian and military police in the event of World War III. After my father and his European counterparts had developed a plan, he had nothing much to do except wait for the war that never happened. So we traveled extensively around Western Europe. My favorite memory from those times is visiting the prehistoric, painted caves of Lascaux, where my interest in people from the past first took root.

During our travels, I learned a lot about history, politics and geography, as well as art and architecture. Much later, I graduated from college (Vassar, 1969) with a major in Political Science, a minor in Economics and enough credits in Art History to have majored in that instead. I went on to a Ph.D. program in Political Science at Stanford with an eye to becoming an expert in American foreign policy.

We were required to take two exams selected from six fields of study, including American Politics, International Relations and Public Law. I chose the first two and, after I passed, began to work on a doctoral thesis. While I was floundering in search of a workable topic, my department chair recommended me as a teaching assistant to a course called "Women and the Law." Ironically, but happily, I found an interesting and important thesis topic in the process.*

After completing my Ph.D., I began to teach at San Francisco State University, which had much to recommend it, including a close proximity to my family. Over the years, I taught critical thinking in the Women's Studies Program, several courses in Criminal Justice and a great many courses in the Interdisciplinary Social Science Program where my specialties were history, politics, economics and geography.

---

* Bessmer, Sue. *The Laws of Rape*. New York: Praeger Publishers, 1984.

At one point, I was assigned to teach a course called "The Individual in a Social and Cultural Context." "What's it about?" I asked. My department chair replied, "Anything you like." I had that summer to prepare and decided to take the opportunity to learn about social and cultural contexts as yet unfamiliar to me. Armed with suggestions from a brilliant classicist, I read the best, most erudite and well-written books on both classical Greece and ancient Rome. They laid the foundation for many years of teaching these subjects and that experience is, in turn, reflected on the pages of this book.

In 2004, the California State University system offered those of us with enough time in service and enough years on the planet a very nice deal to retire. It was not a golden handshake but more like a pleasant shove out the door. I knew I had to take it but I also knew I would miss talking about the subjects I loved. So I looked for another venue.

I found it lecturing on cruise ships purely as a passenger volunteer. I love the experience of doing the lectures. I meet great people, and occasionally I get validation for my professional expertise. Once, after a lecture on "Our Greco-Roman Heritage," a very nice classics professor gave me an invaluable compliment. "As a fellow classicist, I admire your choices of material." To pass as an expert to another expert is worth its weight in gold. Over the years, a significant number of passengers have asked me if they could somehow acquire the material in my lectures. Their interest prompted me to write this book, which contains the following chapters.

The first one is called "Survival," and it rests heavily on a fascinating theory put forth by Robert Heilbroner in *The Making of Economic Society*. He argues that, despite their enormous diversity, societies that exist for a long time do so by employing one or more of three basic economic strategies: tradition, command and markets. By markets he means the sorts of markets specific to capitalism.* Since capitalism did not exist until modern times, this chapter, and the book more generally, focuses on tradition, command and a combination of the two. In particular, we will see how the blending of tradition and command resulted in the success of several ancient cultures, including those of Egypt, Babylonia and Persia.

The next chapter, "Hellas," refers to the name ancient Greeks gave to the places they lived. It first clarifies two important political terms by defining a "nation" and also a "state." Along the way, we will see that an Athenian leader called Peisistratus organized the poorest farmers into a command economy in which he had them growing cash crops such as olives and grapes. He further made it possible for these crops to be converted to oil and wine to be sold abroad. The money they earned allowed them to buy more food than they could produce on their own. Their improved level of economic security and equality was critical to the birth of democracy in Athens.

"Four Empires and a Nation-State" follows the ancient

---

* Markets in general long predate the advent of capitalism. To put it simply, markets can and have existed without capitalism. However, capitalism cannot function without a heavy reliance on markets.

Greeks as they merge into the empire of Alexander the Great and his successors. Next they are subsumed into the powerful Roman Empire. When that empire splits in two, the eastern half, containing the Greeks, gradually becomes what we call the Byzantine Empire. In time, Byzantium falls to the Turks and the Greeks become part of the Ottoman Empire. Finally, they break free and, in 1832, become the small but independent Kingdom of Greece.

"Our Greco-Roman Heritage" examines a phrase that most people have heard but would usually be hard-pressed to explain. In part for that reason, this is one of my most popular cruise lecture subjects.

"Rome and Reflections on Power" looks at the three major sources of power: military, political and economic. It considers how their interplay, their balances and imbalances, drove Roman history. In common with the first four chapters, it also has a marvelous cast of characters, great stories and quite a few twists.

"Slavery" compares and contrasts the practice of people owning people in ancient Greece and Rome with the same practice in the American South. In particular, we will see that in both cases, the experience of being a slave crucially depends on the nature of the work and the temperament of the master. At the same time, there are powerful forces that make ancient slavery and American slavery radically different. These forces are both unexpected and utterly fascinating in their consequences.

After a brief "Intermission," we proceed to a chapter called "Horses and Humans," which discusses the partnership between these two species from the earliest recorded evidence to the medieval European world. In the latter, a hierarchy of mounted warriors dominated political, economic and social life in a system we call feudalism.

This system is often very poorly understood and generally not well explained. Carl Stephenson's slender volume, *Mediaeval Feudalism*, is easily one of the very best books I have ever read, despite his unusual spelling of the topic. Cornell University published this work in 1942 and it remains the gold standard today.

The next chapter, "Church and State," chronicles an epic struggle, of crucial importance to medieval Europe, between a long succession of popes and an equally long parade of German emperors. While grave and weighty issues were at stake, the antics of the various players makes for amusing reading, especially in light of the marvelous tongue-in-cheek prose of a writer you will meet in this chapter.

"Merchant Seamen" tells the story of Venetia, a region that would become Venice but was then a province of the empire we call Byzantine. A central point of this chapter is the crucial role that geography can play in shaping a people, their economy and their political system.

"Venice and the Birth of Modern Europe" takes up that story and describes the changes that led Venice to become an independent Republic, with a mercantile oligarchy and a pivotal role in the commercial development of late feudal and early modern Europe. It also traces the simultaneous rise of various Turkish powers until one of them, the Ottomans, finally conquers Constantinople. This has momentous consequences and will take us to the adventures of Christopher Columbus.

* * * * *

The book has one final purpose and that is seduction. It has been my privilege to read, on the recommendations of friends and colleagues, some of the greatest writers in their respective fields. Most of the quotations found in text are intended to give you a taste of a well-turned phrase, a clever, elegant or incisive argument and to tempt you to read more of that book or other books by that author. So now that you know what to expect, it is time to begin.

# Survival

**I**n order to survive over time, all human societies must acquire or produce, in appropriate quantities, the basic necessities of life. They must then distribute these resources among their members so as to sustain the group from one generation to the next. This much is obvious. While there are a wide variety of specific solutions to each of these tasks, they can be classified into three major categories: tradition, command and markets.*

An especially powerful solution to the problems of acquisition, production and distribution can be found in the combination of tradition and command. A robust appreciation for how they operate together will give us a better understanding of ancient Egypt, Babylonia and Persia, as well as the Minoans and the Mycenaeans.

## Tradition

The old ways, that become so familiar from constant repetition and social acceptance, can exercise a very powerful sway over decisions about acquiring or producing and

---

* Once again, it should be noted that market capitalism did not exist in either the ancient or medieval world.

then distributing both the products of human labor and the allocation of labor itself. This fact is particularly striking in groups that we call hunters and gatherers, who predate history (on the fossil record), and have lasted well into the twenty-first century.

Another example of the power of tradition is found among peasant farmers in both the ancient and the modern world. The fundamental basis for all the wealth and splendor of ancient Egypt was peasant labor because these peasants produced the food that was necessary for every other human activity.

## Command

The great Greek historian Herodotus wrote about a pharaoh named Cheops who commanded parties of 100,000 men to perform each of the tasks necessary to quarry, transport and lay down stones to build a road. He also noted that the men worked for only three months of each year and that the whole project took ten years to complete. It was as impressive to him as the building of the great pyramids.

It is almost certain that these men were peasants, working between the harvest and the planting. During that time, grain was plentiful and the workers could be fed from grain stored in the pharaoh's collection centers. It is highly likely that different groups of peasants were mobilized in each new year. By contrast, one in ten male peasants were conscripted into the pharaoh's army for a long period of service as an infantry man, a notably unfortunate fate. Schoolmasters wrote scathing descriptions of the woes attached to their situation, from the harshness of basic training to the many punishments meted out and the deleterious effects on their health. (All of which is, by the way, an astonishing example of freedom of speech for this otherwise authoritarian regime.)

## Tradition and Command

The central feature of tradition is continuity from one generation to the next. In stark contrast, command is a powerful agent of change, in the building of new pyramids, new roads and other new projects, as well as in the conquest of new peoples and new lands. There would thus seem to be a fundamental conflict between these two tendencies.

There is a small but charming example of a resolution to this conflict in a letter written by a wealthy landowner, away from his lands on business, to his son who was managing the estate in his absence. He tells his son to rent more land from a specific person and to order that it be planted with barley, unless the Nile should happen to flood excessively. In that case, the son should order the planting emmer wheat instead.

If, indeed, the father was right that emmer wheat grows better in soggy soil than barley does, this would be well known to the peasants. They could follow the command without having to deviate from the wisdom born of experience and tradition. Except for such monumental tasks as building a road, what was commanded often matched what people had traditionally done. But what about unusual commands like building Cheops' road?

The key lies in the universal and traditional conviction that the Pharaoh was divine and caused the Nile to inundate at just the right moment, when the fields had been prepared for planting and the rich minerals in the river would fertilize them. This the Nile did ... most of the time. On the rare occasions that it didn't, and hunger or famine threatened, the command institutions, Pharaoh and the various Priestly organizations, supplied grain stored expressly for such emergencies and got the population through the crisis. Who in their right mind would not want to please such beneficent authorities?

The pyramids were not, as previously thought, built by slaves. Slavery played a very minor role in the Egyptian economy and slaves were always foreigners, usually captives in war. The pyramids, like the temples, were built by skilled artisans employed for that purpose. A typical temple complex, for example, would have land attached to it that was worked by peasants. The temple would appropriate by command up to one third of the food they produced and use it to pay for the various artisans needed to sustain a viable community, including those building pyramids and temples. There would be weavers to fashion the linen that would "clothe" the statue of the temple's principal god, but also weavers of humbler clothes, as well as cobblers, bakers, brewers and so many more.

There would also be scribes to oversee the collection of the peasants' grains, to record what they had received and tally the total amount of grain in the temple storehouses. Scribes would also record how much of which products the temple received from the various workshops and pay the artisans their share of the peasants' grain in the form of bread and beer. Since the temple dictated how much grain each peasant owed and how much bread and beer each artisan would receive, this is an example of a command economy. Another term for this is a *redistributive* economy.

The standard economic usage for collecting the peasants' grain is "extracting a surplus," but that is very misleading. It implies that the peasants had consumed all they wanted and the surplus was what was left over. In truth, most extractions were quite painful for the people on the bottom. From the elite perspective, reliable culling of the "surplus" must neither starve the food producers so that there are too few of them to produce food in the next season, nor should the process of extraction cost more than it could collect. What Egypt brought to the task of supporting a hierarchy of people who did not produce food was a system based on the strongest source of power in the world, the power of faith.

## Faith

This is the most effective and least expensive form of social control. Egyptians believed that after death they faced a trial in which they must be able to swear truthfully that they had never committed any one of forty-two prohibited acts. These included such practical matters as never putting out a fire that should be lit or making a breach in an irrigation wall. If they could not so swear truthfully, they would, or so they believed, be eaten by a monster.

Given their belief that Pharaoh brought the sustaining waters of the Nile to their fields, the peasants willingly agreed to provide grain for the Pharaoh, his administrators, his temples and his fellow gods. After death, pharaohs went to live with the other gods and could ask them to look with favor on their former subjects. Egyptians further believed that, if a person's mummy was defiled, something like a soul was destroyed.

Should this happen to a pharaoh, he would no longer be dwelling with gods who could help him to protect the people of Egypt. They believed that the very existence of Egypt depended on keeping secure the bodies and the memories of the pharaohs, wise men and great statesmen. In this way, contributing in any manner to building an extremely secure tomb for the pharaoh was almost literally an act of self-protection. It is for this reason that slaves, captives defeated in foreign wars, did not build the pyramids. They simply could not be trusted with so consequential an act.

## Change

When the most cherished value of a society in general, and its leaders in particular, is continuity, how did the Egyptians handle change at the top from one Pharaoh to another? One of the most dramatic and interesting examples of such change comes with the rule of Hatshepsut. She was, apparently, the daughter of Thuthmosis I, a great warrior king, and Ahmose, his principal wife. Hatshepsut married her half-brother, Thuthmosis II, son of the Pharaoh and a secondary wife. They had no son. Meanwhile, Thuthmosis II

fathered a boy also with a secondary wife. When Thuthmosis II died, his son became Thuthmosis III, but he was too
young to rule. So Hatshepsut, both his aunt and his father's
principal wife, took the reigns as regent.

Evidently she did an excellent job, and, from our point
of view, she also got lucky. The Nile inundated with great
regularity during her tenure as regent. So, when Thuthmosis III grew up, important priests and administrators wanted
her to continue as Pharaoh. They "discovered" that she had
a divine right to rule. According to their story, Amun, an
extremely important Egyptian god, came to Ahmose,
Hatshepsut's mother, in the physical form of her husband,
although she knew that he was really Amun. Together they
conceived Hatshepsut, or so the story went.

Once you enter into the Egyptians' world view, this story
is not at all cynical. Her regency would not have been a
smashing success unless she was favored by the gods as the
daughter of Amun, one of the most powerful among them.

This example is odd only because the smooth transition
involved a female. Often, especially in a change of dynasties,
there are stories about how the successor, while not the child
of the last god-king, was instead the child or the chosen one of
a much more powerful god. This can easily appear disingenu-
ous to us, a religious veneer masking a power grab. But that is
to project backward in time an attitude that would have been
unthinkable to an ancient Egyptian. They believed absolutely
that the gods controlled the material world, that Pharaoh was
a god who controlled the Nile and that continuity from one
ruler to the next was essential to Egyptian success.

Ironically, this world view made changes at the top much less disruptive than they might otherwise have been. A new pharaoh must, of necessity, be the choice of the gods, even when the new ruler was a foreigner. We can call this process *political decapitation* when a new dynasty replaced the old. And political decapitation was not unique to Egypt but was also found in other parts of the ancient world.

## Babylonia and Persia

There were vital differences, however, between Egypt and Babylonia regarding the relative power of the king and the priests. Pharaoh, as noted, was a god who owned everything and stood at the apex of a hierarchy of priests and administrators. Directly beneath him were two viziers, one for Upper Egypt (to the south) and the other for Lower Egypt (to the north and including the Delta). Next came Pharaoh's central administrators, one of whom gloried in the title "Master of the King's Largess."

By contrast, in Babylonia, the king was not divine. The priests of the principle god, Marduk, were more important and powerful than the king, a fact played out symbolically in an annual ritual marking the beginning of a new year. The king appeared, dressed in a simple shift with no crown or other adornments of office, at Esagila, Babylon's greatest temple. There, the chief priest slapped his face and yanked his ears to underscore his subservience to Marduk. If the experience was painful enough to bring tears to the king's eyes, Marduk was thought to be pleased.

This difference meant that Babylonian temples were the

primary economic units of command and redistribution, and that the king received a share of this for his service to the state. The fellow who collected this share was known as the "official over the king's basket," which is a far cry from "Master of the King's Largess."

In 556 B.C., Narbonidus ascended to the Babylonian throne. He was an avid antiquarian, which sounds a bit funny from a modern perspective, but, even back then, Babylonia had a long and venerable recorded history. Narbonidus was impressed by an older god than Marduk and began to praise and worship him. He stayed away from the city of Babylon for ten years and, in so doing, avoided the humiliating new year's ritual. During this time, things were not going well for the city or for the kingdom at large, and blame was placed squarely on the heresy of Narbonidus.

Then, both the city and the kingdom were conquered by Cyrus the Persian in 539. Called "the Great," Cyrus understood and used propaganda wisely. He claimed that Marduk had been searching the world for a proper king, "a righteous ruler," and that he had found one in Cyrus. So under his rule, everything went along just as it had before, with the temples of Marduk dominating their environs in every respect. The only change was that the Persians, or their near relatives, the Medes, took over as the "officials over the king's basket." Here is another example of political decapitation, where change occurs only at the top echelons of society.

For Cyrus the Persian, whose personal god was Ahura Mazda, this was certainly cynical. But, for the priests of Marduk it was real. Here was a new ruler offering to restore the old order of things. He was not a fierce, but rather a tolerant, even beneficent, conqueror. It made perfect sense for the priests of Marduk, and of other Babylonian gods as well, to welcome Cyrus as a savior from the heretic Narbonidus.

Moreover, Cyrus governed wisely. He understood that the people of Babylonia had known civilization for much longer than the Persians or the Medes. Executions were limited to those who posed a clear and present danger to his regime. He vastly preferred cooperating with conquered peoples and living up to his own claims of righteousness, justice, fairness and honor. He "happened" not to be in Babylonia for the new year but he sent his son, Cambyses, as a surrogate, to have his face slapped and his ears pulled. The lessons of the father were not lost on the son.

In 525, during a time of uncertainty in Egypt, Cambyses crossed the desert and made a great conquest, proclaiming himself Pharaoh as chosen by the gods. This worked for him and for several of his descendents until, around 400 B.C., the Egyptians revolted and threw the Persians out, probably because a Persian "Pharaoh" failed to understand the political realities and tried to govern Egypt as simply one of many Persian provinces.

Cambyses conquered Egypt before Herodotus, a Greek famed for his histories, was born. Herodotus writes of this conquest as a terrible, bloody affair, with a half-mad Cambyses violating the most sacred of Egyptian icons, destroying the temples and offending all that was near and dear to Egyptian hearts. This cannot have been true. To insure his own reign and that of his descendents, Cambyses would necessarily have played into the deeply conservative culture of this place.

In any change of regime, there are winners and losers. Perhaps an Egyptian vizier was displaced by a Persian or a Mede. Herodotus might have gotten his information from such disaffected sources. Alternatively, he might simply be expressing a strong anti-Persian bias as a Greek. After all, his *magnum opus* is an account of a series of wars between Greeks and Persians. The former seems somewhat more likely as Herodotus did have some nice things to say about Persia, notably about its extensive postal system and the postal riders.

"Not snow, no, nor rain, nor heat, nor night keeps them from accomplishing their appointed courses with all speed."* This, of course, was adapted to become the motto of the U.S. postal service, "Neither snow, nor rain, nor heat, nor gloom of night stays these couriers from the swift completion of their appointed rounds."

The incredible stability of the Egyptian system, headed by Pharaoh, and the ability and willingness of the peasants to supply huge amounts of grain, as a "surplus," is striking in the march of dynasty after Egyptian dynasty. It is even more amazing that the stability of the system permitted outsiders to come in and take over as Pharaoh without the underlying structures changing in any significant way. Such is the power of tradition allied with command.

* The redundant "no" is in the actual translation as presented in *Bartlett's Familiar Quotations*.

### Command and Consumption in Persia

In the command economy of ancient Persia, a vital feature was a system of roads, known collectively as the king's highway, which allowed people and commands to pass over long distances faster than ever before. It has been called "the original information superhighway." Access to this road was strictly controlled so that no one could use it without a pass, in Persian a *viyataka*.

This pass illustrates two vital elements in the Persian command structure. The first is a rigid system of stratification. Imperial officials were assigned a place in the hierarchy that would then determine the quality of their lodgings, food rations and such as they traveled along the king's highway. Status also determined consumption for ordinary people, animals and even birds. In fact, a low-ranking official might be assigned a smaller ration of wine than one of the king's favorite horses.*

There is an important point to be made here. In a command economy, status determines consumption. By contrast, in modern America, one can enjoy fame and high status simply by owning multiple opulent homes, driving hugely expensive cars and other examples of conspicuous consumption. This difference can make it more difficult for us to fully understand a system in which consumption flows directly from status.

---

* There is a wonderful story about a duck destined for the king's table being fattened along the journey by a quart of wine per day. That must have been one drunken duck.

## Macedonians

Less than a century after the Egyptians kicked the Persians out, Alexander the Great staged a successful coup d'etat. At one point, he was laying out his ideas about the building of a new city, Alexandria, by drawing his vision with grain. Suddenly, a large flock of birds swooped down and ate the grain, obliterating his "blueprint." Alexander exclaimed that this must be an omen of doom for his city. The architect, who doubtless wanted the work, disagreed vehemently. No, no, this was rather a sign that Egypt would feed Alexander's vast empire.

Both were wrong. Alexander died and left as possible heirs a mentally deficient brother and a posthumous son. Inevitably, his empire was divided between his various generals with Ptolemy getting Egypt. He was from a Macedonian Greek family and he and his successors ruled Egypt from Alexandria, a purely Greek city from which Egyptians were excluded. There was, most likely, a considerable fear that close contact might cause the Egyptians to question the very idea of a pharaoh so obviously Greek.

One such, Ptolemy V, commissioned a stone monument to be carved in praise of a favored temple. The writing was in ancient Greek, in formal Egyptian (hieroglyphic) and in Egyptian short hand (demotic). This is now known as the famous Rosetta Stone, recovered in 1799, with identical texts in the known language of Greek and the hitherto undeciphered Egyptian. The correspondence of the three texts provided the key to unlock the mysteries of these two ancient Egyptian scripts.

Cleopatra VII, of Julius Caesar fame, was the last of the Ptolemy family to rule in Egypt. She is often portrayed as an Egyptian but she was a Macedonian Greek. Like other Macedonian pharaohs, she carried on the Egyptian tradition of siblings and half-siblings marrying one another. This was thought to keep their divinity in the family. Apart from this very atypical behavior, they acted and spoke of themselves and the world like Greeks.

In the richness of time, Egypt fell to Rome and its "surplus" grains fed both the city and some of its provinces. Later, when Rome's empire was divided in two, Egypt fell to the eastern half, then governed from Constantinople. With the subsequent spread of Islam, the pharaoh completely lost the status of a god. Allah had taken his place.

## Redistribution

The Bronze Age began in roughly 3000 B.C., when, in Mesopotamia, Anatolia and the island of Cyprus, rich deposits of copper and tin made possible the synthesis of this new metal. For the record, "Mesopotamia" is a purely geographic expression from the Greek meaning "between rivers." A number of political units have occupied this area, notably Babylonia in the ancient world and Iraq in modern times. Anatolia is also a geographic term used to express the place where we, today, find modern Turkey.

From those places, bronze technology spread to a group of islands, called the Cyclades because they make a rough circle around the island of Delos, the legendary birthplace of Apollo, and an important center of commerce for classical

Greece. From there bronze spread to Crete. A millennium later, some eastern horsemen called the Hyksos conquered a horseless Egypt and brought bronze with them. Not surprisingly, they were, for almost a century, able to rule as pharaohs. Here we see yet another example of the flexibility of Egypt's command structure so long as the new rulers go along with the program of pharaoh as god.

### The Cyclades and Crete

The people of the Cyclades were certainly seafaring as we know from the wide dispersion of their artifacts around the eastern Mediterranean. The most famous of these objects are highly stylized figures of nude females with their arms crossed under their breasts, their legs together and their faces at an upward angle with the nose their only feature. Some scholars think that they had stones for eyes and possibly thread for hair.*

As the Cycladic islands faded in importance, a society based in Crete began to flourish circa 2300 B.C. The island had much to recommend it, from good arable land to abundant timber for a variety of uses, as well as lots of wild game to eat. The people also kept goats, sheep and, possibly, cattle. Crete was thus able to be independent and self-sufficient.

In modern times, it became an inviting place for those curious about the past. The great amateur archeologist, Sir Arthur Evans, led the first excavations of a large and

---

* In any case, the starkly elegant way they now appear has inspired modern artists such as Brancusi, Modigliani and Henry Moore.

labyrinthine building at a site called Knossos, which forcefully reminded him of the story of King Minos. According to legend, the king had a wife and he also had a bull and the two fancied one another. Their union produced a creature called a Minotaur, which was half man and half bull, and lived in the center of a labyrinth. Since the most gifted modern genetic engineer could not achieve this mix, we know it is a myth. To make the story even more far fetched, the Minotaur ate people, specifically young and comely Athenians. Very few people eat people and bulls are vegetarians.

Recently, a small and curious fact has come to light that might be the kernel of truth behind this nonsense. Isotopic analysis of copper from Minoan Crete indicates that it was mined near what was or would become Athens. If Athenian traders once visited Crete, they might have inspired some part of this myth but that is mere speculation.

The Minoans had a written language that Evans called Linear A, which modern people cannot read. In his praise of this "high and marvelous" civilization, a wonderful classic scholar called Peter Green writes that the "needs of commerce, and their own native brilliance" led them "through all the main pre-alphabetic systems of writing in a staggeringly short time, moving on from pictograms to hieroglyphs and finally to an advanced syllabary." This advanced syllabary* we call Linear A and the general consensus is that it was not Greek.

---

* A syllabary is a collection of symbols each of which represents a syllable rather than a single letter.

## The Fascinating Minoans

Because we cannot read their writing, we are left to rely entirely on their artifacts. These include the building at Knossos and several more large structures like it, which have been excavated since Evans' time. All have extensive storerooms with a number of large pots for storing oil and grains. From these, we might speculate that Minoan society was another example of a command economy. Conveniently, there are workshops for artisans found in the same buildings. The immediate proximity of non-food producing artisans and stored food, probably for their consumption, has all the earmarks of a command or redistributive economy.

The technical prowess of Minoan builders, artists and artisans indicates that they were specialists and not food producers doing a bit of construction and crafts on the side. In gold work, for example, they developed a technique called granulation, which was lost with their civilization and was so sophisticated that it was not reinvented until relatively recently.

Minoans were also master builders. The theory is that rooms or groups of rooms were added to their structures as needed. In the spaces between these additions, they left areas with no roofs to create light wells to illuminate the interiors. They also did amazing and ingenious things with water, even building a bathroom with running water and the equivalent of a flushing toilet.

Similarly, the existence of writing argues for specialist scribes who also benefited from the redistribution to non-food producers. Even more telling is the fact that accounting of the sort we see in redistributive economies was one of the earliest and most widespread known uses of writing. So much grain came into an administrative center, while X amount of grain or Y loaves of bread were rationed out to the butcher, the baker and the candlestick maker. It is likely, but not certain, that Linear A, as we call Minoan writing, served that same function.

Redistributive is a better word for the Minoan economy than command because we cannot know how that culture was governed. For example, a fresco of a man sitting on a big chair doesn't prove that he was a king. A chairman of the board in corporate America sits in the biggest chair in the room without becoming a king. The figure in the fresco could be a patriarch in a family, a figure being ritually feted before he is sacrificed, or someone holding executive power for a brief time before it rotates to someone else. King is, arguably, a good guess. But it is just a guess and must be recognized and remembered as such.

Another example of a guess posing as a fact is that "the queen had her own private bathroom" in the "palace" at Knossos. Because an adjacent room is beautifully frescoed does not presuppose the existence of a queen. We must be careful about projecting the world as we have known it, with the rich and powerful having exclusive access to the most valued luxuries, onto the artifacts of the past. The beautifully frescoed room could have been a meeting place for decision makers, who also shared the loo.

We do not know and cannot know whether this was a hierarchical society with a king and a court of aristocrats.

We do not know and we cannot know if the large Minoan structures found on Crete were palaces or merely administrative centers for collecting and redistributing food. However, we can be reasonably certain that these were food collection centers because they each have substantial storage areas with large pots to hold oil and grain. The co-existence of artisans' workshops suggests that food was being redistributed to those who did not produce it themselves.

Yet the view that these were palaces, occupied by kings, is widely accepted in the field. Some writers even go a step further by insisting on the existence of a real King Minos despite the absence of any credible evidence. What would encourage otherwise careful and serious scholars to commit to the palace/king hypothesis without stronger evidence?

The most likely answer goes something like this: Arthur Evans is remembered as a giant in the field of archeology. He and his team unearthed a large structure, sumptuously appointed and beautifully decorated, and he succumbed to a very human tendency. When we encounter something new, it is extremely tempting to liken it to something we already know. Surely, he was familiar with the great palaces of Europe and so he called his structure a palace.

There follows the construction of a whole language around this assumption. Evans calls a lovely room the "Queen's Megaron" and so it appears in Janson's *History of Art*. A bathroom nearby becomes the queen's private bathroom. Frescos of lovely women become court ladies. As this naming convention was used and reused, it became more comfortable and accepted without hesitation or reflection.

Since we know that large sumptuous buildings like Louis' Versailles or the Hampton Court of Henry VIII were palaces, it becomes easy to extend this description to the structure at Knossos.

The more interesting comparison goes in the opposite direction. Hampton Court and Versailles were both places where food was collected and then redistributed to non-food producers, including courtiers and kings. Henry VIII had several such redistribution centers and moved his court from one to another because it was, in those days, far easier to move people to food than the other way around. That Hampton Court and Versailles were redistribution centers in command economies is clear. The ways in which these palaces suggest comparisons with the structure at Knossos gives further support to the idea that the Minoans had a king or kings. But this is mere speculation.

So long as we cannot read their writing, we cannot know a lot about the Minoan political organization. However, its levels of innovation and originality suggest that it might have had a social and political system unlike anything else we have ever known.

A clue is to be found in their art. In frescos, men and women are engaged in similar activities, including the very risky business of doing acrobatics on the backs of bulls. This seems so difficult and so dangerous that many suppose the art is not actually imitating life. In either case, for the Minoan mind at the time, there was nothing alien about depicting men and women performing the same daring feats. For those who are seeking gender equality in the modern world, this apparent support from the past makes the Minoans quite appealing.

Moreover, the discovery of frescos in all the buildings excavated on Crete, including those that appear to have been single-family dwellings, argues for a very high level of affluence widely shared. The general historical pattern of economic distribution is that, when power is narrowly held, affluence is limited to the few. However, when power is widely shared, the class of persons who are also well off increases.

Minoan art contributes mightily to the view that they lived in a better society than most. The most pervasive feeling invoked by their art is happiness. The artists, by all appearances, were having fun. They were playing with the images and with those who would see them.

In their art, nature was embraced as beautiful and harmonious, which is in stark contrast to the Greek view of nature as dark and frightening. Even a beautifully realized bull seems almost blissful, despite having an acrobat perched on his head. In his summary of Minoan art, Peter Green writes:

> This delirious dance of colour and the senses, this fascination with plant and animal life, with sex and social intercourse and religious ritual, with the stylized dangers of boxing and bull-vaulting, reveals a life-style clear out of the mainstream of European history.[*]

* *Ancient Greece: An Illustrated History.*

Since they had a culture that was so atypical, perhaps they also had a political system that was equally unusual, even unique. We will never know unless new evidence appears.

The most mysterious artifact found on Crete, and dated from around 1700 B.C., is known as the Phaistos disk. It is a spherical clay object on which some 271 individual characters are divided into clusters by etched vertical lines. With a total of forty-five characters, some being repeated, the assumption is that this is a syllabary and not an alphabet. None of these characters resemble any other signs from any known language, including Linear A. We do not know whose language it was, where its writers originated, if they immigrated to Crete and co-existed with the Minoans, or merely engaged them in foreign trade. Indeed, they might have been a select group of Minoans themselves.

What is also remarkable is that the text is not etched, but is instead produced by pushing raised characters into soft clay. In this way, the disk foreshadows later efforts at printing, and it does so a very long time ago. The next attempt comes 2,500 years later in China and 3,100 years later in medieval Europe. Regardless of who made it, the Phaistos disk shows a degree of innovation stunningly ahead of its time.

### The End

The conventional wisdom about the collapse of Minoan society involves two important events. The first was a volcanic eruption on the not-too distant island of Thera, which is generally dated from 1520 to 1500 B.C. This was a huge eruption, thought to have been, both past and present, the loudest sound ever heard on Earth. To it are attributed "sulphuric acid and fine ash particles in the Greenland Ice Sheet, climate disturbances in China, and frost damage to trees in Ireland and California."[*]

Then, some time around 1450 B.C., there was an earthquake that caused a fire so hot that it baked the clay tablets used for writing Linear A. It also baked the tablets containing a new language, called by Evans Linear B. Because such tablets also appeared at a mainland site called Mycenae, modern scholars have called this culture Mycenaean. Classical scholars were unanimous in the view that Linear B was not Greek ...

## Mycenae

Then, in 1952, Michael Ventris deciphered it and they were all wrong. Linear B recorded a very early form of classical Greek. After an initial burst of excitement, the actual texts were pronounced boring and useless as they were merely lists of things taken in and things rationed back out. Regarded individually, they are boring, but taken as a whole these glimpses into Mycenaean life are immensely useful and informative. With a keen and detailed understanding of the redistributive nature of a command economy, this accounting system fits into a redistribution pattern that we have seen before.

Whether the Mycenaeans invaded and conquered the Minoans, or as one scholar rather fancifully imagines, there

---

[*] April 28, 2006 edition of *Science* magazine.

was a Minoan palace coup that invited a Mycenaean dynasty to come and take over, we can note that Linear A dwindled into nothing while more and more Linear B tablets appeared. So, the three factors thought to lead to the collapse of the Minoan civilization on Crete were a huge volcanic eruption, an earthquake causing massive fires, and an incursion of strangers who took over the place.

As a brief footnote, there is a contemporary debate raging over dating the famed eruption of Thera mentioned above. It seems that for almost three decades there has been a sharp division in archeological circles. Those who match well-documented Egyptian inscriptions with contemporaneous Minoan pots are sticking with the traditional date of somewhere around 1500 B.C. Radiocarbon dating experts insist that the event occurred at least one hundred years earlier, and possibly as many as fifty years earlier still. Two new radiocarbon studies support the older date, but their opponents are not giving any ground.

> Moreover, dendrochronologists have recently come up with an exact date of 1628 B.C. for it. This has surprised the Egyptologists who had been working with a date at least a century later. At the moment they are in denial.*

What makes this so interesting is not the satisfaction of having a fixed date but rather what effect the two different

---

*Dendrochronology attempts to fix dates and chronologies by studying the annual rings on trees. The source is Colin McEvedy's *The New Penguin Atlas of Ancient History* and demonstrates his usual sense of humor.

systems of dating have on our ideas about interactions between the various cultures of the Aegean.

The later pottery-based dates allow speculation that the Mycenaean rise to power and prominence resulted from a strategic alliance with Egypt's New Kingdom. By contrast, the much earlier radiocarbon dates could mean that the Mycenaeans were allied with the Hyksos, the invaders who brought the horse to Egypt and were pharaohs for a time.

The Mycenaean age is thought to be the time of the heroes found in the *Iliad* and the *Odyssey*, which tradition attributed to Homer, but which most scholars now think were long and fascinating stories first spoken by a number of unknown and illiterate bards and only written down when Archaic Greece acquired an alphabet. In any event, they definitely speak of a people whose elite were addicted to war.

Such an addiction is very hard on the treasury, making the demands of this command economy intolerably onerous for the direct producers of food and other useful objects. The eventual collapse of their administrative centers, circa 1200 B.C., may have been the result of this perpetual thirst for war. This led to insatiable demands being placed on the peasants for food, goods and services. This would be met by deep resentment, such that the elites could not trust the peasants to be soldiers.

Tradition then says they were invaded by the Dorians, a tribal people among whom every man was a soldier. This put the Mycenaeans at a distinct disadvantage. Because they were also nomadic pastoralists, the Dorians left very little in the way of an archeological footprint, so we are forced to rely on the traditional view that it was they who brought down the palaces. In any case, writing stops.

This, of course, makes perfect sense. The principle use of writing in a command economy is to keep accounts of the food and other commodities taken in by the center and redistributed to artisans, soldiers, scribes and so forth. Remember all those "boring" lists in Linear B, which taken all together, add their support to the notion that this was a command economy. When the command structure collapsed, the need for scribes and writing collapsed with it.

### Greek Dark Ages

What follows is frequently called the Greek Dark Ages, and it lasts until roughly 800 B.C., when the period known as Archaic Greece emerges with an alphabet borrowed from the Phoenicians and improved upon by the addition of vowels. This was when the *Iliad* and the *Odyssey* were finally transcribed, and that means that they must have been recited again and again over a very long stretch of time.

Writing stopped but the potters went on with their trade. So might spinners, weavers, carpenters, bakers and others whose work left no archeological trace. What is very intriguing about the pottery is that it quickly became superior to Mycenaean ware. This would be much more surprising without the notion that the old system was a command economy.

Most likely, the people reverted to a traditional economy where peasants continued to produce food and artisans continued to work at the crafts that they had learned from their parents. Designing and making pots for your neighbors in return for food, a form of barter, probably inspired greater creativity than turning out X number of pots ordered by a scribe from the palace for the next military adventure.

The illiterate poets that we posit above seemed to have been able to tell stories for their supper. The people must have listened with pleasure to vivid tales of heroes, now that they no longer bore the burden of their "continual indulgence in war."* The scribes, by contrast, could no longer make a living. Once they controlled the peasants by pointing to mysterious markings only they could read. This mark meant that peasant A owed the palace eleven sheep. Their command had been backed by powerful elites. Once these elites were defeated, the mysterious markings lost their power. Scribes were out of a job and writing died. This probably augured well for an improved quality of life for the vast majority of people.

## Market Economy

To solve the economic problems of mobilizing effort, allocating labor and materials, and distributing the resulting products, societies have resorted to tradition, command and a combination of the two. Another solution, however, is the extensive use of markets. By this, we do not mean the barter or retail selling that went on for much of our history as settled farmers. Nor do we mean the exchanges between heads of state that are usually a sort of reciprocal tribute.

---

* The phrase comes from A.R. Burn in *The Pelican History of Greece*.

Instead, we mean a world in which markets are the central organizing features of economic life. In other words, we mean market capitalism.

Exactly what capitalism is and when it came about are two of the most vexed questions in political economy. Fortunately, they are outside the scope of our story. Still we should give a nod to the familiar argument about supply and demand regulating a market for the good of all concerned. To recap briefly, when demand is high and supply is low, prices rise. This causes entrepreneurs to mobilize and allocate resources, including labor, so as to take advantage of these high prices. This then increases the supply of desirable commodities until it equals demand. At that point, prices stabilize. Conversely, when demand is low and supply is high, prices plummet. Low prices drive suppliers out of business until supply and demand are again in harmony. At least that is how things are supposed to work without the intervention of a host of other factors outside our present project.

As all economists know, this argument works best when the resources being moved around are "fungible," which is econ-speak for interchangeable. So electricity can illuminate a shoe factory, a department store, or the red carpet where stars show off their designer footwear. On the other hand the factory manager, the store clerk and the supermodel are not fungible. This is why we use retraining to combat unemployment and why people move to look for a job they are trained to do.

Another well-known hitch in the workings of markets is found in a class of objects that economists call "externalities." Regular people call them rivers, lakes, oceans and air. Without some kind of government intervention, market forces do not and cannot put a price tag on pollution.

Apart from these two exceptions, and they are huge and important exceptions, the interplay of supply and demand does affect prices, in the absence of a third group of exceptions. Monopolies and oligopolies* are able to fix prices for commodities when demand is inelastic, that is to say, when people *must* buy the product from them without regard for the price. All of this means that monopolies and oligopolies can make much higher profits then they could if they faced more robust competition.

## A Disastrous Command Economy

Stalin's Russia is a very good example of a command economy sitting on top of a very traditional base. Indeed, a significant number of Russian peasants were still using wooden plows into the twentieth century. Stalin's intention was to drag Russia into the modern era, and to some extent, he succeeded ... at the cost of enormous, unbearable human suffering.

His plan was to have a Central Committee set important but general goals for the economy over a five-year period. Committees under them would then flesh out the details of how these goals would be met. More specialized committees under those committees would concretize detailed plans.

---

* A monopoly is a single supplier, while an oligopoly involves a few suppliers who can agree to a price other than one established by the market. OPEC is a great example of the latter.

For example, X amount of steel was to be sent to a specific widget factory to be used in the production of 10,000 widgets meeting certain specifications. The specifications would be determined by the ultimate function of the widgets, say as component parts in military tanks.

These were nearly always overly ambitious plans, which stretched the available resources beyond their limits. So, as a general rule, the amount of steel sent to the widget factory was drastically inadequate for the production of 10,000 widgets of the proper size. If the factory manager complained about this problem, or even brought it to a planner's attention, he risked being sent to Siberia. If he produced only the 8,000 widgets that could be made with the allotted steel and also meet the specifications, he faced an even higher risk of being sent to Siberia (frequently under the allegation that he must have stolen the "missing' steel and sold it on the black market). So he had an overwhelming incentive to cheat in one way or another.

He could stretch the steel by adulterating it with some other substance, say sand. This would allow him to produce the requisite number of widgets to the specifications, but they would break easily. Alternatively, he could produce 10,000 widgets that were too small for the next phase of production. So when it came time to build the tanks, the widgets would either be weak or poorly fitted or both.

If the next plant manager complained that he had received inadequate widgets, he also ran the risk of being sent to Siberia. And so it went on and on in a sequence of no-win situations. The only really productive element in the entire command structure was that so many people were sent to Siberia that this once barren region was brought to a kind of civilization by armies of imprisoned slave laborers.

Given the essentially self-destructive and inefficient elements at the center of the Soviet command economy, the notion that there was ever any chance of them beating us in an arms race was based on the worst possible intelligence or the best possible fantasies of acquisition by what Eisenhower called the military-industrial complex. That said, we can now return to the ancient world.

# Hellas

The single most important fact about Greek history is that Greece did not exist as an independent state until 1832. In this chapter, we will focus on the deeply divided Greeks of antiquity. We will explore two important Greek states, Athens and Sparta, becoming familiar with the broad outlines of each political system in the context of their much-heralded differences. We will also discover a surprising, important and hitherto overlooked structural similarity between them that will explain, with elegant simplicity, how they inevitably ended up as allies against the Persians.

Political Scientists distinguish between a nation and a state. A nation is a population with shared social, linguistic and cultural properties. A state is a unit of governance. Modern France is then both a nation and a state, whereas ancient Greece, or Hellas as the ancient Greeks called it, was a nation but not a single state.

As a nation, the Greeks called themselves "Hellenes." They spoke a common language and mocked those who did not, claiming that foreigners spoke "bah, bah, bah," from which we get the word "barbarian." They shared a belief in a pantheon of gods and goddesses and they put great stock in consulting the Oracle of Delphi, despite the fact that the answers were invariably cryptic. "If you do that, it will be a momentous event." This prediction covers anything from a spectacular success to a memorable failure and even a breathless escape from any consequences at all.

Hellenes also shared the notion that war was seasonal and that a moratorium on fighting should accompany the pan-Hellenic games, of which there were four, with the Olympics being the best known to us. Living on Mt. Olympus, one of the gods was called Zeus Olympios. For reasons unknown even to ancient writers, sometime around 1000 B.C., a place beside the Alpheus River in a region called Elis was made sacred to Zeus and called Olympia. There, in 776 B.C., began a festival in his honor that was primarily religious but also included athletic events. Athletes and trainers swore in his name to follow the rules, and were quite sure that Zeus would punish any perjurer with swift and dreadful vengeance.

Politically, the Hellenes were divided into states of varying sizes. Modern scholars usually call these "city-states." The Hellenes called them *poleis*. The singular of *poleis* is *polis*, from which we get words like metropolitan, cosmopolitan, politics, policy and police. The use of the phrase "city-state," while widespread and time honored, has come under criticism in recent years as being seriously misleading. A state is a political unit of governance and the *poleis* were all states. However, the three largest, Sparta, Thessaly and Aetolia, had no cities at all, while the smallest were simply a single village and its immediate vicinity.

The confusion arose, in part, because most of what has been written about ancient Greece focuses on Athens, which fits the "city-state" description, and about which we have the most information. While acknowledging that our Athenian bias is part of the misuse of the term "city-state," Colin McEvedy, a brilliant and multi-faceted scholar, takes the argument a step further. He asks us to consider Megara:

> This was a small state (Greek *polis*) the majority of whose citizens certainly lived in the countryside (*agros*), but which had built itself a dignified little town (*asty*) as its seat of government. But the fact that they had a perfectly good word for an urban centre in *asty* didn't stop the Greeks using the word *polis* for both Megara state and Megara town, as they did for both Athens state and Athens city.*

Where this whole thing becomes problematic for us is when we meld the dual Greek usages of "*polis*" into the single idea of a "city-state." Athens, as we noted, fit that paradigm, but over ninety percent of the other *poleis* did not. They were independent states but entirely lacking in cities. Being very clear about this helps avoid the confusion of comparing ancient Greek *poleis* with the city-states of the Italian Renaissance.

For Hellenes, the ability to participate in political life depended on citizenship. This citizenship had to be in a spe-

---

* Colin McEvedy's *The New Penguin Atlas of Ancient History* (2002).

cific *polis*, and was exclusive to that *polis*. In this way, citizenship particularized the nation and, with few exceptions, depended on birth. So a man born in Athens was a Hellene, and an Athenian, but not a Corinthian or a Spartan. This exclusivity was characteristically Greek.*

Probably the second most important fact about Greek history was the paucity of arable land. This meant that when the population of a *polis* ran out of arable land, the surplus people were usually encouraged, indeed enabled, to leave home and look for land elsewhere. Marseille, in the south of France, was founded by just such wandering, landless Hellenes. Naples, as well, began as a new Greek *polis* called *Neapolis*. These two do not begin to exhaust the available examples of westward movement.

These emigrants are often described as "colonists," and their emigration as "colonizing," but this is again misleading. As soon as the new *polis* was founded, its people lost their citizenship in the *polis* of their birth. They might go back to visit friends and family. They might prefer pottery in the style native to "home," but that was as far as any claim to membership in the old *polis* went. This tendency to divide and then exclude was another trait characteristically Greek.

Hellenes also created settlements to the east, and as far north as the northern shores of the Black Sea. We have a letter from one such emigrant who complains that, for four months out of the year it is very, very cold, and the rest of the time it's winter. These settlements brought the Hellenes

---

* Interestingly, our word "idiot" derives from their word for a man not interested in the politics of his *polis*.

into contact with a people that they dubbed "Scythians." These "Scyths" are widely supposed to be descended from the first people to tame and ride horses. We will see more about that contact later.

Returning to Hellas and the Hellenes, why do *we* call them Greeks? The answer comes from an odd little fluke of history. A tiny *polis* called Graia sent off a group of its landless citizens to found another *polis* and they went west. Along the way, they met some Romans who asked them who they were.* They replied that they were people from Graia, which in Latin became *Graeci*. Later, when other Romans encountered citizens of other *poleis* who looked and sounded like the *Graeci*, they called them that as well. So we call them Greeks because of a Roman mistake.

Their factionalism, their exclusivity and their endless preference for fighting amongst themselves left the Hellenes vulnerable to external conquest. In the time of Alexander the Great, they fell under Macedonian rule. As that empire waned, the Romans took over and made Hellas a province theirs. Centuries later, when the Roman Empire split in half, the Eastern Empire naturally included Hellas. When that empire, which modern historians have called the Byzantine Empire, declined sharply after almost ten successful centuries, the Turks took over.

In the nineteenth century, the notion became wide-

---

* One of the most interesting questions is always how people, speaking completely different languages, manage to communicate on contact. A sort of sign language is the most obvious answer. It is telling that they identified themselves as citizens of Graia rather than as members of the nation of Hellas.

spread that the ideal situation for a people was to have their own nation-state. Of course, this idea would have been repellent to the ancient, exclusive, divisive Hellenes. Nevertheless, in 1832, a state called Greece was carved out of the failing Ottoman Empire. We will revisit this story in more detail later.

## Redivision

Although divided politically and given to fighting among themselves, the Hellenes were a nation, and they shared a common back story. They all "knew" that once upon a time, in the idyllic past, the arable land had been divided equitably. However, by the seventh century B.C., the best arable land was held by the *aristoi*, who also called themselves the *eupatridae* or those having "good fathers."

The latter title clearly asserts that both the possession of good land and the status of *aristoi* were hereditary. It also infers that a good father was an ancestor who claimed the best land, possibly by arriving first. These claims are very difficult to square with an idyllic past when land was divided equitably. Having noted the contradiction, we will press on.

At the next level below the *eupatridae* were less affluent farmers whose land was still good but not quite as good as the land of those with a pedigree. Below them were farmers whose land was adequate to sustain life, and even to be divided between multiple sons. This was ultimately to have disastrous consequences, but initially and, for a time, it was viable.

Finally, at the lowest end of the spectrum were the hill

people, whose land was rocky, barren and best suited for raising goats. Because this type of terrain was, and still is, extremely common in Hellas, these class divisions could be found in nearly every *polis* of any significant size. Therefore, over time, the revolutionary slogan "redivide!" would be a frequent chorus in Hellenic history.

The emigrations described above were usually organized by the *aristoi* as an answer to that demand. The subtext of the organizers' response was "Certainly you have the right to equal land but ... well ... how about someplace else?" An added advantage of exporting both the problem and its solution was that it created "natural" trading partners with access to different kinds of valuable goods. The new *polis* might be closer to ivory or silver or gold and then export or transship these to their old home.

Similarly, since these new *poleis* were often planted on fertile plains, at least some of their citizens could become affluent enough to import luxury goods from home. Among their favorite imports were pots painted in the home style. This pottery has proved durable enough for modern scholars to track some of these ancient trade routes. Rich emigrants might even travel to Olympia, Delphi, Corinth or Nemea to watch the Pan-Hellenic games. The net result was a dramatic increase in the volume of trade and in its velocity, that is the speed with which goods changed hands.

This vital and vibrant economic growth saw the birth of new classes of merchants, ship owners and manufacturers employing up to sixty slaves, a very large enterprise by ancient Greek standards. These new classes objected to their own exclusion from political power and, as is usual in history, the combination of economic power and political impotence was combustible. Revolution was in the air.

Because its roots were mercantile, revolution only came to the *poleis* most involved in trade. Had the *aristoi* been more willing to share power with the newly wealthy and/or had they manifested a high level of class solidarity, these revolutions might have been averted. As it happened, they did neither. They were committed to status rather than wealth as the source of political power, but they were also, in typical Greek fashion, deeply fragmented among themselves into rival cliques.

For this reason, the leaders of these revolutions were often dissident aristocrats who led the discontented new classes and, if successful, enjoyed essentially personal rule for a time, usually with the aid of armed bodyguards, but also with support from the poor. To keep this support, they often engaged in various forms of public works, such as causing an aqueduct to be built. This both brought water into town, which was a service for the residents, but also brought employment to the poor.

Such rulers were called *tyranoi*, which was not a Greek word, and which did not have the negative connotations that tyrant has for us. Instead, it referred to leaders who had not come to power through hereditary right. George Washington or Oliver Cromwell could be *tyranoi* but not King Louis XI of France, one of the wickedest, cruelest monarchs in history. *Tyranoi* is better translated as boss, chief or head honcho.

## The Corinthian Model

The case of Corinth is often cited as a fairly typical instance of this pattern. She was very successful in planting "colonies" in the west, thus creating a large market for her pottery. Sometime around 654 B.C., a man called Kypselos seized power and became a *tyranoi*. The story is that his mother was a noble Dorian of the ruling clan, but that she had been forced by her relatives to marry a man of lower status because she was severely crippled.

Kypselos presided over a redivision, which saw his mother's relations losing land to the allies of the *tyranoi*, who was thus very popular with the people and never needed a bodyguard. His son, Periandros, ruled for forty-four years, kept a bodyguard and lived quite lavishly. In time, his despotism became unpopular and his heir was quickly overthrown. The dynasty had lasted for seventy-seven years. Corinth then evolved into a more moderate bourgeois government in which property, not status, was the condition of political empowerment.

While the case of Corinth was typical of the Archaic period in Greek history, it was not universal. At some time around 580 B.C., the *polis* of Asian Doris sent an expedition to create a colony in the west of Sicily. This was a direct threat to the Phoenicians living there, so they and their allies crushed it. The survivors moved on to the Lipari Islands,* where they created a *polis* whose constitution mandated the redivision of the land every twenty years. The resulting lack

---

* These are a cluster of small volcanic islands off the north coast of Sicily in the southeast Tyrrhenian Sea.

of class conflict drew envy from some other Greeks.

The Lipari experience was facilitated by its aggressive treatment of non-Greeks. This brought plunder from abroad that could be used to buy off unrest at home. At the same time, the level of tension between Greeks and non-Greeks was rising, with Phoenicians uniting behind Carthaginian leadership and forming alliances with other non-Greeks like the Etruscans.

The periodic redivisions found on the Lipari Islands make merely a footnote when compared to the other two major deviations from the Corinthian paradigm described above. Athens and Sparta would dominate Greek history in the classical period, and neither of them followed anything like the Corinthian model.

The *polis* of Sparta dominated the region known as Laconia, just as Athens dominated the region called Attica. In this, they were similar. All the other regions of Hellas supported a number of *poleis*, some more powerful than others. None of these, however, enjoyed the local monopoly on power characteristic of Sparta and of Athens.

Indeed, the general view is that, apart from being Hellenes, this monopoly on local power was all that these two superstars of their day had in common. For each of them, the political and social arrangements they evolved were unique to themselves and radically unlike the other. However, when considering how they confronted the Persian threat, we uncover another telling characteristic that they have in common: they were *both* governed by their own citizen-soldiers in what was collective rather than personal rule. The vital significance of rule by a citizen-army will be developed later. For now, we will look at each of these players individually.

## Sparta

Spartan dominance was military. Some of the smaller hamlets in Laconia were allowed to keep their personal freedoms so long as they acknowledged Sparta's special status. Others, especially those who resisted the Spartans, became reduced to a condition called helotry. Helots are often compared to medieval serfs, but there are, as we shall see later, enough differences to look for an alternative. A less elegant but more accurate analogy is a tenant farmer who has no choice but to farm a particular patch of land and give over fifty percent of his yield to the land owner.

At some time, probably around 630 B.C., the helots of Messenia, who had once been free, revolted violently with help from Arcadia, and the Spartans were literally fighting for their lives. In the end, the Spartans won and the Messenians were forced back into helotry. They were systematically humiliated and degraded, but they never forgot that they had once been free and the urge for revenge was never far below the surface.

In response to this hostility, Sparta refurbished its constitution. The traditional two kings had their power reduced. They were monitored by five ephors,* elected annually and sworn by an oath of allegiance to uphold Sparta's unwritten

---

* Ephor is sometimes translated as "overseer."

laws. They would be, in effect, the executive branch. However, the ephors had to consult with an elected council of twenty-eight men over sixty years of age. Only especially noble families could stand a candidate for election and, if he won, he served for life.

The traditional two kings continued to be leaders in war, defenders of property and judges of issues involving the transfer of property when no obvious male heir could be found. In practice, this generally meant deciding which kinsman got to marry the heiress.

The assembly consisted of every man thirty years old or older from the few thousand full citizen families. Such families are often referred to as Spartiate families. They elected the ephors and the council and they voted on all important decisions, including matters of war and peace. Since these men constituted the citizen army, their voice in questions of war or peace would be absolutely necessary. However, they were constitutionally required to vote a proposal up or down in its entirety. The assembly had no right of amendment.

This is vitally important because the power to propose is always greater than the power to decide. Shall we go to war today or tomorrow? Shall we go to war or rally our allies in a display of force? Shall we go to war or pay the tribute demanded by our enemies? The power to delineate the available choices is always greater than the power to choose among them. This is one of the most important general points one can make about politics and its significance and universality can not be underscored too heavily.

Because of the natural precariousness of a minority

Spartiate land owning class, facing a substantially larger number of oppressed helots, the government usually got its way. What might then have looked, on paper, to be a democratic system (at least among the elites) was actually a very reactionary one. For the remainder of her history, wherever Sparta intervened, she would always champion the forces of conservatism and oppose inclusive democracy.

In a small but humorous aside, Sparta has to have had the oddest system of voting in all of human history. As was typical among Hellenes, politics took place outdoors. Whether voting a proposal up or down or voting for candidates for the council or for the ephors, the method was by acclamation, that is, by shouting out one's choice. In Sparta's case, this common practice had a real twist. A group of men shut up in a nearby building had then to decipher which preference was the loudest. It was rather like a secret ballot where all the voters knew who had selected what and the secret was kept only from those who must decide the outcome. This may not be quite as crazy as it appears. After all, the Spartans valued strength and power above all else, so basing a decision on volume rather than on numbers was consistent with such values.

In her efforts to keep her lands and her helots, Sparta also developed a set of social customs promoting strength, solidarity, patriotism and militarism. New babies were presented to the ephors and if they appeared weak or sickly they were exposed, that is left out in the open to die of hunger, thirst or the ravages of wild animals. In some cultures that practiced exposure, other parents with other priorities could rescue these babies. This was absolutely not the case in Sparta. The rejected babies were pitched off a precipice, so they rarely lived, and never as a desirable adoption prospect.

Boys that passed the test and were reared at home left their mother at the age of seven. They were assigned to small bands led by older boys and overseen by carefully chosen exemplars of adult Spartan perfection. The boys had minimal creature comforts, which included rough beds, one tunic for summer and winter (which was frequently very, very cold), an amazingly unappetizing diet and not nearly enough of it. They were expected to improve their lot by stealing from the helots. If caught, they were not punished for stealing but rather for the ineptitude of being caught.

They were taught reading, counting and patriotic songs and dances, which helped them to master the coordinated movement required by a military unit. Each band of boys played against one another in rough ball games and organized fights in order to give each unit a sense of solidarity. Older boys were then given more explicitly military training.

At the age of twenty, a young man had to be elected, by a unanimous vote, to a group that would be his unit in the army. Their barracks would be where he ate and slept most of the time, even after he married at age thirty. Not to be elected would be such a catastrophe that it doubtless motivated these boys to extreme stoicism under the fiercest challenges.

All this makes clear why our word "Spartan" denotes the most uncomfortable and minimalist accommodations or fare. It also explains the extraordinary heroism and determination of the three hundred Spartans who stood against the Persian hordes at the pass of Thermopylae.* Famously, a Spartan mother, learning of the death of her son, said that he died for Sparta, "As I bore him to do."

The Spartans of classical Greece attributed their improved constitution to a single law-giver, Lycurgus. Modern writers range from treating this as a pure myth to accepting it as an accurate instance of collective memory. In the words of the brilliant classical scholar, A.R. Burn, 'Spartan realities are difficult to discern through the mists of the great Spartan patriotic myth."

There is also a theory that the Spartans adopted their system from some Dorian *poleis* on Crete, which had powerful magistrates and soldier-citizens who took their meals with their military unit. These Dorian aristocrats ruled a much larger subject population held in a form similar to or perhaps identical to helotry. To retain their power, they had to turn to militarism. In both Sparta and Dorian Crete, early promise in the arts collapsed in the face of this cultural choice.

Spartiate rule did not manifest a commitment to Dorian ethno-centrism. Sparta was badly beaten by the Arcadians of Tegea, and this was her last attempt at conquest. She had

---

* Leonides, the Spartan leader, had three hundred Spartans, but not the usual young men. Instead, he brought only men with healthy sons so that their families would not disappear at their death. Each Spartan had seven helots, perhaps three of whom were armed. He also had men from five other *poleis*, for a total of seven thousand armed men. Nevertheless, they were vastly outnumbered. One version of the story says that when the Spartans knew the end was nigh, they sent the others home and bought Hellas time with their lives.

plenty of land and a surfeit of helots. Instead, after avenging the beating, she made an honorable alliance with Tegea and also Elis, home to the sanctuary of Olympia. Other alliances with Arcadians meant that, around 540 B.C., the Spartans or, as they are often called but variously spelled, the "Lacadaemonians," with their allies, controlled the Peloponnese.

Spartan policy was inevitably conservative, even reactionary. She was determined whenever possible to support aristocratic government, oppose the rise of popular and populist *tyranoi* and, failing that, to work tirelessly to topple them. In these respects, Sparta stands in stark contrast to the other great power of the day.

### Athens

"Early Athens has no history, only archeology and legend."* The essential reason for this was that, by Greek standards, Athens had an unusually large amount of arable land. Thus, there were no occasions to export surplus people, and no revolutionary pressures to underwrite an Athenian version of Kypselos. After 600 B.C. that changed quickly.

As more and more peasants were trying to eke out a living from the foothills, with its rocky, inhospitable terrain, hunger was becoming a steadily increasing problem. This contrasted vividly with the fact that the rich were exporting grain to feed an increasing demand for luxury goods for their own conspicuous consumption. The unexpected consequences of the adoption of money, a Lydian invention in

* A.R. Burn

the time of King Croesus, further fueled the flames.

As more time passes since the last harvest, more and more people run out of food. In the past, they had borrowed a quantity of grain in a neighborly fashion and returned the same quantity after they brought in their harvest. With the adoption of money, however, the poor had to borrow the cost of a quantity of grain. They had no theory of the effects of supply and demand. Nevertheless, they could know from experience that, as grain supplies diminish, the price will go up. By the same token, they could understand that after the harvest, when grain is plentiful, the price will drop. This was exactly what happened, with disastrous consequences.

What that meant for the borrowing poor is obvious. They got much less grain for a much higher price when they were buying, and they had to sell much more grain to repay the monetary debt. Thus, they were getting further and further into the hole at an ever-increasing pace. They would then find themselves in the condition of debt bondage. This gave the debt holder permission to mark off their land with stones, indicating his right to seize this land for non-payment and sell its owner into slavery.

The tremendous drawback with this cycle, not only in terms of the misery of the less fortunate, was that Athens, like all Hellenic *poleis*, depended on citizen soldiers for her defense. Meanwhile, as we saw in Corinth, commerce had brought new classes of merchants, sailors, ship builders and manufacturers who had no claim to a say in politics. We have already seen how this leads to political instability.

The ruling Athenians, quite brilliantly and a bit surprisingly, elected a dictator to sort out these problems. Their choice was Solon, who had the confidence of all classes. He was descended from kings, but was only modestly rich. He had traveled as a merchant and was famous for his poems decrying the plight of the poor and excoriating the rich for their greed.

No agreement exists on the exact year of his ascension to the dictatorship, but the most favored candidates are 574 or 572 B.C. Naturally, he did not redivide the land as the poor had hoped he would, and as the great landowners who had chosen him knew he would not. He did cancel all existing debt, which led to an orgy of tossing away the hated boundary stones. Further, he forever banned the selling of free Athenians into slavery. Finally, he organized a project to repurchase all Athenians sold into slavery whose whereabouts could be traced. We do not know how this was financed, but, in view of his writings about the greed of the rich, they probably paid handsomely.

Solon also banned the export of grain. No longer were the rich to increase their fortunes abroad while, at home, their neighbors were starving. Naturally, all this was pleasantly cathartic for the would-be revolutionaries. However, these measures were only temporary solutions to a much deeper problem, the sharp inequities in the quantity and quality of the land held by Athenian citizens.

When the poor again needed to borrow money to buy grain in the waning days before the harvest, that grain would be at its scarcest level and therefore at its most expensive price. Forbidding the rich to export grain would make it less

scarce and thus lower the absolute price. It would not, however, lower its relative price. The poor still needed to borrow
money to buy grain when grain was dear, and sell grain to
pay the money back when grain was cheap. This is precisely
the opposite of the traditional advice on how to get rich: buy
cheap and sell dear.

As a small aside, Sparta never adopted money, largely
because her government was reactionary by instinct and
wary of any of this newfangled stuff. Also, money was frequently used to buy luxury goods from foreign sources, and
Sparta was on a perennial austerity program. As it was,
Sparta dodged the bullet of a problem it could not have fore-
seen and would not have understood.

Solon also overhauled the Athenian constitution, which
was equipped with the usual archaic features. It had an
elected executive, nine archons (meaning regents or rulers)
and a Council made up of "the *best men*," or *eupatridae*,
who got together to discuss the important issues of the day
as they had done since Athens was a village. They met at a
rock called Areopagus and the Council was thus sometimes
referred to as the Areopagite Council and its members as
Areopagites.

There was also an assembly of "the people," by which
was meant male citizens having a specified amount of land.
They had to be consulted about important decisions and
could approve or disapprove. This was not just a façade.
These men were the army. If they strongly disliked the decisions of the Council, they would not fight for them. However, the assembly had no initiative, no power to propose,

and, as we have seen, this is by far and away a greater power than the power to decide. Moreover, the high prestige and esteem enjoyed by the men of the Council, and the humble nature of the Assembly, meant that the former usually, but not always, got their way.

Solon, instead, gave the Assembly real power and influence. He dictated that all free men were to be part of the Assembly, even those with very little land, like the farmers on the barren hills, or none at all, like the newly well-off merchants, shipbuilders and such. He decreed that a man with enough *landed* property to support a warhorse could run for archon. A wealthy merchant could buy land if he fancied a spot of politics or had an axe to grind. Elected archons then served for a year, at the end of which they had to account for their actions in both general and financial matters. Only if a man's conduct in office passed muster with the Assembly, could he then pass into the Areopagite Council.

This changed the balance of power in Athens enormously. Men who were once influential because of their pedigree and inherited wealth had to be popularly elected and then had to account for their actions to this same electorate. Since these men had extreme contempt for both tradesmen and hill farmers, they were quite unhappy with this turn of events.

Solon also created a second council, the People's Council, which took over the old functions of the Areopagite Council to discuss issues, make proposals and recommend candidates for archon. This People's Council consisted of one hundred men from each of the four tribes that could be found in Athens, and that were represented in all the classes. Membership in the People's Council excluded the poor, but the middle farmer, who was a member of the armored infantry, would have been eligible.* Since the councilors were chosen by lot, it was not necessary to be famous to win a place in this august body.

The Areopagite Council was kept as a sort of Supreme Court, to use a modern American analogy. They were the "Guardians of the Laws," and could probably charge, convict and punish anyone whose behavior, in private as well as in public, contravened the strong mores and customs of Athenian life. They also acted as a brake on any rash or drastic innovation. Importantly, however, they had lost the initiative, lost the power to propose, to the People's Council.

By trying to please everyone, Solon pleased no one, and so he threw in the towel, reminded the Athenians that they were bound by a solemn promise to cleave to his dictated constitution for ten years, and left town. He had given the fractious Hellenes of Athens whole new lines of political division. Before his reforms, aristocratic families, with their hangers-on of lesser folk, duked it out for power and prestige in the old Areopagite Council, which only they could join.

By giving political rights to the middle and poorer classes, Solon created new opportunities for new factions. Class rivalry could blend with the old clan rivalry and even older local rivalries. Moreover, the economic woes of the

---

* The term "middle farmer" is widely used to refer to a man with enough resources to equip himself for infantry duty, but who fell below the class of wealthy landowners who comprised the powerful aristocracy.

poor, which had led to debt bondage and slavery and all the rest, had only been swept away for the moment and were bound to reappear. Various strong men, *tyranoi*, tried to rise to the top only to find opposition from other contenders. Instability abounded. In some years, the archon list read *anarchia*, "no archon elected", from which we, of course, get the word anarchy.

Around 570 B.C., Megakles, head of an important aristocratic clan, made a bid for power that was opposed by a coalition of other nobles. In a bold move, he declared himself a champion and defender of Solon's constitution. Wealthy merchants and ship builders, a so-called "Coast" party, flocked to his side to oppose the elitist and reactionary *eupatridae* of the "Plains" party. Before much happened, a third party, the "Hill" party, appeared on the scene led by another ambitious *aristoi*, Peisistratus. These were men left free and with a vote under Solon's constitution, but still agonizingly poor.

Peisistratus made two failed attempts to seize power in Athens, and left after the second to seek his fortune with a band of his followers. He was gone for ten years during which he established rich gold mining concessions. These gave him the wealth that bought a private army of Scythian bowmen, who later became the Athenian police force. With them, he returned to Attica in 546B.C., and beat, somewhere between Marathon and Athens, a citizen army that had been sent against him.

He instituted a modest ten-percent tax on everything and used the revenue to bolster the economic situation of his followers, and to solidify his one-man rule. For the poor farmers with okay land, he made loans to buy a plow and oxen. These loans were soon repaid as a result of the increased yields on these farms. The poorest farmers were those working rocky land on the side of a hill, trying to eke out a living growing grains. He provided them with long-term loans to be used to plant grape vines and olive trees, which can do well under such conditions.

To understand the dynamics here, one must understand the larger world in which Peisistratus functioned. By far the best way to do that is to be found in the historian and geographer William McNeill's *The Shape of European History*.* McNeill begins with the Mediterranean Sea and its contiguous seas, the Black, the Aegean and the Adriatic. He notes the relative ease of their navigation, particularly as compared to the storms and tides of the Atlantic Ocean and its connecting seas. Nevertheless, the Mediterranean produced enough turmoil during the winter months that few ancient mariners would sail at that time. Instead they sailed only from May to October, and then hugging tightly to the coastline.

Since the harvest typically occurred in May or June, the import-export trade in grains could be done by sea in that season with favorable currents. Athens had to import grains, which would only be possible if it had a hinterland where food producers could be compelled or induced to part with a surplus in grain and possibly other food staples. For Athens,

* Quotations in the ensuing section are from McNeill.

the local hinterland in Attica had hill farmers unable even to feed themselves.

Instead, the larger hinterland of the Mediterranean, especially to the north where the climate favors neither grapes nor olives, would be a likely source for the exchange of grains for luxury items such as wine and olive oil. And so it proved to be. McNeill argues that the great "palace" centers of Minoan Crete were early examples of the symbiotic exchange of a large amount of food staples for a much smaller amount of wine and olive oil.

Here is McNeill's argument. In the grain-producing regions, local magnates would extract the surplus by force or by the threat of force. As we noted in discussing Egypt, extracting a surplus by faith is much cheaper than by force. Force means feeding the non-food-producing enforcers, and that means less surplus for the magnate "playing the role of landlord." Some of this surplus the magnates consumed locally, and some of it was exchanged for luxury goods imported by seafaring merchants. McNeill makes the point that the numerical advantage of the local people usually made it impossible for foreigners to seize the goods they wanted, such as grains, metals and timber. Instead, they were forced to trade for them.

He then notes that olive oil and wine could serve as luxury exports because they required some "capital," since the first crop would not bear fruit for several years in the case of grapes, and decades in the case of olive trees. McNeill then adds that some "skill and fairly elaborate machinery" is needed to convert grapes and olives into wine and oil.

Yet once the uses of wine and oil became familiar, landlords and chieftains of the backwoods areas of the ancient Mediterranean, wherever they lived, were willing, indeed eager, to exchange grain and other products of the fields and forests for the precious wine and oil.

Naturally, the terms of these exchanges favored the producers of luxury goods, which he refers to as the "civilized center." He does not review the supply and demand issues here, but the argument is implicit. These "barbarian" northern leaders really, really wanted the wine and olive oil, so demand was high, supply was scarce and the price was steep.

He extends that argument by comparing the relatively small acreage needed for the production of enough wine and oil to the much larger quantity of land required to grow adequate supplies of grains and other food stuffs.

In effect, the pattern of trade enlisted the active cooperation of thousands of distant landlords in the delicate and difficult task of squeezing unrequited goods and services from the peasantry. Only after local magnates had collected a quantity of goods in demand at the civilized center, could they hope to exchange such goods for the wine and oil they came to prize so highly.

McNeill argues that the "special quality of Athenian culture in its Golden Age" was owed profoundly to this "unique geo-economic balance" between wine and oil exporting Athens, the civilized center, and the local magnates of the non-Greek hinterlands eager to provide whatever was demanded by that center in return for the magnate's access to wine and oil. McNeill further argues that the participation of Athenian farmers in public life was enhanced by their role in growing the trees and vines that yielded olive oil and wine. City dwellers, however aristocratic, could not belittle or ignore the producers of the prosperity that benefited the entire *polis*. Neither could they neglect the part that these hill farmers played in Athens' army.

> In this fashion, a firm bond between urban and rural segments of the Athenian citizenry could be maintained. The agricultural producers of Attica, instead of sinking to the level of excluded and oppressed peasantry (as seemed to be happening before Peisistratus [d. 527 B.C.] organized production of wine and oil for export) instead came to embody the very essence of the Greek ideal.

McNeill then reminds us that all the freedom and civil equality of Athens in its Golden Age rested on the "labors of distant cultivators" that actually produced the grain and other goods that sustained the Athenians' high standard of living, and who received nothing in return. He calls this the "collective exploitation of distant communities" and argues that it is no less, and perhaps even more, oppressive than their exploitation by local landlords. McNeill makes a robust argument here. However, he does not specify what local landlords he has in mind.

That said, he returns to his obvious admiration of Athenian society and says that the "real measure of the city's wealth was the leisure its citizens enjoyed without starving." A leisured citizenry of several thousand provided the ideal audience for theater, poetry and practical or theoretical discussions so that "literary, intellectual and artistic creativity has never been so concentrated before or since."

It should be noted that McNeill is attempting to write a history of Europe that relies as little as possible on the doings of great individuals. Instead, he suggests that the meeting of disparate cultures was the real agent of change. In the whole of his book, McNeill rarely names a political leader or a powerful general. He names Peisistratus. This is a measure of the importance of his ability to see an economic opportunity, organize his *polis* to seize it, and channel the resulting affluence into his commitment to the arts.

When Peisistratus induced the Attic farmers to shift their crops to grapes and olives, when he organized the production of wine and olive oil and arranged for their export in exchange for grains and other staple foods, he was creating a command economy. However, unlike the command economies of Egypt, Babylonia and the like, his did not sit on a traditional base of peasants who could provide a "surplus" and still keep themselves alive.

Traditionally, the hill farmers tried to subsist on the grain they could grow and frequently they failed, which is why Peisistratus had to use radical measures. He changed the base. He brought to subsistence farmers the ability to raise cash crops. In addition to planting vineyards and olive trees, these farmers also took up beekeeping, thus producing another luxury cash crop, honey. While they waited for their cash crops to mature, they were kept busy and fed doing a variety of public works, which Pesistratus financed with his modest ten percent across the board tax, and some of his own money as well. This is also a command structure, and it also changes the base. So this is a great example of command as an agent of change, not simply at the top with a change of personnel, but throughout the society as a whole.

McNeill did not write about the command economy aspect of this development because he was probably not familiar with this concept. Pesistratus, doubtless in concert with friends and allies, developed a plan to solve a specific set of problems. It was a good plan, and it worked, partially because Pesistratus and his allies were able to give Athens a generation of social peace while the vines and trees matured.

McNeill's essential argument is both clear and cogent. He was writing *The Shape of European History* against a backdrop of books that posit, explicitly or implicitly, the idea that history is made up of great actors doing momentous deeds. He wanted, instead, to present history as having patterns and structures and constraints. To repeat, his basic argument is that change happens when disparate cultures collide. It is a very sound argument.

History also has accidental fortuitous events and random disasters. From time to time, just the right person lands at just the right place and actually makes a difference. People do innovate and change the world, but they do it under the conditions in which they find themselves.

To illustrate this point, let us return to Athens at the

time of Peisistratus. The poorest peasants of the hills had long had their own rituals, apart from the larger *polis*. One recognized the suffering of Dionysus, the god of wine, who shed his blood in the service of men. It consisted of choral songs, mimic dancing and the sacrifice of a goat, hence the name *trag odia* or goat song.

With these peasants playing a much greater role in politics and the economic health of Athens, other social classes began to be exposed to these ritual songs that they had never previously heard. This cultural exchange, combined with Pesistratus' funding of the arts, most notably of poetry and drama, as part of public life, yielded rich fruit. Within a generation or a bit more, these goat songs reappear, changed beyond all recognition, as tragedy, in the hands of three of its four greatest practitioners ever to live. These were Aeschylus, Sophocles and Euripides. The fourth, of course, being Shakespeare. Meaning no disparagement to the Bard, he was, after all, standing on the shoulders of giants. They, by contrast, were taking a ritual expression of the deepest despair of the poorest among them and raising it to an exultant art form.

If the hill farmers of Attica had remained so marginalized and starving that they died out, and with them their goat songs, would we ever have had an art form called tragedy? Would the world have ever produced a theatrical experience of the same nature but with another name? We can never know the answer to that question because it didn't happen that way.

Before we leave Peisistratus, there is a lovely small story

about him that takes the tyrant out of the *tyranoi*. He very much enjoyed walking in the countryside both as recreation and to check on how things were going with the hill farmers, which we would now call "his political base." One day, he saw a peasant trying to clear his land of lots of large stones. He sent his one attendant to ask the man what sort of products he was getting from his land. "Only aches and pains," the peasant answered, "and of these Peisistratus will be wanting his ten percent." Laughing, Peisistratus introduced himself and promised, as he did not want the aches and pains, to return to town and strike that farm off the tax roles. This he did.

Peisistratus reigned as a *tyranoi* from 546-528 B.C., bringing peace and prosperity to Athens. In these conditions, other innovations in art also flourished. Somewhere around 535 B.C., there was a revolution in vase painting called red figure pottery. Until then, the unadorned pot was red and the designs, often including human figures, were painted in black. Then the details within the figures, like eyes or a mouth or musculature, were etched with a sharp object so that the red color underneath was revealed. This is called black figure pottery.

The new idea was to paint the outlines of the figures in black, leaving the figure itself in the red clay. Then it became possible to paint all the small details within the figures in black. Obviously, painting details gives the artist more control than attempting to etch them out. The designs soared in their creativity and incredible beauty.

Peisistratus, by organizing the production of olive oil

and wine and by facilitating a process by which Athens and Attica could import enough food for prosperity and social peace, played a huge role in one of the most interesting periods in human history. Peter Green summarizes his reign beautifully:

> The main elements we associate with classical Athens were being established–piquant paradox--by a rich dictator who could afford heavy cultural investments without any immediate or tangible returns. Healthy international trade ... coupled with active promotion of the arts made a dynamic formula.

There is no evidence that any Athenians in this period, including Peisistratus, had a "theory" of supply and demand. Instead, they dealt with the empirical reality on the ground that they could trade wine, olive oil and honey for much more grain than the same land could produce. This solution to the poverty of hill farmers created the material foundations for the development of Athenian democracy, as we shall see.

## Democracy in Athens

In 508 B.C., the issue du jour was citizenship. Under Solon's constitution, foreigners with money or useful skills were welcomed and offered the unusual opportunity for citizenship, so long as they settled their families in Athens and formally attached themselves to one of the old Ionic tribes. A coterie of nobles set out to examine the voting roles and found that many of these newcomers had failed to join tribes and were thus, technically, not citizens. The nobles wanted as limited and exclusive suffrage as possible and proposed purging the role of these scofflaws. Ancient law favored their position. Thousands were struck off the list and many more feared to be.

Cleisthenes, a scion of an old aristocratic family, became the champion of the disenfranchised.* He proposed before the Assembly that all free men living permanently with their families in Attica should become citizens by an act of the Assembly. The problem could be solved by tossing out the old Ionic tribes and creating new ones. This practice was common among Greek *poleis* wishing to incorporate a large new immigrant population. Apparently many in the Assembly feared a return to oligarchy, to the rule of the few, and so the measure passed.

It had been vehemently opposed by the archon, Isagoras, who declared the measure to be revolutionary. He then called upon his friend, Kleomenes, one of the two Spartan kings, to come and restore order. The Spartan came, with bodyguards, and he joined Isagoras in denouncing Cleisthenes to the Areopagus, the ancient Athenian version of a Supreme Court, as acting against the constitution. Cleisthenes did not stick around to see what the outcome would be and left to bide his time until his enemies, almost inevitably, reached for too much power.

Backed by the Spartan King, Isagoras and the Areopagus

* Cleisthenes is sometimes spelled Kleisthenes, but that spelling is apparently less popular with modern writers.

banished more than seven hundred households from Attica, all of Cleisthenes' aristocratic clan and their allies. They went on to abolish the People's Council because the Council had to have approved Cleisthenes' proposal before it was put to the Assembly. It was too much for the people to swallow.

Their leaders had been banished, but they had grown accustomed, under Solon's constitution, to governing themselves and to prosperity and good times under the *tyranoi.*[*] The People's Council refused to disband. The men of Athens came out with arms and a will to win the day. Vastly outnumbered, Isagoras and Kleomenes fled with their backers to the Acropolis. The men barricaded them in and, as they had no provisions, on the third morning, they surrendered. Kleomenes departed with his Spartans, leaving behind their arms and, save for Isagoras who was smuggled out with them, their Athenian allies. These were tried before the People's Council and executed under the terms of the law. It is the first recorded case of a people, without leaders, taking military initiative on their own, not as a mob but as a militia. It was only a two- day siege, but it changed the world. As A.R. Burn puts it, with delicate irony, "A minor action, really – like the fall of the Bastille."

Cleisthenes was then free to return and implement his reforms. As promised, he abolished the four old tribes. Citizenship was thereafter based on membership in a small, local political unit called a deme. The immigrants were probably already incorporated into these local institutions,

---

* Peisistratus and his two sons who succeeded him one after the other are the *tyranoi* referred to here.

each of which had a headman and a small treasury to finance local projects. Cleisthenes, as inventive and imaginative as Solon, grouped these demes into thirty units, which he called "Thirds." He then built ten new tribes, assigning each of them three "Thirds," one from the plains, representing landed interests, one from the coast, representing commercial and shipping interests and one from the hills, Peisistratus' former political base.

He sought above all else to create *polis* unity. Each tribe cut across traditional class barriers. Each contained three non-contiguous "Thirds," which undermined any parochial ties. Each tribe was named after an Attic hero and the names were selected and assigned by the Oracle of Delphi. To further legitimize these ten new tribes, they engaged in competitions in both athletics and music. Each tribe also provided a regiment in the army, electing new officers, the Generals, to command them under the war archon.

Any demesman could nominate another for the new People's Council, enlarged from four hundred to five hundred members. The fifty councilors from each tribe were selected by lot from among the nominees. The year was divided into ten parts (roughly thirty-six days each) and each tribe's fifty councilors took it in turn to be "in presidency," with the order again decided by lots. During their time in office, they were called "the Presidents," *prytaneis*, and the period of time was called a *prytaneia*. They acted as a sort of steering committee during meetings of the full Council or the Assembly.

Every afternoon, the *prytaneis* chose, by lot, one of their number to be the Duty Officer, who held the office from sunset to sunset, with a chain of office, custody of the state seal and the keys to the Treasury. For that day, the Duty Officer lived in a mess immediately adjacent to the Council Chamber with sixteen councilors from his tribe whom he selected. No one could hold the position of Duty Officer more than once, nor could he sit on the Council more than twice, and not in consecutive years.

All this added up to two very important things. At any given moment, a huge portion of the male citizen population had direct experience of day-to-day administration, and there was always, at any hour of the day or night, a Duty Officer and a committee to be found in the event of an emergency. They could decide quickly whether to convoke immediate meetings of the Council and the Assembly, and to alert the war archon and the generals.

*Kratos* is power in Greek, and because the demes had *kratos*, the system came to be called a democracy. However, some elements of the old system remained in place. As per Solon's constitution, only men who could support a warhorse were eligible to be one of the nine archons. If their term in office was deemed satisfactory by the Assembly, they then joined the Areopagite Council for life. This body continued to be a sort of ultimate court that could declare legislation unconstitutional. As it contained all of Athens' primary political, military and religious experts, its views commanded general respect.

The following spring, the Spartan king Kleomenes, still smarting under his "mistreatment" by the Athenians, and convinced that this democratic revolution was dangerous, was joined by his fellow king in rallying the armies of the Peloponnesian League to crush Athens and its revolution. Other *poleis*, smelling a chance at plunder, joined in. The Athenians, determined to stand against all odds, faced their main enemy with their ranks in order and their heels dug in, only to experience what must have seemed a miracle.

The enemy did not advance. Perhaps they had expected a rag-tag mob and were stunned by the Athenians' discipline. In any case, the Corinthians, sometime allies of Athens, developed qualms of conscience and withdrew. Then, the Spartan king, Damaratos, expressed doubts about the wisdom of his fellow king, Kleomenes, and his plan to get revenge. Their allies, seeing the kings in dispute, decided to give up. "Without a blow struck the great Peloponnesian army went home." A.R. Burn called this "Athens' revolutionary war," and he quotes Herodotus on the subject:

> It shows how splendid a thing is political equality; the Athenians under the tyrants were no better soldiers than their neighbors, but once they were rid of them they were far the best of all … Once they were free, every man was zealous, in his own interest.

Part of the self-interest of each free Athenian fighter was to submit to a collective discipline, which might frighten off their enemies, and failing that, would stand them in good stead in the face of an attack.

## The Persians

During the intimidating run up to Kleomenes' invasion, Athens, under the guidance of Cleisthenes, had asked the Persian Satrap at Sardis for Persian protection. The response was absolutely predictable. Of course, Persia would help so long as Athens would offer up earth and water, symbolizing the gift of all her territory to the Great King. Feeling quite desperate, the ambassadors agreed to the deal. Once they returned home and found the crisis had passed, they tried to repudiate their promise, but Persia was having none of that.

The ensuing wars between the Hellenes and Persia's polyglot armies have been nicely chronicled by many fine writers, including Burn. Tom Holland's *Persian Fire* reads very much like an adventure story. The two best known and probably most important land battles involved, respectively, the Spartans and the Athenians. These were the battle of Thermopylae and the battle of Marathon. Holland provides a detailed and yet stirring account of both events.

At the pass at Thermopylae, three-hundred Spartans, with some help, in truth, held off the Persian hordes for days and might have been able to do so indefinitely. Sadly, but inevitably, a Hellene, with an itchy palm, literally sold them out by agreeing to show the Persians an obscure path around the pass, which required local knowledge. In this way, the Persians got behind the Spartans and killed them all. Two men blinded in earlier fighting had been sent home, and it is from them that we have a great story. When Xerxes, the Persian king, said that his minions would fill the sky with arrows, a Spartan replied, "Good, then we shall fight in the shade."

At Marathon, democracy was put to the test. For the first time, Athenian regiments were made up of the new tribes, not the old local alliances led by powerful, aristocratic clans. They fought in a formation called a phalanx, where each man's shield overlapped the shield of the man beside him. If anyone fell back or, worse, ran away, the whole line was fatally weakened. Democracy held the high ground against wave after wave of attackers. Fortunately, the ground was too rocky for the Persian chariots. Giving up, the Persians first loaded their horses onto their ships. Seeing this, the Athenians counterattacked and it was a complete rout.

The story goes that a famous runner was sent to warn the townspeople that the Greeks had won against incredible odds, so that those left at home ought not to surrender the city. This run gave its name to the marathon race of today. The race is, indeed, the same length as the distance between the plain where the Greek victory took place and Athens proper. However, and more stunning than a lone heroic runner, the whole army raced home to make sure no traitor accepted a bribe to open the gates of the city.

Xerxes could not conquer Hellas without destroying the Athenian fleet. This he attempted at Salamis (480 B.C.) and not only failed, but was compelled to watch his own fleet destroyed. He went home, leaving half his expeditionary force behind. Meanwhile, Athens had been burned to the ground and was at her lowest point. The next year, the Spartan army, with its Peloponnesian allies, joined forces with eight thousand Athenians and six hundred refugees from Plataea, which had also been torched. They found the Persians still at Plataea, and in a battle beautifully described in Holland's *Persian Fire*, they evicted the Persians from Hellas forever.

The story of how the belligerently reactionary Spartans and the democratically progressive Athenians came to be allied is often recounted in rich detail. What no one appears to have noticed is that, behind these lavish accounts, there existed an essential structural similarity between the two states. Indeed, the structural similarities in their systems of governance are fundamental to the histories of both Athens and Sparta when they each confronted the Persian threat. They were both governed, in large part, by collectives rather than individuals subject to bribery or political decapitation.

Moreover, Sparta and Athens were each governed by the identical type of collective. In each, the Assembly, which was also the army, voted on issues of war and peace. The fact that each had an assembly that was made up of its army cannot be emphasized too strongly. Faced with the demand for complete submission to Persian authority, Sparta and Athens had the same reply. There was no way the army in either *polis* would vote themselves into Persian slavery. They would, of course, fight. Whatever this one said to that one or how this or that detail played out, the results would always be the same. The Spartiate class and the Athenian citizenry would always vote to fight. As they had a common enemy in the Persians, and two systems of government having in common their collective nature, this enemy could not win except in battle. So, despite their many differences, once they faced a common threat, Sparta and Athens would, perforce, both chose active resistance and thus be allied.

## Proud and Mighty Athens

After the Persian defeat, the Spartans returned to their parochial concerns, while the Athenians set out to exploit their newly discovered military might. Right after their victory at Salamis, the Athenian fleet seized the Hellespont, the ancient name for the Dardanelles, denying Persia access to Macedonia and Thrace, and opening the Black Sea to Greek shipping. Then, over several years, the Athenians "liberated" Hellenic settlements along the northern and eastern coasts of the Aegean, only to enroll them in an anti-Persian league dominated by Athens.

As a maritime power, Athens could not take on the Persians inland, and so the avowed purpose of the league was achieved with the recapture of the Hellenic Aegean islands. At this point, it should have been possible to transform the league into an alliance among equals. Instead, Athens, retaining her dominance, rededicated the league to Aegean peace and the extension of trade. The Aegean peace was to be enforced by an Athens strengthened by tribute from her allies. In fact, the tribute monies were largely spent funding public works at home, most notably the construction of the Parthenon. At the same time, the Athenian merchant classes were the prime beneficiaries of trade protection.

Athens then began throwing her weight around peninsular Hellas in a way that riled the Spartans. As McEvedy puts it, they were not "prepared to tolerate indefinitely the repeated needling of the greedy, cocksure Athenians." Four wars ensued, known collectively as the Peloponnesian War. On the sidelines, the Persians gleefully fueled the conflict. Athens was a power at sea. Sparta was superior on land. For the third of these conflicts, the Persians bought the Spartans a fleet, and they used it to upset the balance of the Athenian league. Then, when Sparta began to beat the drums of an anti-Persian campaign, Persian gold was re-routed to Athens and Thebes. At the end of the fourth war, won by Sparta, it was evident that both sides were exhausted and lacked the political will to fight on.

Still, generations of Hellenes were schooled to war, and many of them rented themselves out as mercenaries. One such group included Xenophon, an Athenian writer of decidedly conservative principles. In *A March Up Country*, an intriguing account of his experiences, Xenophon recounts the heroic Greek fight for the throne in service of the Persian king's younger brother. The Hellenes brought victory to their cause, but their prince died just as his would-be throne was won. His other supporters melted away, leaving a group of ten thousand Greek mercenaries in a sea of Persian soldiers.

Their leaders approached the Persian headquarters under a flag of truce, and they were unscrupulously murdered. Only one managed to stagger back to camp to warn the others. Leaderless, in a strange land with no maps or guides, these men were in trouble, and Xenophon had a dream in which he was called upon to lead them. The next day, he gave a stirring speech in which he invited every man to make suggestions, and then caused the group as a whole to vote on these.

Every morning, while they marched toward what they hoped would be home, several parties would explore in different directions, and each would return with a report. The group listened and then voted on which way to proceed. Someone had the bright idea of leaving their war spoils behind and letting the Persians carry these for them.

Xenophon bullied and cajoled them into never giving up, and in this way kept them going. The great irony of this tale is that a very conservative gentleman, with a strong disdain for democracy as a system, turned to it when his back was to the wall. Let everyone speak and let the best, most effective ideas win. Thus they made it home safely. Moreover, in the final confrontation, they took back all their possessions, which the Persians had been packing during their long pursuit. It is an extraordinary story.

The Hellenes remained a nation, though divided in their political ideas and preferences. They never did come together as a single, unified government, as a state. National characteristics of exclusivity, prickly local patriotism and almost unending internecine warfare made the creation of an Hellenic state a virtual impossibility. Instead, as we shall see next, they were forcibly brought under unitary political rule by a succession of empires. We turn to that story next.

# Four Empires and a Nation State

**IN** the last chapter we examined the concepts of nation and state using examples from ancient Hellas to flesh out the details. In this chapter we will focus on defining what is an empire and what is a nation-state. One again we will focus on the Hellenes as they go through the phases suggested by the title.

Empire is a word with many meanings. A captain of industry, especially a monopolist, might be described as having an empire in the commodity being monopolized. Thus one can speak of a bubblegum empire or a slot machine empire and there is nothing really wrong with that usage. However, it absolutely does not work for our purposes.

Instead, we will define empire in narrowly political terms to refer to a unified, usually hierarchical, system of governance in which the governed consist of more than one nation. If the subjects were all of the same nationality, the political unit would be a nation-state. Empires are a kind of state, a unit of governance, but of a special type that warrants its own category, with an emphasis on national diversity. So, with a clear idea of what is meant by empire, we will see the Hellenes fall under the dominance of another group of Greek speakers.

### The Macedonians

Macedonia lies to the north of the Hellenic mainland and has both rugged mountains and a fertile alluvial plain. The mountains produced wild, deeply divided peoples who were governed by their own strongmen. However, by the early years of the fifth century B.C., a family called the Argeads founded a royal dynasty to govern the plain and to organize its defenses against repeated predation by the mountain folk and others. Peter Green gives us a glimpse of their political history:

> Alexander I steered Macedonia through the Persian Wars by collaborating with both sides as occasion dictated. Perdiccas II spent much of the Peloponnesian War switching his allegiance with dizzying rapidity, and selling shipbuilding lumber simultaneously to Athens and her opponents, like some primitive armaments consortium.

Green goes on about kings, named and unnamed, to describe a situation of ever- increasing danger from ambitious neighbors coupled with "Borgia-like intrigue at home." This was the mess inherited by Philip II, the first king with real relevance to our story. However, before we press on with the details, we must know a bit more about the Macedonians and their relationship to the Hellenes.

Except for certain elites, like Philip, they spoke only an extremely rustic form of Greek that was beyond the comprehension of the Athenians and, for this reason, many of their writers insisted that the Macedonians were not related to the Hellenes at all. This we know to be false. They did, however, differ from the Hellenes in several important aspects, enough to be considered a separate nationality.

First, they did not divide themselves up into *poleis*. Macedonia was a kingdom. This was a truly huge difference. Aristotle argued that living in a *polis* was essential to any definition of what makes a person a person and not a barbarian. To fully appreciate this issue we turn to A.R. Burn:

> It must be added that our maps usually underemphasize the disunity of classical Greece, since the appearance of the Greek names of regions, such as Arcadia, Boiotia, Ionia, with boundaries drawn between them, but not between the cities within them, gives the impression to a superficial glance that these regions at least are states. Except Laconia, under the rule of Sparta, and Attica, they were not. Achaia contained twelve small *poleis* or cities, Phokis as many as thirty ... Boiotia fourteen, some of which had over ten thousand inhabitants, no insignificant figure by Greek standards.

Such was the fragmentation and exclusivity that characterized Hellas. How profoundly it contrasts with a single, unified kingdom cannot be emphasized enough.

As they had to fight constantly with the barbarian Thracians and Illyrians, the Macedonians had maintained a "Homeric" style monarchy with a strong king charged with both political and military leadership. As noted above, the first of these that figures in our story was Philip II, who ascended the throne in 359 B.C.* He was a brilliant soldier, an able orator, a charming and witty companion, and according to Burn, "the greatest diplomatist in the Greek world, which was full of that craft."

He was a great advocate of prisoner exchanges. In an early example, he traded the mercenaries and Athenians he held captive for Macedonian prisoners of war. In this way, he made his enemies less implacable and his troops profoundly loyal. A rarity among the world's most successful generals, he was prouder of his diplomatic than his military victories.

The discovery of gold allowed him to buy a large mercenary army, and he used it to fight the Illyrians and Thracians all year round, honing his troops to perfection. Any lull in the fighting was occupied by drills designed to keep them in top form. He borrowed successful strategic moves from the best, and invented a few of his own. His absolute failure to recognize or respect the notion of a limited fighting season not only made him different from the Hellenic citizen-soldiers who fought only in season, but also was deeply resented by them.

---

* He had served under his older brother, yet another King Perdiccas, who died. Philip then became regent during the minority of Perdiccas' young son. When the Macedonians had realized his extraordinary talents as a leader, they acclaimed him king.

In his final battle against the combined forces of Athens and Thebes, Philip positioned one flank of his men with their overlapping shields well below the high ground of a sloping hill. As the Athenians charged, he ordered his men to retreat a foot at a time until the Athenians were exhausted. When the Athenian generals shouted for their troops to keep up the assault and drive the Macedonians back home, Philip reportedly growled under his breath, "Amateurs!"

The Athenians had held the high ground, a strategic advantage, but they left it to pursue the "retreating" Macedonians. This, in turn, caused them to lose touch with their Theban allies and to leave a weak and vulnerable hole in the middle of the Greek line. As we know from the last chapter, keeping their overlapping shields perfectly aligned was essential to the success of a Greek phalanx. The ensuing debacle spelled the end of Greek independence and its first taste of imperial rule.

This was the famous Battle of Chaeronea of 338 B.C.. In its aftermath, all the *poleis* were compelled to join the Pan-Hellenic League, a creation of Philip's that placed them directly under his command. He announced that its purpose was to launch a massive invasion of Persia, which had briefly lost its mastery of Egypt only to retake control. What made a huge difference in Philip's calculations was that this reconquest, like all Persian victories over the previous century, had been accomplished by using Hellenic mercenaries. Philip knew he had the finest Hellenic army ever assembled, and he was utterly confident in his victory.*

Sadly, his confidence was premature. In 336 B.C., he was assassinated, some argue by the connivance of the Persians and others by order of his wife, Olympias, mother of Alexander (later called "the Great"). Openly polygamous, his most recent marriage had just resulted in a son who might have challenged his older half-brother's claim to the throne. As it was, young Alexander showed his mettle from the start and was quickly accepted as a worthy replacement for his father.

It was Alexander who set off to conquer Persia, and he succeeded exactly as his father had expected to do, had he lived. He pushed his army further east than the eastern frontier of Persia at its largest, and he was only stopped when his troops refused to budge another step. In Bactria, in the vicinity of modern Uzbekistan, he left a number of troops too wounded to travel, and they became the local elites, an Hellenic outpost in central Asia.

Some scholars argue that Philip's death was a disaster because he would have accepted the Persian offer of everything west of the Euphrates River, while Alexander did not. This would have meant a smaller and more manageable territorial addition, and one that might have remained attached to the Mediterranean world by virtue of its proximity.

As it was, Alexander made no innovations to the Persian political structure, merely placing Macedonians and Greeks

---

* Burn provides the following anecdote. "'A wonderful people are the Athenians,' said Philip; 'they produce ten generals every year; I have only found one in my whole life, and that is Parmenion.' He refers to his right-hand man, and the only man of his generation to approach his own military prowess."

in all the top positions of power. It was another classic case of political decapitation. He used that same technique in Egypt by having an important priest name him the son of god, and hence pharaoh. In Persia, Alexander did make one dramatic attempt to merge the Hellenic and Persian peoples by insisting that his officers marry noble Persian women. When he died, most of these marriages were dissolved.

The key problem with Alexander's reign was that, despite frequently risking his life, he made no provision for the governance of his people after his death. He died in Babylon in June of 323 B.C., perhaps of malaria, possibly of poisoning, or, equally possibly, of alcoholism. In any case, he died young and left only a posthumous son and a retarded brother. It was not long, then, before his generals began to fight over the spoils. It is not an edifying tale.

So, the first empire to subsume the Hellenes was the Macedonian empire forged by Philip II. His son, Alexander the Great, ruled Hellas and the many nations that had once comprised the Persian empire. At his death, Hellas ceased to be part of an empire and became, at least in theory, a kingdom ruled by one of Alexander's generals, a Macedonian Greek. The "in theory" part refers to the complete inability of the king to prevent endless warfare between the various *poleis*.

This fighting was reflective of the Hellenic traits of exclusivity and belligerence toward their neighbors. They did not, as the saying goes, suffer one another gladly. To this was added the problem of massive external provocation. Another Macedonian general, Ptolemy, ruled as pharaoh in Egypt. He wanted to extend his rule to cover Hellas and Macedonia, so he bribed various *poleis* to fight one another, and thus destabilize his rival's realm. In the richness of time, all this chaos brought another player onto the stage, one for whom order was the most important element in safety and trade.

## The Romans

Rome had been involved in two wars with Carthage, the other great power in the western Mediterranean. These were called the Punic Wars because Carthage was a Phoenician city and *Poeni* is Latin for Phoenician. In the Second Punic War, Hannibal, their most formidible general, had been a nuisance to Rome, to say the very least, although the Romans won in the end.

During this period, Philip V of Macedonia was busily trying to topple his rival in Egypt. He failed, but he did scoop up some Aegean islands, to the dismay of the biggest players in that region, Pergamum and Rhodes. They appealed to Rome for help, and since Philip had been allied with Hannibal, and victorious Rome now had resources to spare, they agreed to teach him a lesson. In 198 B.C,. a Roman army landed in Greece.

What happened next is beautifully described by Colin McEvedy in *The New Penguin Atlas of Ancient History*:

> Philip had only one card to play, the brute force of the Macedonian phalanx. An experienced Roman general was later to say that the onslaught of a phalanx was the most frightening thing he had ever seen in his life, but

it was no longer the war-winning weapon it had been. A Roman legion was a more flexible formation, and once its swordsmen were in among them, the lines of Macedonian pikes quickly lost order and discipline.

Philip was driven back into Macedonia proper and forced to promise to stay there. The Roman Senate declared the rest of Greece to be "free," or at any rate, free to do whatever it pleased, provided it had asked for and received Senatorial approval first.

This was the beginning of a huge change in the complexion of the Roman Empire. Its annihilation of Carthage had given Rome western boundaries extending along the Mediterranean coast to what is now France and Spain, as well as some inland territory in both. Rome also gained fertile coastal property in North Africa, such that her boundaries touched those of Ptolemaic Egypt. In these areas, the language of trade, the *lingua franca*, would become Latin, or a "rustic" version of Latin called *lingua rustica*.

By contrast, Greek was the *lingua franca* of the new eastern territories, all once governed by Macedonian elites. The decades after Alexander's death saw the rise and eventual triumph of "Hellenism," the name we give to both an aesthetic and a lifestyle that were intrinsically Greek . New towns were built along Greek lines and old towns were reshaped to resemble, as much as possible, the Greek ideal. At the same time, the language was spreading from the elites to the bureaucracy and the marketplace. It may well have seeped down to become the speech of the common people, but, until very recently, their voices were not often part of the written record. The Roman Empire, at its height, was almost evenly divided between the Greek-speaking East and the Latin- speaking West.

From 171-168 B.C., the Romans had to deal with Macedonia again. They abolished the monarchy and divided the territory into four parts. In 148 B.C., there was another outburst. Rome crushed it and annexed the country for direct rule by Roman officials. Greek factionalism on the Balkan Peninsula, in old Hellas proper, continued unabated to the great irritation of the Senate. In 146 B.C., it too was brought under direct Roman rule.*

## Byzantium

Jumping ahead to the fourth century of our era, the Roman emperor Diocletian took the imperial title by force and then tried to stabilize an Empire that had suffered the scourge of civil war between generals for several generations. One step was to divide the Empire into Western and Eastern halves, each with its own Augustus (head man) and Caesar (second in command). Thus began the third empire to rule over the Hellenes.

His successor, Constantine, chose, as his eastern capital, a small Greek settlement, strategically placed at the

---

* On a much lighter note, Mel Gibson, the director of *The Passion of the Christ*, was asked why he had the Roman soldiers in the Levant speaking Latin instead of Greek. He offered two reasons. First, Latin is a more familiar language to American viewers, and second, we do not know how Greek of that period was pronounced. In fact, we have no way of knowing how ancient Latin was pronounced either. Oh, well ...

head of the straits leading to the Black Sea. It was called Byzantion in Greek, and Byzantium in Latin. Constantine renamed it for himself as Constantinople or Constantine's *polis*. He relocated his government to the much richer Eastern Empire and caused the "surplus" grain from Egypt to be rerouted from the city of Rome to Constantinople, which played a huge part in the subsequent collapse of the Western Roman Empire.

In the fifth century of our era, as the West was falling, some Latin-speaking Senators fled to Constantinople, where they demanded to be recognized as the primary rulers of all that bore the name of Rome. As Greek speakers dominated every element of governance, these upstarts were soon put in their place. This resulted in a rather peculiar situation. For the next several centuries, Greek-speaking rulers of Greek-speaking people would call themselves "East Romans" and their empire "East Rome."

This makes so little sense to the modern mind that some-one, somewhere decided to call this the Byzantine Empire and the name stuck. However, it must be noted, indeed insisted upon, that they never called themselves Byzantines. To their way of thinking, they were "East Romans" and everybody living in the west were "Franks."

## The Ottoman Turks

By 1453, the Ottoman Turks controlled all of the East Roman Empire except Egypt and the Levant, which belonged to the Mamluk Sultanate, and the city of Constantinople, the last stronghold of the dying Empire. Mehmet the Conqueror was determined to blow down the walls, which had stood for almost one thousand years. He had canons built at the site of the siege for just this purpose.

Finally, the walls began to crumble and the Turks were able to get into the city. They taunted the Greeks with the cry, "We're in the city! We're in the city!" In Greek, *Is tan polis! Is tan polis!* The only problem was that they didn't get the pronunciation quite right. So Constantinople became Istanbul.* With the fall of Constantinople, there was no longer any state, any unit of governance, in which Greeks governed themselves.

Greek speakers often did very well in the Ottoman world, even rising to positions of political power, but only as "slaves" of the Sultan, and only as individuals. The Vizier, the highest political position after the Sultan, was the Sultan's slave, as the Sultan would say that he, himself, was the "slave of Allah." A number of Viziers were Greek speakers, as were many other civil servants, merchants and diplomats, and they were increasingly found in parts of the Ottoman Empire other than Hellas. Similarly, over the centuries, other peoples ruled by the Ottomans wandered in and settled in Hellas. This would have important consequences several centuries later.

### The Nation-State

By the early nineteenth century, a new age was dawning

---

* Foreigners usually ignored the change and persisted in calling it Constantinople. So, in 1930, the Turks issued an edict officially banning the use of non-Turkish names for the city.

with a new vision of how people should be governed. The French Revolution and the rise of Napoleon had set Europe ablaze with wars and shifting coalitions. In the end, Great Britain, Austria, Prussia and Russia emerged as the so-called "Great Powers" who had beaten Napoleon and sent him off to an obscure and isolated island to die. The Great Powers then set about framing the conditions of their newly won peace.

One of the ideas that had emerged was the notion that the proper unit of governance was the nation-state, a government staffed by people sharing the nationality of the governed. Napoleon had ignored this idea completely. He gave Spain to his brother and parts of Italy to other family members. Now that he was gone for good, a general European housecleaning could be undertaken. It would include a highly politicized version of the "nation-state."

For a variety of reasons, the Ottoman Empire was decaying badly, though it would limp along until the end of the First World War, where it would choose the losing side. A number of its component nations hoped to win support for independence. For the most part, the Great Powers did not look favorably at carving up the Turkish Empire because each worried that another would then have new allies and the delicate balance of power might be tipped against them. The one exception was Hellas.

## The Philhellenes

The educated classes of Europe and America were brought up to revere Classical Greece, producer of Aristotle,

Sophocles, Plato, et al. These included virtually every important political elite. They were therefore more willing to take a favorable outlook on the recreation of Classical Greece in a modern nation-state. Ironies abound here. The whole notion of a nation-state would have been an anathema to ancient Greeks, who were convinced that the *polis* was the most perfect unit of government.

Moreover, the Greeks seeking independence were "Greek" only in the sense that they were divided into a great many factions, arguing fiercely with each other about how and when independence should come about and what form it should take. Many of their supporters, called Philhellenes, which means lovers of the Hellenes, believed that they would be liberating the descendents of Solon, Pesistratus, Cleisthenes and those who had lived alongside of them, had heard their speeches and seen them in action.

This was not so. A plague in the seventh century had wiped out most native Hellenes, making way for a huge immigration of Slavic peoples. This remains, to this day, a very unpopular fact to bring up to Greeks. A wonderful incident illustrates this point. In 1910, a British diplomat asked a peasant about his nationality. The peasant replied, vehemently, that he was a Greek. However, he said it in Albanian.

When a war of independence broke out in 1821, a number of these Philhellenes turned up to volunteer. For the most part they were worse than useless. The Germanic ones were forever challenging each other to duels, so they came to be called "etiquette soldiers." Their attempts to introduce European fighting tactics were a disaster. These "Greeks" had for some time developed successful guerrilla tactics, which most nearly resembled those of the Afghan mujaheddin.

The single most helpful Philhellene was the poet Lord Byron. He arrived in Greece in January of 1824, with an entourage of nine servants, a personal physician and an untold number of handsome uniforms. He ran from pillar to post attempting to unify the disparate factions. He failed completely, but, and this is a huge but, he died trying. The dominant sensibility of the age was Romanticism, and what could be more romantic than a great Romantic poet dying to insure the rebirth of Hellas?

It galvanized European public opinion and the people clamored for their leaders to induce the Turks to give up at least a part of what had been classical Hellas. Given the Ottoman's weakness, that was not too difficult. In 1832, at the Convention of London, Greece was made the "independent" Kingdom of Greece, under the protection of the new trio of powers, the United Kingdom, France and Russia. Naturally, her "protectors" endowed her with a king of their own choosing.

He was a Bavarian, which was actually a bit less nutty than it sounds. There was no Greek royal family extant. They could not elevate one of the major players in Greek politics to royal status as this would cause all the other factions to unite against that choice. Neither could they let the factionalized Greeks decide for themselves because that would result in either a stalemate or a civil war. Either would defeat the purpose of liberating Hellas.

They chose Otto, the seventeen year-old son of Ludwig

of Bavaria.* Otto's reign was not especially successful, and in 1862, the "protecting powers" urged him to leave. Indeed, they actually held a plebiscite to see who the people wanted as their next king. The overwhelming victor was Alfred, the second son of Queen Victoria and Prince Albert, largely because the British navy still controlled the eastern Mediterranean.

From a Greek perspective, the advantage here was that the British might use this power to induce the Turks to release more of the land that once was Hellas, so that the Kingdom might be made larger. From the perspective of the French and Russians, the precise disadvantage of Alfred was that the British already had too much power in the region, and to have a son as King of Greece would guarantee them yet another ally. So, they vetoed the choice of the people and brokered a deal amongst themselves.

They hit upon the choice of a Danish prince, William of Holstein-Sonderburg-Glucksburg, whose father became King Christian IX of Denmark the very next year. William would rule as King George I, King of the Hellenes. The change of title from "King of Greece" was a definite signal that he wanted more of "Hellas" liberated from the Turks. In this, he was aligning himself completely with the one shared aspiration of every Greek faction, more territory under Greek control.

We have now come full circle and explained why the single most important fact about Greek history is that there

---

* For the record, the Ludwig who built the fanciful, extravagant castles in Bavaria was a different Ludwig.

was no such country as Greece until 1832. Failure to appreciate that fact makes any little tidbits one might read about Greece unintelligible. So, for example, the writer of a history of Greece for a guidebook to Greece found out that the Ottoman Turks took Constantinople in 1453 and wrote that the result was that the State of Greece disappeared for several centuries. A thing that did not exist cannot disappear.

In the ancient world, the Hellenes chose to be divided into separate political units, into *poleis*, and given the view that living in a *polis* defined you as human, they were unlikely to change on their own. However, as a result of those divisions, they were recurrently conquered by much larger units into which they were subsumed. Our four empires, of course, are the Macedonian, the Roman, the East Roman or Byzantine and the Ottoman Turk.

Three facts came together to make possible, in 1832, the creation of the Kingdom of Greece. The first was the growing organization of Europe into nation-states, and the consequent view that this was the proper order of things. Now, it is not at all clear that the residents of Hellas comprised a common nation in 1832, as evidenced by the chap who announced he was Greek in Albanian some eighty years later. On the other hand, he did "get" that the international community wanted to see the Greeks as a nation. This community was deluding itself at the time and for some time in the future. However, delusions can be powerful incentives to action. The nation-state momentum was not going to be derailed by a glitch in the nation part of the equation.

The second factor in the birth of Greece as a state was

the make-up of the political elites in Europe and America, though the latter played only a peripheral role. They came from a cadre of men for whom a classical education was the mark of a "gentleman," and who had enough leisure time to acquire one. Ironically, one would suppose that a classical education would have made them aware of how committed the ancients were to the *polis* ideal, and how repugnant they would have found the whole notion of a nation-state. Then, too, it is easy enough to see the past through the prism of a popular value system of one's own era.

The third factor powering Greece toward statehood was a fluke, and accounts less for the facts and much more for the timing. The death of a great Romantic poet at a time when all art was dominated by Romanticism brought the "liberation" of the noble Greeks to the forefront of the popular imagination. And thus, in 1832, there was a country called Greece for the very first time.

With the introduction of universal public education and the institutionalizing of the Greek language and modern Greek culture in the mid twentieth century, she became a nation. So what does it matter that many of them had Slavic ancestors? Nationality has to do with language and culture, not with the gene pool. Greece, today, is a modern nation-state.

## A Pause to Chuckle

The succession of King George I of the Hellenes invites a small addendum, which happens to be a very funny story. Some decades later, King George was back in Denmark for a family reunion. Present were his older sister and her husband, Edward, Prince of Wales, usually known as Bertie. Also present were his younger sister and her husband, Alexander III, Tsar of all the Russians. These three gentlemen, no longer young, decided to take a gentle constitutional. Along the way, they became so caught up in their discussion of European politics that they lost sight of the time.

When they caught sight of it, they realized that they had strayed much too far from home to get back in time for dinner. Parenthetically, it speaks volumes for the time and place that three such important men could stroll around the countryside unattended. As luck would have it, an old Danish farmer with a horse and cart happened by and agreed to give these gentlemen a lift.

As they were riding along, it occurred to George that it might be fun to have the farmer on, as the British say. So he proceeded to introduce himself and his companions. "I am George, King of the Hellenes. This is my brother-in-law, Edward, Prince of Wales, and my other brother-in-law, Alexander, Tsar of all the Russians." The farmer smiled, tipped his hat, and replied, "Glad to meet you, gents! I'm Napoleon Bonaparte!"

# Our Greco-Roman Heritage

**IN** 1981, Greece entered the European Union. At that time, and for more than two decades to come, she was the only member state to have no shared borders with any other member state. The decision to bring in Greece well before any of her neighbors reflected the western assumption that Greece was an integral part of the west. In turn, that assumption rests on the notion that Europe was built on a Greco-Roman foundation, and thus has a Greco-Roman heritage.

European colonists brought that heritage with them to North America and it is still present today, at least as a vague, amorphous notion. Unfortunately, it is a notion increasingly divorced from any real understanding of what it actually means and, importantly, what it does not mean. At my first mention of that heritage, most of my students looked reproachful. "Not you, too," their faces seemed to say, as I used a phrase they had heard before but never understood. There was also an element, especially from

Asian, Hispanic and African American students, of pressing and serious doubt that they had any such heritage at all.

Before trying to flesh out what the concept does and does not mean, I needed to persuade the students that they actually engaged in behaviors that could be traced back to Greece, while other elements in their lives had their roots in Rome.

I posed a series of questions to them. Could they name several countries in Western Europe? As a group, they did very well, with England, France, Italy, and Germany being routinely selected. Could they also name several countries in the Far East? Again, they did well as a group, which was not surprising given the number of them who were Asian-Americans.

Now, if you were going to travel from California to Western Europe by the most proximate route, would you head east or west? The geographically challenged would shout out "west!" Others, taking more time to think, or perhaps relying on personal experience, gave the correct answer, which is, of course, east. Similarly, if you were to travel from San Francisco to the Far East by the most proximate route, you would head west.

None of this makes any sense at all except in the light of our shared Greek heritage. We use directional designations that worked for ancient Greeks, but make no sense at all in terms of America's geographic position in the world. Western Europe was and is west of Greece. The Near East was east of Greece and quite close by. The Far East was east of Greece and far away. The Middle East was between these two extremes. Modern Americans talk about the world's geography in terms inherited from the ancient Greeks.

Moreover, rarely do any of us notice this geographic peculiarity, which illustrates how fundamental and how transparent these habits have become.

Having made this point, there must also be evidence that we have a Roman heritage that comes into play in our modern lives. It is most easily revealed in the Latin roots of so many common English words. For instance, the Romans placed great value on *industria, disciplina* and *frugalitas*. Romans deeply respected and admired people with lots of *auctoritas* and *dignitas*. None of my students had the smallest difficulty sorting out the English meanings.

The tricky bit is that neither of these examples involve anything Greco-Roman, because they do not have properties that are *both* Greek and Roman. The geography is purely Greek. It has no Roman roots. Similarly, the Latin words, which are so accessible to English speakers, have nothing to do with Greek. The Greeks and Romans both spoke Indo-European languages, but they were not closely related to one another.

The English language, however, is deeply Greco-Roman because it has words derived from both Greek and Latin. We know that *polis* gives us politics and policy. The Latin *levitas* gives us levity, a trait the Romans despised. They were, by contrast, great fans of *gravitas*, of taking things that mattered quite seriously.

## A Dangerous Cliché

As a cliché, however, references to our Greco-Roman heritage can be extremely misleading. One obvious danger lies in mistakenly assuming that Greeks and Romans were more similar than dissimilar. This is extremely well illustrated in a question asked by a fellow cruise passenger during a walking tour of Rome's Colosseum.

"What's the difference between Greeks and Romans?" At first, it was hard to imagine what family of answers this question could have. The Greeks have bigger feet? It seemed, in fact, a very silly question. However, having spent a career reassuring students that there are no stupid questions (which, to be honest, isn't entirely true), it seemed only fair to try to understand what prompted his question.*

Upon reflection, it seemed very likely that, having heard the phrase "our Greco-Roman heritage" a great many times, this man might have come to the not-unreasonable conclusion that Greeks and Romans were rather like one another. Certainly, when Americans speak of their "Irish" heritage they are making, probably unconsciously, two key assumptions: that Irish people have a set of common cultural features, and that these identify them as a nation.

Nothing could be further from the truth about the Greeks and Romans. They were, in fact, as different as chalk and cheese. As we explore their differences, we should note that, as is frequently the case in discussions of "the Greeks," the actual data comes largely from Athens. We already know, from an earlier chapter, a great deal about these Hellenes. We are quite aware of their divisions into separate units of governance, their *poleis,* and we know that citizenship was exclusive.

* This musing led to a cruise ship lecture called "What can be misleading about our 'Greco-Roman heritage'?"

This exclusivity will be a key difference between them and the Romans. One of the most basic facts of Roman history is that, over time, the unit of governance came to include peoples of many different nations. Ruling over more than one nation is, as we have discussed, a defining feature of an empire. Rome does not start with this striking inclusiveness. She acquires it gradually and for very specific reasons. We will turn to this story now.

### A Brief Gallop through Roman History

Roman history is commonly divided into three periods, that of the kings, of the Republic and of the Empire. The traditional date for the founding of Rome is 753 B.C. At some later date, the Etruscans conquered Rome and provided a series of kings, the last of whom was ejected by the Romans in 510 B.C. Thereafter, Romans harbored a deep loathing for kings, which would have an important effect at a much later date. The oral tradition behind this account is legendary, but it has been culled by archeology down to these bald facts: that the Etruscans were overthrown and that Romans ever after hated kings.

The second period, the Republic, lasted from 509 to 27 B.C. It was a time of stunning expansion. It involved leaders honing their political and administrative skills and learning from other cultures. In this period, Rome went from a city-state on the Seven Hills to a vast dominion encircling the Mediterranean Sea, which they called *Nostrum Mar* or "Our Sea." In his masterpiece, *The Romans*, the historian R.H. Barrow writes that the core means by which she acquired and maintained that dominion ... was her singular power of turning enemies into friends, and eventually into Romans, while yet they remained Spaniards or Gauls or Africans. From her they derived 'Romanitas,' their 'Roman-ness.' 'Romanitas' is a convenient word used by the Christian Tertullian to mean all that a Roman takes for granted, the Roman point of view and habit of mind.

This statement might seem very odd to any reader whose primary exposure to the Romans comes in the context of their persecuting Christians. However, the Christians, who do not appear until the next phase of Roman history, represent a unique case that we will discuss later. The overarching principle, however, is that a polytheistic religion can absorb all or parts of other polytheistic religions, which the Romans did, while monotheistic religions such as Judaism and Christianity cannot be absorbed because their core is all or nothing.

In all other cases, the Roman expansion in both the Republican period and later in the Imperial period was, often after some internal struggle, basically inclusive. Rome became the first power in Italy by force of arms, although she did not win every battle she fought. She also made many unequal alliances that justified "defending" her allies against others and, as part of their defense, taking them over. It was a long and protracted process. When it was done, the "Italian allies" asked for citizenship. Some powerful Romans wanted this request denied and they won the day.

The Italians then rose up in a rebellion called the "Social War," which lasted from 91 to 88 B.C. Rome won on the battlefield but not in the court of public opinion, so in the end the Italians were granted Roman citizenship. This was not just important because of the franchise. In Roman courts, a Roman citizen had powerful advantages over non-Romans. Moreover, and of vital importance, it was unlawful to enslave a Roman citizen.

The reign of Augustus lasted from 27 B.C. to 14 A.D., and began the third period in Roman history, called the Empire. During this time, Augustus reorganized the army by placing legions on the frontiers and creating auxiliary legions to back them up. These auxiliary legions were staffed by local men who became Roman citizens at the end of their service, along with one wife and their children. This fact was recorded in Rome and the soldier received confirmation on a double tablet, called in Latin a *diploma*.

We have now jumped ahead of our story to make a point. The political history of Rome was inclusive. There were hiccups along the way, such as the Social War, but the trend overall was inclusive. The new citizens whose fathers were auxiliary legionnaires became the next generation of "Roman" legionnaires, while another group of local men made up the auxiliary legions. Citizenship thus expanded with each generation, all around the Empire. In the west, this also promoted the diffusion of Latin and the planting of cities organized along Roman lines, with a forum, public baths, a theater and other typically Roman amenities.*

Barrow turns out to be right, of course, that, with the exception of monotheists, the Romans had a talent for "turning enemies into friends, and eventually into Romans." The Greeks, by contrast, were drastically exclusive. They were Athenians, Spartans, Corinthians, etc. who could make friends but only as part of the ever-changing alliances against each other and the occasional outsider. This season's enemy might be next season's ally and vice versa. In this respect and others, Romans and Greeks were thoroughly different. "Our Greco-Roman heritage" definitely does not mean that they were two peas in a pod!

Barrow attributes Roman inclusiveness to a favorite word among Romans, *humanitas*, which had a two-sided meaning. One's humanity provided a special dignity, which one was entitled to defend and protect. At the same time, every other human being also had a special dignity equally worthy of defense and protection. Barrow concludes that "this recognition implies compromise and self-restraint and sympathy and consideration." Also, in the end, it argues for inclusion.

## Roman Values

"What manner of men were the Romans?" Barrow poses this question and answers, first, that they would be willing to be judged by their deeds. The "Latin for 'history' is simply 'things done' (*res gestae*)." However, a recitation of Roman

---

* Citizenship did not promote the spread of Latin in the east where the *lingua franca* remained Greek.

deeds would paint an incomplete picture for us unless we grasp the extraordinary power that Romans attributed to forces beyond their control. It was vital for a Roman to subordinate himself to these forces, a conviction that might be better understood by using an analogy to a river with a strong and rapid current.

If a man wanted to swim upstream, he was destined to fail. If he wanted to get from one bank of a river to the other by swimming straight across, he would also fail. Only if a man swam with the current could he be elevated to a collaborator and thus have some chance of success. Victories in battle were followed by a parade through the city led by the victorious general. These "triumphs," as they were called, always ended at a temple. Once there, the general acknowledged that his successes were entirely due to his own submission to the God of War as well as the submission of the army and the people of Rome.

For this reason, Romans desperately wanted to know where the forces were headed, and they looked for answers in omens and signs. The most basic unit of Roman society was the *familia*, which was a larger unit than the nuclear family of our world. The *paterfamilias* was the head of the *familia* and also its priest. He studied the signs in order to read the forces, which were Gods. He also had memorized, precisely, an incantation or recitation specific to his *familia*, which had evolved over time and proved useful because, after all, the *familia* was still there, and perhaps even thriving.

As the years and the centuries passed, the meaning of

these ordered sounds was lost. The same was true of the recitations given in public to celebrate and advance the cause of the second key unit in Rome, the state. As with the family, so with the state. The smallest flaw in the pronouncing of the sacred syllables could mean either starting over from the beginning or courting disaster. When he was in power, Sulla, a powerful and important Roman general and dictator, appointed a man, notorious for stuttering, to recite the most sacred of public incantations. If he made a mistake, he would have to start over. Apparently, Sulla enjoyed watching the listeners waiting with bated breath for that very real possibility.

### Greeks versus Romans

The recitation by rote of ancient phrases without intelligible content would have been unthinkable to a Greek. Certainly Greeks believed in forces larger than themselves, but the manifestation, the sensibility, was quite different. Consider the opening of the play *Oedipus the King* by Sophocles. The chorus laments that religion is dying because people are losing faith in the gods. The gods had decreed that a king would be murdered by his son, who would then marry his own mother, two dastardly sins to the Greeks. Apparently this had not happened. As the play unfolds, in truth, it had. It was just that no one knew that yet. So religion was dying, not because the gods were so callous as to decree such a fate for an unborn son, but because these gods had (seemingly) failed to pull it off.

The venerable classicist, Edith Hamilton argued that the real religion of the Greeks was not their mythology but rather two essential beliefs. If you could see that something was the right thing to do, why would you not do it? If you can recognize excellence, why would you not pursue it? The impetus to proper behavior was *internal* and involved recognition and appreciation of virtue. These questions had a moral and spiritual aspect, which was completely absent in the incomprehensible Roman incantations. As we shall soon see, the Greeks and Romans were dramatically different from one another in their religious lives.

## Republican Virtues

Returning to what later Romans called "the old ways" of the early Republic, Barrow lists the religious virtues Romans admired. First among these was that a man must recognize the obligation to subordinate himself to some *external* power that bound him to behave properly. The Latin term for this was *religio*, and it entailed *pietas*, which was an element of that subordination. You were *pius* to the gods, to your parents, your elders, your children and your friends when you admitted that they have claims upon you based on the sacred nature of those relationships. Of all this, Barrow wrote:

> The demands of *pietas* ... constituted in themselves a massive and unwritten code of feeling and behavior which was outside the law, and was so powerful as to modify in practice the harsh rules of private law, which were only a last resort.

Additional Roman virtues include *gravitas*, which meant appreciating what was important and acting responsibly. It was the opposite of *levitas*, which meant flippancy, instability or being silly when one should be serious. This was a trait Romans despised. *Gravitas* might be combined with *constancia*, sticking to a purpose, or with *firmitas*, tenacity. It might be leavened by *comitas*, which combats grim seriousness with graceful manners and good humor.

*Genius* was also a Latin word, but it had no association with individual brilliance, imagination, creativity or speculation. Instead it was used to explain groups like a *familia* or a legion, which were more than the sum of their parts. That extra dollop was their *genius*. The *genius* of Rome was, in her own eyes, her ability to work in unison with the forces to ensure her successes and her endurance.

The early practice of rite accompanied by formal invocations and crystallized into a sacred law helped to develop that genius in law which is Rome's great legacy; and the law of the state borrowed a reflected sanctity from its sacred counterpart. Law presupposed obedience and was not disappointed. The position of the head of the family, the respect given to the mother ... were confirmed and strengthened. The validity of moral ideas was securely established, and ties of natural affection ... were made firm by a code of behavior which lay outside legal obligation and was of compelling power.[*]

[*] *The Romans* by R.H. Barrow.

The formal nature of Roman religion provided neither warm personal feeling nor the danger of hysterical ecstasy. Perhaps its very formality led Roman officials to tolerate Roman citizens' attraction to more emotionally satisfying rituals from the various civilizations that became part of the empire. The only condition was that these Romans also respect the forces. They should stand up at the proper occasions and show respect for that state religion that had, after all, seen Rome grow to ever-greater power.

This the Christians would not do. Moreover, if a conflict arose between the wishes of the family and the teachings of Jesus, a true disciple should always follow the latter. So, it was the political implications of Christian distain for the claims of the *familia* and the state, the two main institutions holding Rome together, which deeply offended Roman officials. It was never an issue of their private faith, but rather of their public conduct. Christian persecution by Roman authorities was seen by those officials not as a religious act but rather as political reaction to what was understood by them as treason.

So far, we have seen that Greeks and Romans differed in two critical arenas of life. The Greeks were exclusive in matters of citizenship while the Romans were inclusive. Moreover, the Greeks' religion was powered by an internal conscience that was expected to recognize and appreciate virtue and excellence. The Roman was bound to piety by external forces to which he must, albeit willingly, submit. We will notice other, less significant differences as we proceed.

### Greeks versus Romans Redux

A student of mine once wrote a paper contrasting Greeks and Romans and she came up with a very clever title, "Greco-Roman Wrestling." Rules about plagiarism preclude me from stealing it. What it captures was the fact that they were opposites in so many ways and that they actively disliked one another. Romans admired the art and literature of the classical period and a "gentleman" in Roman society must speak some Greek. On the other hand, the Greeks they were encountering in real life were nothing like their classical forefathers. So the Romans despised them all the more for not living up to the standards that had been set for them by their ancestors. As it happens, with the passage of time, the Romans also fell away from the *mores maiorum*, the customary conduct of their ancestors. We will discuss this in more detail later.

The Romans were team players, always regarding themselves as part of a larger unit, the family or the legion or the state. But, especially for those on the lower end of the scale, the state was too distant to feel like a satisfactory group. So, slaves, freedmen and poorer freeman created clubs for themselves. These clubs, which might include men of all three classes, had a religious aspect, often a task to perform (such keeping the crossroad clean) and the pleasures of a social or dining club. They sometimes even provided for the members' funerals. Barrow describes such a group as "church, social club, craft-guild and funeral society."

They recorded the rules of the club and kept minutes of

meetings, some of which are still extant. They had elected officers who took an oath at the beginning of their term and provided an accounting of it at its end. New members were admonished to read the rules and understand the sort of conduct expected of them. These rules, naturally, were a reflection of values and standards expressed by Roman law in general. There were provisions for what sorts of food and wine were appropriate for members' dinners. All of which speaks to the very Roman desire to socialize with others, but in an orderly, rule- based way and in a formally constituted organization.

It is essentially impossible to imagine Greeks doing anything of the sort. This is not to say that the Hellenes didn't socialize. They did. They just didn't organize and lay down rules about it, have dues or keep minutes. Greeks were at once too spontaneous, too imaginative and too quarrelsome to pull off anything as stolid as a Roman club. They were quirky individualists. There was Diogenes strolling around at midday with a lamp searching for an honest man. Pythagoras may have become famous for his theorem, but he was also deeply committed to founding a new religion on the tenet "Thou shall not eat beans."

Greeks and Romans also differed in their approaches to art and architecture. The Greeks, as Edith Hamilton put it, "loved beauty with economy." A tiny, exquisite wine cup was painted with delicate vines and Dionysus in a boat surrounded by dolphins, which had been pirates before he neutralized them. It was fashioned for the moment, to make its owner smile as he sipped some wine amidst good conversation. It is quintessentially Greek, and we are lucky that this cup is still with us.

In writing, being sparse and succinct was also highly prized by the Greeks. After the defeat at Thermopylae, the Spartans had a poet make an inscription commemorating their sacrifice. It is variously translated but one clear example would be "Passerby, tell the Spartans that we lie here according to their laws."

Romans reveled in great, huge things like the Colosseum and the colossal statue of Nero beside it (that gave it its name). Romans built roads as straight as possible. In *Everyday Life in Roman Britain*,* the authors wrote of driving along winding country lanes, then snaking through a congested city only to emerge on a beautiful straight road, the foundation of which had been laid down by Romans. Romans built aqueducts which are still standing today. Romans built for the ages.

Greeks certainly engaged in monumental building. The Parthenon comes to mind. However, to an ancient Greek sensibility, her splendor was displayed in her elegant proportions and almost organic beauty, not in her size. For Greeks building with a focus on bigger is better, we are driven to consider the Colossus of Rhodes. It was built some years after the reign of Alexander the Great and reflects a new sensibility that was influenced by his eastern conquests, including Egypt. As it is the only example of Greeks trying to

---

*This is a book written in the 1930s intended for British children. The authors noted that these children might have read the admirable biography of Agricola by his son-in-law Tacitus. This is not nearly as likely among most American college students in the twenty-first century.

impress with sheer size, it is arguably the exception that proves the rule.

Romans were extremely clever in practical matters. Their walls often had inner and outer sides separated by a space. They then built fires at strategic openings from which warm air flowed through the spaces between the sides, heating the house. After Rome fell, home heating in Europe did not again equal Roman standards until the nineteenth century.

Greeks were imaginative in speculation, in theory and philosophy. Romans were imaginative in solving practical problems based on experience. This matters because of the way in which cultural exchanges work. When Romans "borrowed" elements from the Greeks, they "borrowed" them to use as Romans. Barrow describes it thus:

> For some of Greek thought the Romans had little use, as, for example, metaphysical speculation; some they appropriated in part, as, for example, the practical bearing of mathematics, but not its theoretical foundations; a great deal they put through their robust and matter-of-fact minds, modified, and handed over in a shape which was adapted for everyday use by the peoples they governed.

Romans liked things to be down to earth and profoundly disliked speculation or abstract philosophy, both mother's milk to the Greek* mind. Here, again, we see the stark differences between them.

* This, of course, did not apply to the Spartans nor to those for whom hard work precluded the leisure of abstraction and philosophizing.

## Comedy

For a people who seem as dour as the Romans, it is ironic that their first writings preserved for us to read should be comic. The first Roman writer we have is Plautus (254?-184 B.C.), who has a great deal to tell us if we read him properly. Most scholars seem to have gotten off on the wrong foot, except for a brilliant treatment by the classicist Erich Segal. Because Plautus set all of his plays in Greek locations and gave the players Greek names, he is widely thought to have lifted the plots from some obscure and unknown Greek comic playwright. As we shall see, their comic sensibilities mark so major a difference between Greeks and Romans that no such transfer is possible.

As an aside, some of my students had great difficulties with the idea of setting a play somewhere else. I had some success with the following example. If we were on Broadway watching a revival of the musical *Oklahoma!* the play would be "set" in Oklahoma, but we and all the players would be in New York City. It is very odd that prominent scholars would have the same problem with the idea of setting a play elsewhere.

So, there was nothing to prevent a Roman writer from setting his original plays in Greece or from assigning his characters Greek names. Had Plautus borrowed Greek plots, he could easily have changed the characters' names into typical Roman names. The core evidence that he did not borrow from Greek plots is that the characters are Roman in every other respect. They have household Gods, which the *paterfamilias* attempts to assuage with memorized and inchoate incantations. They go to the forum. They are subject to Roman law. They display Roman social mores. In fact, Plautus' players are all, by common cultural attributes, and thus by nationality, Roman. No Greek could have fashioned these plots or created these characters because of the massive differences between the two cultures.

Indeed, argues Edith Hamilton in *The Roman Way*, the plays would not work and would not be funny if the characters were culturally inaccessible to the Roman audiences. So why did Plautus chose to set his plays in Greece and give his characters Greek names? Segal's answer to that question is clear and persuasive. Plautus feared setting them in Rome.

The most important official in Republican Rome was the censor, and one of his primary functions was monitoring public morals. Cato the Elder, as censor, had a Roman Senator banished from the Senate for kissing his own wife in public. Segal tells us that at least one playwright was executed for diminishing the *auctoritas* and *dignitas* of a prominent and powerful Roman. So, Segal argues, Plautus made his players Greek to avoid any identification of these characters with a specific living Roman, and thus to avoid the censor's wrath. That this was his motive is made more obvious by the fact that his plots skewer the petty conceits and other failings of the rich, powerful and well connected.

This is an infinitely more plausible explanation than the alternative. The "proof" that Plautus stole his plots from Greek comedies rests almost entirely on their being set in Greek places and peopled by folks with Greek names. Examined in detail, however, the plots reveal essential Roman qualities at every turn.

Segal, in *Roman Laughter*, calls Plautus' humor "the comedy of inversion." In such comedy, everything is turned on its head. The protagonist, who sets all the other players in motion, cleverly pulls their strings and triumphs in the end, is always a slave. Often the play opens with one slave meeting the "clever slave" and reacting with surprise. "I haven't seen you for a long time!" The clever slave then explains that he was sent to the mines for his last escapade and he is only just back. As no slave ever returned from the mines, we know we are now in a fictional world, or, with an eye to the censor, in Greece.

In *The Braggart Soldier*, Plautus created an outlandishly boastful soldier, Pyrgopolynices, and his worshipful toady, Artotrogus.* In the opening scene, as translated by Segal, Artotrogus is flattering his idol:

By Destiny's dashing, dauntless, debonair darling,
A man so warlike, Mars himself would hardly dare
To claim his powers were the equal of your own.

To this a preening, "Prygo" queries him:

Tell me – who was that chap I saved at Field-of-Roaches
Where the chief of staff was Crash-Bang-Razzle-Dazzle,
Son of Boom-Boom-Smash, you know, Neptune's nephew?

---

* When dealing with difficult names, nicknames work well. For me, these two became Prygo and Art. After that I could just read the play and enjoy the humor. Also notice that Mars is a Roman God.

"Art" replies:

Ah yes, the man with the golden armor, I recall.
You puffed away his legions with a single breath
Like wind blows autumn leaves ...

For Romans, such utterly nonsensical braggadocio would not be funny if the general were one of them. It is hilarious when the braggart is a despised little Greekling.

The plot is extremely complicated and very funny, and it hinges on a rule in Roman law. Essentially, the clever slave, Palaestrio, hires an actress to pose as a wealthy widow and lure the soldier into a compromising situation in which another actor, playing her husband, invokes his legal right to castrate the seducer of his wife. At which point, all the brave talk deserts the soldier and he is left pleading:

And my beating up today – I grant it was my just reward.
As a favor, let me leave with testimony to my manhood!

In the end, "Prygo" realizes that he has been tricked by the clever slave into relinquishing a beautiful young slave girl who is the true love of Palaestrio's former master. The three of them have run off to somewhere else to live happily ever after.

In the final monologue, "Prygo" asks for pity and adds:

Now I see I've been bamboozled. Oh, that rogue Palaestrio!
He enticed me into this. And yet ... I find the verdict's just.
(philosophically)
There would be less lechery if lechers were to learn from this;
Lots would be more leery and less lustful. (to his slaves)
Let's go in. (to the audience) Applaud!

There are additional reasons for believing that Plautus wrote these plots himself rather than borrowing them from a Greek. They rest on two further differences between the cultures. There was a censor in Rome who actively practiced censorship. Nothing like that constrained the great Athenian playwrights. No subject seems to have been off limits.

When Athens and Sparta were at war, and Athens was having a rough time, Aristophanes wrote his profoundly anti-war comedy *Lysistrata*. This would never have been permitted in Rome. Moreover, the comedy, in which the women of Athens and Sparta unite, swearing not to have sex with their husbands until they stopped fighting, was a huge success! In this respect, Americans are far more Roman than Greek. It is nearly impossible to imagine a successful T.V. sit-com using comedy to criticize a war the U.S. was fighting at the time, even if there were wide-spread public opposition.

### Women

In addition to having very different notions about censorship, Greeks and Romans had very different attitudes about women and paternity. Greeks attempted to ensure that their children were their own by sequestering "their" women. Respectable women did not go out to dinner parties or any public entertainment, and they had a separate part of the house so that they were not on hand when their husbands entertained. This actually created a problem when Athens had to be evacuated in the face of a Persian siege. Respectable women, even though swaddled in draperies, were reluctant to venture outdoors. Yet Greek comedy has jokes aplenty about keys being stolen, locks being broken and windows being climbed through. Apparently, this was funny.

As an aside, Xenophon tells a story about a dinner party that Socrates attended. The iconic philosopher said that his entire object in life was to get along with people. One man asked, "Then why did you marry Xanthippe?" The other men thought this was hilarious. Socrates replied, "Because I figured, if I could get along with her, I could get along with anybody." One wonders, if women were so hidden away, how did these men know Xanthippe was a shrew?

There is considerable controversy over the whole business of sequestering women among scholars of classical Greece. Sarah Pomeroy, in *Goddesses, Whores, Wives and Slaves* argues that sequestering is further evidence of Greek devaluation of women. Conversely, James Davidson, in *Courtesans and Fishcakes*, contends that sequestering gave wives an alluring mystique that was pleasing to both their husbands and themselves.

Davidson further assumes that men, especially intelligent and educated men, relish the conversation of smart and learned women. It is to this enjoyment that he attributes the rise and popularity of the courtesan in ancient Athens. These women could go to dinner parties and entertain in homes, which were often bought for them by their patrons. They existed in a realm separate from the wholesomely respectable, but not actually tainted by the stain of prostitution. The most famous of these was Aspasia, who lived with the great Athenian orator Pericles as man and wife until he perished in a plague. They could not marry because she was not an Athenian citizen. Some of their contemporaries even claimed that she wrote his speeches.

The whole business of sequestering women when possible and wrapping them up to the point of invisibility, when impossible, was reflected in their pottery. Men lived outdoors. As farmers, most worked outdoors and, and as soldiers, they drilled outdoors. They assembled to discuss politics and/or philosophy under the bright Greek sun. As a consequence, men were always depicted on pots as having very dark skin. Sequestered women, by contrast, were always portrayed with extremely fair skin.

So here we are. Hellenes tried to "solve" the paternity problem by sequestering their wives. At the same time, they not only tolerated comedies that hinged on the ways to find access to sequestered women, they actually found them funny. This is an enigma.

By contrast, Romans believed a woman's chastity was her greatest possession and to lose it was, literally, a fate worse than death. A famous Roman story lauds a father for killing his daughter rather than allowing her to be ravished by an enemy. Cornelia, the daughter of the famed soldier Scipio Africanus, was renowned and revered for her chastity. She was probably born not long after Plautus died. She married well, bore twelve children and was widowed while still retaining her beauty. Any number of rich men, even princes and kings, asked for her hand in marriage. Her reply was always the same. "I am already married." For this conduct, she was idealized as a role model for other women. Women utterly committed to chastity were then allowed to dine out, go to public entertainments and enjoy a freedom unknown to women in Hellas.

There was, of course, absolutely no expectation of chastity or fidelity for Roman men. Plautus reflects this double standard in his plots and yet he seems, in a very subtle way, to mock it. In one play, the son finds platonic love with a slave girl. His father wants to seduce her. The mother, fiercely protective of her son's feelings, gets wind of the plot and her loyal, clever slave substitutes himself under the "wedding" veil. A Roman audience, deeply disgusted with actual homosexuality, roars with laughter as the besotted old lecher woos his own male slave.

Three things were never turned on their heads in Plautus' plays. The mother was always revered, the wife was always faithful and the daughter was always modest and chaste. So vital was the ideology of the "good woman" to Roman morals that Plautus either engaged in self-censorship on this point, or, more likely, internalized the Roman moral code so thoroughly that making mockery of those values never crossed his mind, even as he inverted so many other cultural norms.

Yet another difference between Greeks and Roman has to do with women and heroism. In the magnificent Athenian tragedies, women do unutterably brave things, frequently from the highest principles, and (rightly in my view) get no extra credit for being female. Women in Roman literature are praised to the skies for heroically defending their chastity, but they are not presented as capable of heroism in any other context.

With respect to modern American attitudes towards women and heroism, we are truly Greco-Roman, that is to say self-contradictory. We recognize that women can and do engage in acts of real heroism. Women protesting bread shortages marched and were killed in pre-Revolutionary France. Women figured prominently in all the resistance movements in Nazi-occupied Europe. However, until very recently, they got an extra dollop of surprise, wonder and credit because they were heroic and also female. That seems to be changing, if slowly.

For now, we can return to the unknown tourist at the Colosseum and his question, "What is the difference between Greeks and Romans?" This is a question that can best be answered by another question: "How much time have you got?"

## On Being Old Fashioned

The Hellenes were not of one mind about extreme female modesty in clothing. Spartan men apparently made no special fuss when Spartan women played athletic games in short tunics, presumably outdoors in front of everyone. Their fellow Hellenes wrote off this peculiarity by saying that the Spartans were "old fashioned." This seems a very odd notion to the modern Western sensibility. After all, we have gone from the puritanical, prudish clothing standards of the Victorian age to a widespread acceptance in the west of skimpy bikinis and even nude beaches.

That was, however, not the reality of the ancient world. Anthropologists note that members of hunting and gathering bands have absolutely no privacy whatsoever. In ancient Egypt, public nudity by both men and women was perfectly normal and excited no comment, except by visiting Greeks, like Herodotus. Moreover, unmarried Egyptian women were free to select any sexual partner they fancied, and should they get pregnant, their status improved as motherhood was venerated. So the trend in the ancient world was from no modesty and few inhibitions to more and more of both. Thus the women of Sparta, in their skimpy tunics, were, indeed, old fashioned

# Rome and Reflections on Power

There is nothing simple about power. It can be as culturally determined as beauty or as elusive as charm, and both charm and beauty have changed the details of history. In this chapter, we return to the theme of the interplay between economic power, military power and political power. When the systems by which these powers are distributed are mutually complimentary, the society is likely to be quite stable at the very least, and extremely successful under the best of circumstances.

In Athens, when the aristocracy monopolized political power to the exclusion of wealthy commoners, civic unrest boiled up and was met, in the end, with Solon's constitutional reforms allowing new men to enter the political arena. When the militarily important Attic farmers faced starvation, Pesistratus mobilized the state apparatus to bring them economic relief. The details and outcomes in Rome were quite different from those in Athens but the basic patterns were identical. When political, economic and military sources of power are out of alignment, things change. The shifting balance of these three sources of power as they played out in Rome will be the primary focus of this chapter.

## Early Rome

What we know about the early political stirrings of the Romans comes from their own traditions and some logical deductions based on what we know came next. There was a Senate made up of the *patresfamilias** of each of the important extended families who had founded the community. These families came to be called "patricians." They proposed a new king and their choice was confirmed by the entire male community. Membership in the Senate was for life. The king kept charge of the "sacred things," except during times of transition when this job fell to the Senate.

The Etruscans conquered Rome and thrust three kings upon her, which, after the last was banished, left Romans with an intense loathing toward kings. The top executive responsibility passed to two consuls who had the power to veto one another. Their mutual vetoes acted against change, which completely suited the profoundly conservative early Romans. However, in the event of a real crisis, a dictator could be brought in for a limited time and to serve a very specific purpose.

The consuls, who must be patricians, held office for one year. They were elected by all the male citizens in assembly, and it was from them that the consuls received their *impe-*

* This is the plural of *paterfamilias*.

*rium* (a particularly comprehensive form of political power). In addition, over time, lesser executive positions were created and the magistrates holding these positions, like the consuls, were selected from among the patricians.

All the while, new people had become part of Rome. As the city expanded in area, it enclosed neighboring villages and their populations became Roman citizens called "plebeians." They had citizenship and the franchise (the right to vote), but they were excluded from every important political office, including all those with the power to propose various choices in public policy. As we saw in "Hellas," the power to propose is always greater than the power to decide.

Importantly, the categories of patrician and plebeian referred to castes into which a Roman citizen was assigned by birth. At first, it was unlawful for a patrician to marry a plebeian, so that newborn babies had a clear designation as to their caste membership.

Both patricians and plebeians were citizens and members of the assembly, and both enjoyed an equal franchise, their differences were enforced by custom.

Patrician magistrates named patrician successors and presented their choices to the assembly for ratification. Moreover, legislation presented to the assembly by patrician magistrates and accepted by the assembly had to be ratified by the patrician Senate. So it had been and so it would be, for Rome had no written constitution and relied entirely on the old ways or *mores maiorum*, "the manners of one's ancestors, which are among the most potent forces in Roman history."*

Patricians were the founding families of Rome and their names were listed for all to see. Plebeians, by definition, always became Romans after these founding fathers. Many of them were involved in trade because Rome, under Etruscan rule, had become a commercial center linked to trading partners over both land and sea.

Patricians, a landed aristocracy, shared a distain for commerce as not quite clean. Witness Cicero's assertion, noted in "Survival," that the merchant who buys goods at the dock and charges more for them in his shop was a "thief." This radical rejection of commerce provided an opportunity for the plebeians to seize, and seize it they did. Over time, some plebeians, or plebes as they are sometimes called, grew wealthy, sometimes very wealthy. At the same time, some patrician families fell on hard times. Yet the latter continued to monopolize the all-important powers to propose legislation, to nominate executives and to ratify the decisions of the voters.

As we saw in Athens, such a situation was extremely volatile and the pressures to change it were great. The earliest concerns expressed by the plebeians had to do with protection against the unfettered powers of the consuls. First, they were promised that no Roman citizen would be put to death without an appeal to the people. This could work well enough in Rome. However, argued the patricians, who, alone, were the generals, this would not work in matters of

* R.H. Barrow, *The Romans.*

military justice. When an army was in the field and disobedience or treachery required the ultimate punishment, the people were not on hand to be consulted.

This delaying tactic resulted in a threat by the plebes, partially enacted, to found a separate city and withdraw their willingness to serve in the Roman army. Not only did some plebes have wealth, but they far outnumbered patricians, making them vital to Roman military success. The concessions the plebes won over time were political. By contrast, what Pesistratus gave to the Athenian hill farmers was much-needed economic assistance that, over time, turned into political power. The common point, however, is that political power, economic power and military power must achieve some sort of equilibrium or instability and civil conflict will follow.

So, bit by bit, over roughly a century and a half, the patricians reluctantly but finally conceded political power to the plebeians. Along the way they created a series of new political offices such as tribune of the plebes. In the end, the shift in power was complete. No patrician could be a tribune of the plebs, but a plebian could hold any one of the offices once reserved for patricians.

By 267 B.C., it looked as if Rome might be headed toward a system of government that could reasonably be called democratic. Sadly, the Punic Wars, fought against the Semitic Carthaginians, arrested this progress towards a democratic Rome. At least that was the story popular among Roman oligarchs, and it is still doing well among historians of Rome.

By this point the Senate, once the patricians' exclusive club, had changed its character with the political ebb and flow. Instead, it had become a final political resting place for victorious generals and/or former magistrates who had successfully climbed the "course of honor." This *cursus honorum* consisted of a series of magistracies ranked from least important to most important. After completing the circuit, a man passed into the Senate.

Because successful generals were often also magistrates, this meant that the Senate had a monopoly on the most experienced leaders of Rome. So, the argument went, wars could not be fought by the voters. They haven't the knowledge and they are too unwieldy to make the sorts of instant tactical changes frequently needed for military success. Athens gave us democracy while Rome told us that, in a crisis, it will not work.

Essential to that difference was size. Athens could win against the Persians and still be democratic because the *polis* was small and thus more maneuverable. Moreover, the percentage of adult male citizens with direct experience of governing at an executive level was substantial, and they were therefore able to understand situations and make decisions about them with a high level of skill and success.

Political scientists distinguish between three types of democracy. When the "people," however designated, collectively make the final decisions, this is called "direct democracy." One modern example would be a town meeting where the citizens vote for a new traffic light or some school renovation. The existence of the Electoral College prevents the election of an American President from being a case of direct democracy.

At the other end of the scale, there is "representative democracy." The people do not decide directly, but rather cede this power to "representatives." In the case of the U.S. House and Senate, the members are chosen by the voters. A traditional defense of this sort of system is that it represents the best of all possible worlds. On the one hand, the voters have some say in who will represent them, while, on the other hand, the office holder, with superior knowledge of the situation and more experience, is free to do or not do what a majority of the constituents might want. The validity of this argument varies with the wisdom, probity and objectivity of the office holder. It also varies with the ignorance, corruption or bigotry of the office holder. That is to say, this defense of representative democracy is both very true and completely untrue, depending entirely on specific circumstances.

Athens represented something in between these two. The voters as a whole did not rule directly in many cases. However, because Athens was relatively small, everyone knew at least one of their representatives well enough to approach him and explain their point of view on critical issues of the day. This power of persuasion, made possible by familiarity and accessibility, was closer to direct democracy than to the representative sort. So, political scientists gave this exceptional example its own category of "classical democracy."

At best, Rome might have become a representative democracy. Unfortunately, as things turned out, her unwritten constitution came strongly to favor oligarchy, which is rule by the few. These were the few, some patrician and some plebian, who made it through the *cursus honorum* and then into the Senate for life. Along the way, the plebeian majority created a new status, that of *nobilis*, which meant that serving in high office ennobled a man, and, if he made it to consul, also ennobled his children.

*Nobilis* absolutely did not imply the sort of high minded, disinterested altruism captured in the French phrase *noblesse oblige*. Instead, it denoted superiority, fame and the quality of being formidable. This was clearly how they saw themselves. At the same time, however, the term also applied to animals, especially wild animals. *Nobilis ferae* was used to describe the most dangerous and most easily provoked animals, which may have reflected how Roman elites were seen by the victims of Roman provincial plunder.

Everyone continued to believe that being a patrician was "better," and this left two interesting sources of income for patrician families. One was to sell your daughter to a nobody who wanted to enhance his status with the acquisition of a patrician wife. The other was based on the fact that Roman law restricted inheritance when the heir was childless. Thus, a man coming from great wealth needed an offspring to keep the money in the family. If his wife produced no children, it behooved him to adopt and, by preference, to adopt a male patrician. Being practical, the Romans would never adopt babies because that was a risky strategy. How would the boy turn out? Instead they adopted young men or old teenagers. This will be an important tidbit for our story down the road.

Given a Senate that was made up of all the most experienced soldiers and statesmen, it was the obvious institution to manage the Punic Wars. Quoting Barrow:

> ... the "opinion of the Senate" now became "the decree of the Senate"; as a body it ceased merely to discuss the problems submitted by the magistrate and now initiated discussion, and so it gathered into its hands practically all state business. Its conduct of affairs during the hardest years of the war was in general excellent; if later it fell from its high standard of efficiency and moral integrity, it was for reasons which we have presently to consider.

The greatest of these reasons was that, in the course of the wars, Rome had acquired territory that it was, at first, reluctant to make into provinces. Instead, the Romans were content to disarm these places and then tax them. In time, however, these evolved into provinces with an implied need for a provincial governor. A handy way to supply these governors was found in the consuls. After their year was up, each would be made a pro-consul and sent to govern a province. Technically, the pro-consul was bound by the terms of Rome's agreements with each province, which were usually quite generous to the locals. In practice, however, without supervision, he need be only as scrupulous as his conscience demanded.

Like consuls, pro-consuls served a single year in office. Unlike consuls, they served alone and not in pairs with the power curb each others' actions by a veto. The single year was supposed to limit the pro-consular power, but it usually had the opposite effect. With only a year to enrich himself at the expense of the province, more pro-consuls than not became especially rapacious. When they finished their year, they passed into the Senate, which was the only agency with authority to call them to book for violating the terms of provincial rule. Not surprisingly, the Senate routinely failed to do so.

Of course the actual governing of each province involved many more Romans at hand than simply the pro-consuls. However, to go into great detail about their various titles and responsibilities merely confuses the issue. The important point is that they had neither the power to limit the pro-consuls' plundering, nor the will to do so, as they often got a share of the spoils.

All this involved a marked shift in the relationship between economic and political power in Rome. After 146 B.C., when provincial government began, political power abroad provided a platform for extracting the wealth of great temples, palaces and estates, and then carting it home as one's own. While this brought political and economic power into alignment for individual people, it resulted in very bad governance in the provinces. At home, it also led to more intrigue in the competition to be appointed provincial governor.

Magisterial candidates were increasingly buying votes to make their way up the *cursus honorum*, which made the "honorable course" a good deal less honorable.

Size had something to do with that as well. The smaller

the electorate, the fewer the resources needed to meet and greet most of them. The current buzz word for this is "retail" politics.

Conversely, the larger the electorate, the more resources are needed to build name recognition and a following. We are now calling this "wholesale" politics. It was not an accident that the first rung on the course of honor was the role of *quaestor*. He was a financial officer who was also personally responsible for funding the games to entertain the public. The more lavish the games, the greater the positive perception of their organizer. So the *quaestor* who wanted great political success must either be rich himself or attract the attention of rich backers.

Great military success could also be the basis for winning over the electorate. Publius Scipio elevated himself to heroic stature by conquering New Carthage, the capital of Punic Spain in 209 B.C. He then conquered the rest of Carthaginian Spain three years later, and returned to Rome to stage a lavish triumph and to insist that Rome finish the job by invading Africa. Such was his charisma that he got his way. With two legions, he won a series of battles culminating in his victory over Hannibal at Zama in 202 B.C. Carthage had to surrender to him, and, thus gave him an additional name, Scipio Africanus.

### Heroes and the *Mores Maiorum*

What is telling about this is that Roman generals had won important victories in the past without becoming individually lionized. Barrow attributes the change to the translation of Homer's *Odyssey* into Latin, which was done by a Greek slave for his master's children. It soon gained a much wider audience. Homer's heroes, at once godlike and human, were decidedly not Romans in the *mores maiorum*. These were not generals who triumphed "through" the gods, but rather through their own heroism, skill and might.

In the old ways, the *genius* of a legion was collective, in the sense of a whole that is greater than the sum of its parts. This was a view of the world that was arguably anti-heroic. Then, too, the notion that forces beyond a man's control cause his success, because he has subordinated his personality and will to them, is not an heroic formula, either.

Homeric heroes were existentially Greek, and thoroughly inconsistent with the Roman *mores maiorum*. They did, however, fit in with the new emphasis on personal wealth and power in place of obligation and duty to Rome. Scipio Africanus harnessed these Greek heroes to fashion a Roman leader of a new type that found strong opposition in supporters of the old ways.

Marcus Porcius Cato was born in 234 B.C., and grew up on the Sabine farm he would later inherit from his father. He was the very epitome of the old-fashioned farmer-soldier. At twenty, his legion faced Hannibal, and he stayed in the army until the end of the war. At thirty, he was *quaestor* to Scipio in the province of Sicily, and was also with him in Africa. He was consul in 195 B.C. and censor in 184 B.C. It was he who drove Manilius from the Senate for kissing his own wife in broad daylight in front of their daughter.

Cato, also called Cato the Elder or Cato the Censor, was

famous in Rome and in the provinces for his extreme austerity. As a general, he had marched with the ranks and carried his own weapons. As the provincial governor of Sardinia, he abolished the traditional entourage that came with
that role and caused great expense and hardship to the local
people. Later, as censor, he fashioned one law after the other
to limit, by high taxation or prohibition, the luxury encouraged by Rome's growing wealth. He was absolutely convinced that luxury and self-indulgence were making Romans
soft and selfish, thus putting Rome in danger.

He fought with all his intellect and with the power of his
office against the trend toward the Hellenistic idealizing of
the individual as a hero, for it scared him. According to
Barrow:

> His ideal is a citizen of high moral principle, based on
> tradition, realizing himself in the commonwealth and
> its business, and so creating a triumphant government
> pre-eminent for enlightened policy and massive integrity
> ... Young oligarchs should not be trained to luxury, nor
> democrats to the belief that freedom is doing whatever
> you please. 'A man should not think it slavery to live
> under the constitution; he should think of it rather as his
> salvation.'

He was, therefore, deeply disturbed when he saw Scipio
Africanus manipulate the people with the sheer force of his
personality and his accomplishments. Once, when Scipio
was under fire for misappropriating funds, he had the public

accompany him to the temples to celebrate his victory over Hannibal at Zama. That day happened to be the anniversary of that victory, and Scipio dodged the charges. Later, he was convicted but his popularity was such that no one dared arrest him. For Cato, the ardent lover of law and justice, it was all a very bad omen of what was to come.

We began with the premise that political, economic and military power must be distributed in ways that are congruent with one another. By the time of Scipio Africanus, Rome had achieved such a balance. Military success in the field could translate into political success at home, which could then be used to exploit the wealth of the provinces. Conversely, severe social unrest would arise when wealth could buy votes and a politician so elected could get himself appointed general. Military skill and experience cannot be bought. They must be earned. This truism would soon matter a very great deal.

## The Senate and the People

Traditionally, public business in Rome bore the initials SPQR, which stood for *Senatus Populus Que Romanum*, which indicated that both the Senate and the People of Rome* approved of the official, the decree, the law, etc. This pact between the Senate and the People was often strained, particularly as they worked out removing the patrician monopoly on political power and accommodating well-to-do plebeians into the power structure.

* When used as an institutional title, "People" is capitalized. When referring to the citizenry as such, it is not.

The next major challenge to Roman stability would come from two forces. The first was a marked reduction in the proportion of farmer-soldiers in the citizen body of Rome. The second was a marked increase in the use of successful politicians to lead armies despite their lack of military experience or savvy, and their intense drive to enrich themselves without any real thought for the welfare of their soldiers.

Farmer-soldiers as a group were heavily and negatively impacted by the new colonies won in conjunction with the Punic wars. In the beginning, Roman farmer-soldiers fought campaigns not too far from home and were thus away only during the fighting season. They could go home for the harvest in the fall, sire their children, take care of their chores and join in the spring planting before returning to their legion.

After their successes in the Punic wars brought Rome colonies, much of the subsequent fighting was overseas and the farmer-soldier could not get home. His wife could not manage the farm by herself and, more and more, she could not bear him children because of his prolonged absence.

As their farms went under, the land was most often acquired by the wealthy to create large holdings, on which they grew, surprise, surprise, olives and grapes to make oil and wine. The wealthy had the capital to wait for these crops to produce, where the small farmer did not. They imported armies of slaves, won by the victories of the very farmers they were displacing, to do the actual work. Moreover, these wealthy families were also those controlling the Senate, and they had no incentive to act as Peisistratus had acted in

Athens to save the farmer-soldiers from financial ruin.

Two exceptions, two brothers, fought to change this pattern of depopulation in the countryside, and the loss of Roman farmer-soldiers. They were Tiberius Gracchus and Gaius Gracchus and they were surviving sons of the famously faithful widow Cornelia. In addition to refusing to remarry, she was also praised as "the mother of the Gracchi.*" Unhappily, the Roman constitution, oligarchic to its roots, was structured to protect the interests of the wealthy land speculators and not the poor farmer-soldiers.

Tiberius Gracchus violated that constitution and seemed likely to get away with his aims by the justice of his cause and his personal charisma. He was murdered instead. Nine years later, his younger brother met the same fate, but not before passing a much needed law. It stipulated that farmer-soldiers could retire after ten years or six full campaigns. This law still left the family vulnerable to losing their land because the farmer-soldier was not deployed close enough to home to defend his family's rights.

It once seemed odd that the sons of a woman so representative of the "old ways" should be constitution-busting radicals, but with a deeper understanding the apparent irony disappears. The Gracchi were trying to preserve the old ways, the days when Roman soldiers were also farmers, learning the old values from working their land.

Farmers knew that forces beyond their own actions determined their fate. They knew that they could plant,

* Gracchi is the Latin plural of Gracchus and refers to the two brothers, Tiberius and Gaius.

weed and tend their crops, but that a cold snap could suddenly kill their crop, or a cloud of locusts quickly consume it. They possessed the desire to submit to Rome's gods in Rome's service, and represented all that was good about the *mores maiorum*. Gradually, as they lost their land, they also began to disappear as a type of Roman citizen.

As the now-landless farmer-soldiers migrated to Rome, they frequently could not muster the necessary means to join one of the five recognized classes. The censor, who organized the census, used data on wealth to assign families to the various classes. At the bottom were those with so little that the censor simply had their heads counted. Thus they became known as the *capite censi*, or the head count population.

As more and more former farmer-soldiers, once the backbone of the Roman army, poured into city, the traditional pact between the Senate and the People began to fray. The erstwhile farmer-soldiers, turned *capite censi*, knew that they had served Rome well and expected some help in return. Colin McEvedy sums up the situation in *The New Penguin Atlas of Ancient History*:

> The People had acquired an agenda of their own, with land for veterans and bread for the urban poor as the lead items; the Senate had its doubts about the necessity for either and was grudging in its response. Just as important, the People tended to idolize successful generals and vote to continue their commands, something that struck at the root of the Senators' collegial principle.

The Senators' worst-case scenario was the emergence of a military hero, along the lines of Scipio Africanus, who would also be prepared to champion an organized Peoples' party. Such a party would support land for veterans and cut into the land-grab by wealthy estate owners. They would also demand bread for the poor, while curtailing the ability of the Senate to replace the popular general with one of their own. Since the general controlled the spoils of war, Senators feared for their share.

### An Imbalance of Powers

A series of events conspired to bring a Peoples' party into being, beginning with the migrations of two tribes, the Cimbri and the Teutones.* Sometime around 115 B.C., they left their homeland on the middle Danube and went to search for somewhere else to settle. No one seems to know why. Eventually, their peregrinations took them close enough for Rome to send out an army to stop them.

At its head was Marcus Junius Silanus, who had recently completed his stint as one of the consuls. It was a purely political appointment. Silanus was such a military incompetent that the Roman legions, sent out in Rome's defense, were slaughtered in droves. To be beaten by nomadic Celts, burdened down by their families, animals and belongings

---

* Some scholars have designated these tribes as "Germans" because the Romans of the time referred to them as such. However, Roman usage was geographic not ethnological. These two tribes were Celtic but had been living in an area east of the Rhine and north of the upper Danube which Romans called Germany. Clearly, their artifacts mark them as Celts.

was a disgrace. Nor was this was to be the only Celtic rout of once mighty Rome. It was a sorry testament to a system that had so politicized military office that the appointment of generals was wholly devoid of any consideration of military experience or competence.

At the same time, an equally well-connected but militarily inept former consul had been given command of a Roman army in North Africa. He was charged with quelling the troubles on the provincial border with Numidia and with its king, Jugurtha. This general, too, wasted the men under his control in senseless exercises in futility. His name was Quintus Caecilius Metellus, and he had on his staff Gaius Marius, who would become one of Rome's greatest generals.

All this needless slaughter of badly led Roman soldiers contributed to the already acute shortage of farmer-soldiers, a slowly disappearing breed. In response to those shortages, the Senate nullified the *lex Sempronia* of Gaius Gracchus limiting the number of times a veteran could be called back. Marius opposed the nullification because he appreciated the contributions and the hardships of these veterans. Indeed he informed Metellus of his opposition and his determination to return to Rome and run for consul. Metellus pointed out that, as his legate, Marius could not leave Africa until he did. Marius countered that Metellus could give him permission, but Metellus would not hear of it.

Rome had its own Numidian candidate to replace the troublesome Jugurtha. He was only too willing to organize a letter-writing campaign to the People enumerating the damages being done to Roman interests by Metellus. It was hugely successful, in large measure because the complaints were heartfelt and real. Giving important military commands to well-connected political hacks was never a good idea. The letters also described how the talents of his two senior legates, Gaius Marius and Publius Rutilius Rufus, were being frittered away because Metellus could not hold a candle to them in military experience and was, as a consequence, jealous and spiteful.

When Metellus' family and supporters made it clear just how badly his reputation in Rome was being damaged by the letter campaign, he realized he had to let Marius go. Still, he waited until it would be too late for his nemesis to get home for the next election. As luck would have it, favorable conditions at every stage of the journey allowed Marius to beat the odds. In 107 B.C., he was elected the junior consul, in large measure because of his military reputation and his opposition to nullifying limits on how often a veteran could be called to service.

The People then demanded the recall of Metellus from his commission in Africa Province and the substitution of Marius in his place. Tradition had allowed the Senate to make such decisions. However, as a constitutional matter, pre-dating the Punic wars, the People had the legal right to appoint and remove office-holders. The problem for Marius was that Metellus had every right to bring the army back to Rome with him. Once there, they would be conscripted for use against the Cimbri, the Teutones and their growing number of Gallic allies. Marius had the command, but no army.

When he took office as consul, he made a dramatic

announcement. Given that Rome and Italy were radically depopulated of farmer-soldiers able to equip themselves, he intended to raise a new army from the *capite censi* and have them equipped at the expense of the state. The Senate howled and refused the whole idea. Marius took it to the People and won. Thus he created the first professional army in the west.

While Marius and the head count army were keeping Jugurtha on the run in Numidia, another political appointee, Lucius Cassius, had taken the six armies Metellus brought home from Africa and led them against the Celts and their Gallic allies. His first encounter with them convinced him that they were disorganized barbarians. So when he decided to pursue them, he did not take even elementary precautions, such as tightening the ranks or marching in a defensive formation. As a result, he and his army were caught in a carefully laid ambush, and he and an estimated thirty-five thousand Roman soldiers died. That is a huge number in terms of ancient populations.

After making short work of Jugurtha and returning to Rome triumphant, Marius was chosen by the People to defend Italy from those same Celts and their Gallic allies. Emboldened by their victories over Roman armies, they planned a two-pronged attack on Rome. Marius and his head count army, brilliantly trained by their innovative leader, annihilated the horde that took the coastal route. In so doing, he had to let the other half reach the Po valley via the Alps. The next year, 101 B.C., he caught up with and crushed them as well.

By that point, Marius had been elected consul by the regular means in 107 B.C. and again in 104 B.C. in *absentia*, a completely extra-constitutional act. He was re-elected by more conventional means in 103 B.C., 102 B.C. and 101 B.C.. After saving the city, Marius was rewarded with another victory as consul in 100 B.C.. It was unprecedented and it outraged the oligarchy.

To make matters worse from their point of view, Marius demanded land for his veterans from the public lands, the lands that once belonged to other nations before they were conquered by Rome. The oligarchs had long been, quite unlawfully, selling or leasing that land for their own profits. By complicated, and rather dull, parliamentary maneuvering, they managed to resist his demands and to push him out of the public eye.

### Civil War

The Senate had its own rising star, Lucius Cornelius Sulla, a patrician loyalist who had learned to fight with Marius, but broke with him over matters of policy. Allied Italians fought a war with Rome because she refused to grant them citizenship despite their having fought several wars on Rome's side. Sulla prosecuted this war, usually called the Social War, on behalf of the Senate, while Marius had very little to do with it, most likely because he agreed with the Italians. They had died in droves in the failures of Silanus and Cassius, and he was always a fair man, especially to veterans.

Meanwhile, Mithradates, an eastern potentate, was

playing havoc with Roman interests in Asia, and Sulla, the Senate's favorite, got the coveted eastern command. Before marching east, Sulla used his legions to buttress the Senate, and drove Marius into exile in Africa. Mithradates had taken advantage of the Social War to take over Anatolia (modern Turkey) and even to attack Greece. Sulla drove him back, but settled with him leniently. Mithradates kept his kingdom because Sulla was anxious to get back to Rome.

Marius returned to Rome with a faithful army of irregulars, overturned the Senate, and established exactly the sort of popular government that the oligarchs had long dreaded. Sulla dashed home only to find that Marius had died of natural causes. Sulla's experienced legions made short work of Marius' levies, and Senatorial power was brought back with the appointment of Sulla as dictator. Sadly, the restoration was considerably bloodier than the Marian coup d'etat.

The Senatorial government that Sulla rebuilt got by reasonably well in the years after his death in 78 B.C., but they faced some problems they could not solve by themselves. There was a rebellion in Spain to be quelled, rampant piracy in the Mediterranean, which threatened the city's grain supply and, yet again, trouble with Mithradates. As McEvedy writes in *The New Penguin Atlas of Ancient History*:

> In each case, the Senate turned to Pompey, the ablest of Sulla's lieutenants. He did not disappoint. He put down the Spanish revolt (76-71 B.C.), swept the pirates from the seas (67 B.C.) and then moved against Mithradates ... Pompey's victories were quick and conclusive: he followed them up

by making the direct settlement of eastern affairs that the Senate had been avoiding for the last century (64 B.C.)

He had eliminated the most important enemies of the empire while greatly extending its territory and increasing its annual revenues from 8,350 talents to 22,500 talents. The Senate should have been grateful but they weren't. The essential problem was that Pompey had accomplished so much that their political reflex was to cut him down to their size. They waited until he disbanded his army before denying the very reasonable demands he had made for his veterans.

Embittered, he was an easy target for recruitment into the camp of the Senate's enemies, chief of whom was Julius Caesar. He had led an army in the conquest of Gaul and written dispatches home to the Senate and the People describing his victories. These greatly enhanced his prestige, or *auctoritas*, and scared the Senate witless. McEvedy writes of him:

> The man who had gone into politics to pay his debts returned to Rome with the Empire in his pocket and Cleopatra ... on his arm. Caesar's political administration was like his generalship, active and efficient, but behind the urgency of the reformer lay the restlessness of an opportunist.

Having the Empire in his pocket was a mixed blessing, but a queen on his arm was an unmitigated disaster. Romans hated kings and Caesar too nearly resembled someone aspiring to that role. As a consequence, he was assassinated in 44 B.C. One might have expected a Republican reaction, but the Republic was dead in all but name only. Instead, Caesar's heir, Octavius, and Caesar's lieutenant, Anthony, joined forces. In a single battle in 42 B.C., they defeated what the remaining Republican forces.

Octavius and Anthony then divided the Empire into three parts. Anthony got the more troublesome east because he was the more experienced general. Octavius got the west. Africa went to Lepidus, described by McEvedy as a "myopic grandee whom Anthony and Octavius had been carrying around with them to reassure the conservatives."

Anthony found solace in the arms of Cleopatra and used his exhausted and diminished legions to win back her Ptolemaic kingdom. Not surprisingly, when the inevitable rift between Anthony and Octavius resulted in a military showdown, his legions deserted him. He committed suicide, as did Cleopatra after her capture, while her son by Caesar was killed so that Octavius' claims as Caesar's heir were undisputed. McEvedy then writes:

> With unchallengeable hegemony, and the new name of Augustus, Octavius now gave the Mediterranean world what it had lacked for so long, internal peace and sensible frontiers.

In addition, Augustus reorganized the army, and stationed the legions at the frontiers, where they were least likely to meddle in Roman politics. He reorganized the bureaucracy along much more efficient lines and gave himself a variety of small but key offices within it. He respected the middle classes and recruited them as his administrators and provincial governors, receiving in return their undying loyalty. He made fashionable again old notions of devotion to duty and selfless service.

Augustus rebuilt the temples and encouraged poets and other writers, such as Horace and Virgil, to revive the old values, the *mores maiorum*. He referred to himself as the first among equals, and he was first not so much because of his power, but because of his legendary *auctoritas*, a concept with a long Republican history. What he restored was not the Republic as it had been in the past. Rather, he restored a respect for good government, which had been lost. He succeeded because that was what most people wanted.

Rome began with the rule of an elite patrician caste. Over time, access to power opened up to the plebeians, who had exclusive access to some important political institutions, as well as growing access to positions from which they were previously barred. Some plebeian institutions even acquired sovereignty, which is the final right to rule.

However, that sovereignty had lapsed, not by law but by custom, in the rigors of prolonged Punic wars. Rome thus became, *de facto* but not *de jure*,* an oligarchy of the rich, both patrician and plebeian. As that oligarchy acquired

* These are Latin terms for in fact and in the law. Which one is which is obvious to an English speaker.

provinces to plunder, under the guise of governance, their economic, and with it their political power, hinged on the ability of Roman armies and their generals to win still more provinces.

## The New Order

When wealth and political clout began to cause total incompetents to be given important military appointments, serious civil strife was the obvious next step. With Marius, Sulla, Caesar and Pompey, we see a return to balance. Great generals win huge victories that benefit Rome and she rewards them with the top political jobs.

Augustus played that game and won. Then he changed the playing field. As McEvedy explains:

> Caesar's dazzling talents had kept the Mediterranean world in turmoil: the grey genius of Augustus created peace and prosperity, and the machinery for its continuance. He used men wisely, shunned the spectacular and died in bed.

His creation of a machinery for continuity, stability and good government cannot be emphasized too strongly. He was succeeded by the dour Tiberius, the insane Caligula, the old but honest Claudius and the outrageous Nero. Through all this the basic structure of governance in Rome and in the Empire survived largely intact. Highlighting the value of the structure and the failure of the man, McEvedy writes of Nero:

> His position required little more of him than the

appearance of gravity, yet this was a role that Nero, the self-described actor, was never able to sustain ... The end came ... when the governor of Spain proclaimed the Emperor's unworthiness and marched on Rome. Besides the Praetorians, Nero had a newly raised legion in Italy ... [But] he was unable to interest either in his survival and the last of the Julio-Claudians died by his own shaky hand.

One general replaced another as Emperor until Vespasian, the general in charge of quelling the Jewish revolt, won and established the next major dynasty, the Flavians. They returned Rome to the professional government instituted by Augustus. Vespasian also ordered the construction of the Colosseum, which was finally completed by his sons Titus and Domitian.

Domitian had no heir so the Senate stepped in and appointed a highly respected old man who, to please the soldiers, adopted the gifted general Trajan to succeed him. Trajan then adopted, as heir, his cousin Hadrian, also an able military man. Hadrian reorganized the army in such a way that defense of the Empire was less costly than ever before. He also adopted another respected adult, Antoninus Pius, who then adopted Marcus Aurelius. The period from Hadrian to Marcus has been hailed as the golden age of the Empire. The Roman practice of adopting adults allowed political power and military prowess to combine in a system of stable succession.

Marcus Aurelius abandoned this system and Rome suffered. McEvedy writes:

Marcus (161- 180) spoilt the sequence by bequeathing the purple to his foolish son Commodus, whose assassination provoked a civil war similar to that at Nero's death. The British, Danubian and eastern armies each proclaimed their candidates; not surprisingly it was the choice of the biggest battalions, the Danubian commander Septimius Severus, who made good. He ruled from 193-211; the Empire then passed through an increasingly alarming series of his relatives, the last of whom was assassinated in 235.

Before explaining what happened next, it might be wise to recap the overall patterns to this point.

In the time of Gaius Marius, political hacks were set up as generals who saw their first duty as filling their own coffers. Their repeated failures set the stage for change, for a military man to win political office and lead a professional army with agendas having to do with rewarding veterans. This offended the oligarchy and thus caused a series of civil wars that Augustus ended by reorganizing the government with an eye to order and continuity. With a few glitches, he succeeded in structuring a very stable administrative apparatus, which could even sustain the occasional truly disastrous emperor.

Another piece of Augustan reorganization worked as follows. We remember that he instituted the practice of locals manning an auxiliary legion and becoming, at the end of their service, Roman citizens. From then on, the armies garrisoned in each province were actually local people with a stake in local defense. The governor of a Roman province would have satisfactorily completed a series of military and civilian jobs, the *cursus honorum*, and as governor, was general to the army garrisoned in that province. Remembering that public office holding conferred *nobilis* on a man, these governor generals were also "aristocrats." So the Senate did not mind very much when an army elevated its general to the purple as he would, by definition, have the required credentials. In McEvedy's words, "the move was illegal but the piece was orthodox."

Then, in 235, the legions of the Rhine broke all the rules. They murdered the last relative of Septimius Severus and proceeded to declare a Thracian soldier, Maximin, with no political office at his back and thus no *nobilis* (and worse obscure birth), as their choice for Emperor. The Senate was outraged and armed Italy against an invasion. They held off Maximin long enough for his army to doubt his credentials as their leader. The soldiers murdered him and the Senatorial candidates as well. As McEvedy explains:

> After an uneasy pause, compromise prevailed in the Emperors Decius, Gallus and Valerian, who were generals and gentlemen (244-260). Their total lack of success destroyed the prestige of the old Imperial system and with it resistance to frank military despotism.

Military power had bested political power decisively and would dominate so completely that the Roman Empire would know very little other than chaos for the next two decades and more. From 235 to 284 there were at least twenty Emperors with Senatorial blessing, and that number or more without it. Armies not only proclaimed their generals Emperors, but, in order to improve their pay, armies put themselves up for auction to the highest bidder.

## Diocletian

While all this was going on, nations on all of Rome's frontiers began to seep into the Empire. As the holes in its borders were enlarged, whole migrations were allowed to pass, often unobstructed, as "Roman" armies fought one another for primacy. In 284, another general, Diocletian,* came to the fore, in what seemed likely to be but another episode in the ongoing saga of civil war. Diocletian, however, was different. Like Augustus, he reorganized Rome with an eye to stability and continuity.

*Aspects of Antiquity* is a glorious collection of essays by M.I. Finley, who writes like a dream. "The Emperor Diocletian" is so thoughtful, so measured and so elegant that it is very hard to take up the subject without quoting him extensively. I shall not make the attempt.

> The secret of Diocletian's survival lay in his simple realism. He accepted the Roman world as it was, he reduced its problems to their simplest possible terms, and he made simple solutions, applied with untiring energy, great attention to detail and total ruthlessness. The army

* Rightly or wrongly, we pronounce this Dye eh klee shun with the emphasis on klee.

was the key, both for good and for evil: the protector of the empire against external enemies and against revolts within, on the one hand, and on the other hand the nursery to pretenders to the throne.

Therefore, he set out to change how the army was structured in relation to the state. Diocletian divided the Empire into two, an eastern and a western half. He gave himself the east, the richer, older, more civilized half, and appointed another *Augustus* for the west, endowed with slightly less power and considerably less *auctoritas* than Diocletian himself. Indeed, he took advantage of the eastern proclivity for god-like rulers. He always dressed lavishly and had his subjects kiss the hems of his garments. Dividing the Empire in half made each part more governable, not only because of the considerable reduction in size, but also because the two halves were thoroughly and importantly different, and so presented importantly different problems. It is not clear that Diocletian fully appreciated this second advantage.

To each *Augustus* he assigned a *Caesar*, or second in command, who was the heir to the throne. The idea was that, if each *Caesar* knew he would succeed his particular *Augustus*, he would then be vigilant on his behalf. Each *Augusti* had a Prefect, who was drawn from the Praetorian Guard, a special legion assigned to protect their person. Diocletian thus took provincial government away from the generals. The Empire was then divided into much smaller units, each headed by a civilian, called a *Dux*. These were grouped into various Dioceses, which were governed by another civilian *Vicarius* or Vicar, who answered directly to the Praetorian Prefect. This civilian chain of command insulated the Emperor from military "pretenders to the throne." As Finley notes:

> Diocletian enlarged the army, reorganized it, improved the pay and promotion system, and subordinated everything to its needs. To supply the army's food, clothing, weapons and transport, he vastly extended the system of compulsory contributions in kind, embracing the majority of the population of the empire.

Diocletian also attempted to make a set of sweeping changes to the economy without any clear ideas about how it worked. He failed to curb inflation, which was his primary goal, but he did contribute to major social changes that deserve our attention, but at another point in this book. While we are here we might note that the civilian organization with Vicars and such was the model for the Christian Church when it was finally and formally institutionalized.

The author of more than a dozen books on ancient Greece and Rome, Moses Finley deplores the tendency of modern writers to extract dire "lessons" for the modern world from the example of Diocletian's bureaucratic failures. He argues that the situations are so radically different that such applications cannot stand.

> Modern values and moral judgements are confused with practical judgements. The plain fact about Diocletian's

reign, whether we like it or not, is that it was a great success. He saved the Roman Empire, so completely that in the east it lived on, much along the lines he laid down, for more than a thousand years – for Diocletian may properly be called the first Byzantine emperor. How many states in history have had a longer life?

To this line of reasoning, Finley adds, many modern scholars retort that he saved a state that was not worth saving. Finley agrees that "Diocletian's world was an appalling one ... shot full of brutality." In support of this, he cites the writings of a Christian, highly critical of Diocletian's fellow *Augusti*, Galerius, who probably engineered the various persecutions of the era:

I have read nothing more disgusting than his long, detailed and complacent description of Galerius' slow, agonizing death from some loathsome disease. It was a world without freedom, without creativity, and without hope: men looked for salvation in the after-life, not here on earth. It was a world of mass servitude alongside outrageous wealth, of bombast and ignorance and dreadful superstition.

However, Finley argues, this was not entirely nor even mainly Diocletian's fault. He accepted the Roman world as he found it and as it had been for centuries. Finley uses the marvelous phrase a "political policy of calculated frightfulness" to describe other moments in Rome's history. He cites particularly the destruction of Carthage at the end of the last Punic War, the reprisals Sulla took against the defeated followers of Marius and the crucifixion of 6,000 slaves after the defeat of Spartacus.

Yet these were extraordinary moments: the end of a foreign war, the end of a civil war and the end of an uprising that threatened the very foundation of Roman life. Diocletian also seized power at an extraordinary moment, a moment when the whole enterprise that was the Roman Empire was tottering on the brink. He could have been just one more in the long list of contenders for the throne. Instead, he was a man with the particular qualities needed to end the dominance of warfare over statecraft. Had he not come forward and taken the reigns, the empire would have crumbled before her enemies on all sides. Diocletian's restructuring saved the East Roman Empire and laid the foundation of what would follow in the west. That story is embedded in the lives of another set of players not yet seen on our stage, the horsemen. They will come later. But first ...

## Her Hand in Marriage

Alliances can be an element in political, economic and military power. The principle tool in forming alliances, until fairly recently, was matrimony. Romans had a number of forms of marriage, but the important ones for this discussion are with or without *manus*, the Latin word for "hand." The *mores maiorum* had the *paterfamilias* give away the *manus* of the bride to the *paterfamilias* of her new husband. She was then just as fully subject to the wishes of that *paterfamilias*, whether her husband, his father or some other senior male as she had been to her birth *paterfamilias*.

This is a system completely congruent with the notion that a woman marries once and for life. We remember Cornelia, mother of the Gracchi, whose husband died and who refused all subsequent proposals with the assertion "I am already married." She had, on the occasion of her marriage, joined another family to whom she was now permanently attached.

However, over time wealth and power became more abundant and fortunes became more changeable. This gave rise to many more marriages without *manus*, such that the bride remained under the control of her birth *paterfamilias*. If the husband's family suffered a reversal of fortunes, whether economic or political, the woman could be snatched out of that situation and married to a more advantageous ally. All of which makes hash of the ideal of a woman marrying once and for life.

As we know, Roman women could go out to dinners, parties, the races and other places where they encountered men. What was to stop a discontented wife from pursuing her own vision of a more prosperous, more powerful or more congenial partner? The great Augustus himself fell pray to a scheming married woman. As it happens, her husband was her *paterfamilias*, so this was a marriage with *manus*. Nevertheless, Livia made a complete conquest of Augustus and her husband, wisely, saw this as an opportunity. He was right. His son with Livia, Tiberius, succeeded

Augustus to the purple.

Using the women in the family as marital, and thus sexual, pawns in the pursuit of power had, ironically, the force of empowering these women as the case of Livia clearly illustrates. Without *manus*, the husband she lived with cannot invoke his family's claim to their right to govern her conduct because they have none. The genie was out of the bottle as far as the self-enforced chastity of women. Augustus kept trying to stick it back into the bottle by exhorting the *mores maiorum*. It never worked.

The contemporary poet, Ovid, wrote a marvelously wry, sly and funny book called *The Art of Love*. It includes quite a bit of advice about the seduction of married women and Augustus exiled Ovid, probably for this reason. Some think Augustus was also motivated by Ovid's failure to tell him about his daughter Julia's reputation. Augustus had forced his stepson, Tiberius, into divorcing his much-loved wife and marrying the fiery and difficult Julia. She rebelled against her father's wishes on an extravagant scale, apparently earning a reputation of unbridled sexual license. In the end, Augustus exiled her as well.

Prior to that, he had insisted that his wife and daughter spin yarn, weave cloth and fashion it into garments that Augustus wore. It was part of his campaign for the *mores maiorum*, but it may have had a canny ulterior motive. He looked like a complete country bumpkin and not at all like the most powerful man in Rome. Since he did not wish to follow in Caesar's footsteps, avoiding any appearance of becoming a king suited him to the ground.

## Family Matters

It is commonplace to say, "It isn't what you know; it's who you know." What is meant here, of course, is that knowledge and expertise are too often trumped by insider connections. Indeed, this is so. However, there is another way to consider the relationship between what you know and who you know. What you know is heavily dependent on who you know.

To use a personal example, my grandfather used the word pusillanimous* in ordinary speech. When someone annoyed him, one of his epithets was, "He's just a pusillanimous mass!" In my experience, this word has appeared in two books by Colin McEvedy, the S.A.T. test and the Graduate Record Exams. Thanks, Grandpa.

To use an historical example, consider Lucius Cornelius Sulla. He was a patrician very much on the skids with not the smallest chance of achieving either political or military power. All that changed when a young patrician girl, living nearby, decided he was the one for her. Her name was Julia, but she was called Julilla in the family as her older sister was also named Julia. To the outside world, they were Julia Major and Julia Minor. Similarly, all the women in Sulla's patrician family were called Cornelia.

Julia Major married a much older man, her father's choice but very much to her liking, who was the sensible yet brilliant general and consul, Gaius Marius. When Julilla got her way and married Sulla, their joint father-in-law per-

* It means cowardly.

suaded Marius to advance Sulla's career. Thus, through this very small quirk of fate, Sulla learned military matters from, by far and away, the best general of his generation.

Julia, Major and Minor, had two brothers. One was called Gaius Julius Caesar, and he had a son that he named, to no one's great surprise, Gaius Julius Caesar. The son was the chap who got himself assassinated, in part, for having a queen on his arm. He was thus nephew to both Marius and Sulla. However, Julilla died young and the Sulla connection was broken. It would be Gaius Marius who would mentor young Caesar and turn him into the greatest general of his generation.

Meanwhile, Pompey was the most talented of Sulla's lieutenants. When he became disillusioned with the Senatorial party, he and Caesar joined forces. Although the two men were quite near in age, their bond was sealed by his marriage to Caesar's daughter. Her name, of course, was Julia, and she had quite the crush on Pompey. His exploits vanquishing pirates had made him the Roman equivalent of a pop star. Julia's death would drive an intractable wedge between these two men who had both so dearly loved her.

Mark Anthony was a protégé of Julius Caesar, and so learned his fighting skills from the best of that generation. Unfortunately for him, he did not understand the Cleopatra mistake, and that lost him the support of his army. Mark Anthony's ally, enemy, and ultimately his downfall, was Octavian, the great nephew of Caesar.

Augustus, as he dubbed himself, learned military tactics and techniques from his great-uncle Julius, but he also learned from his dire example not to embrace any of the trappings of kingship. Indeed, he insisted emphatically that he was never any more than *primus inter pares*, first among equals. It all worked out very well for him. What you know very often depends, in very important ways, on who you know.

# Slavery

**IN** much of ancient Greece and all of ancient Rome, slavery played a significant role. It is, therefore, important to understand how this practice worked. Unfortunately, what most of us know, or think we know, about ancient slavery is clouded by two serious misapprehensions. The first is that slavery was more widespread in antiquity than it actually was. The second and more misleading error lies in assuming that slavery in ancient Greece and Rome was very much like slavery in the American South. In crucial ways it most certainly was not.

To understand the first issue, we might begin by looking at the distribution of slavery in the ancient world. While slaves existed in the great agricultural empires of antiquity, including Egypt, Babylonia and Persia, they were not an important element in these economic systems. In fact, slaves were vastly outnumbered by the much more important traditional peasant farmers.

By contrast, where slaves were present in ancient Greece, they were typically a central element in the economic picture.* The same was true of the city of Rome, of the large private estates in her western imperial provinces, and also of most aspects of the government apparatus itself. For our purposes, phrases such as "slavery in antiquity" and "ancient slavery" are limited to these highly significant Greek and Roman institutions.

## The American Comparison

It is tempting for modern people to look to the experience of slavery in the American South as a model for understanding slavery in the ancient world. What makes this particularly tricky is the fact that there are ways in which the two are basically similar, and other ways in which they are totally different. We will begin with a critically important difference. American slavery co-existed with a modern economic system that we call capitalism. Ancient slavery did not. Not having capitalism in the picture explains, in crucial ways, why slavery played a much larger role in antiquity, across a much wider array of activities, than was true in the American South. To understand this, we must take a brief detour.

An essential element in capitalism is a market in abstracted labor. The ability to buy three-quarters of an hour of a plumber's time is an example of abstracted labor. So is the ability to buy an eight-hour day with provisions for overtime. Another example of abstracted labor is the ability

---

* As we noted in "Hellas," the primary exception is found with the helots, who performed the arduous and menial tasks for Spartans, which were elsewhere consigned to slaves.

to engage a skilled technician to be on call around the clock, for a single day, in the event of an emergency, but, who is paid only for the actual hours worked.

Having a market in abstracted labor was an element in the economic revolution that contributed enormously to the development of capitalism. How, when, where and why that revolution took place are all hotly contested issues. Fortunately, they are also outside the scope of this story. We can all agree, however, that one of the features defining capitalism is the presence of a market in abstracted labor, and that this market is possible only if we can assign a monetary value to various kinds of labor.

The ancients did not have markets in abstracted labor. They had, indeed, no notion that labor could be abstracted, and certainly no notion that this abstracted labor could have monetary value. Let us look at a marvelous example of the disconnect between the way the ancients thought about commerce, value and labor and the understandings that we completely take for granted. For Cicero, the great Roman thinker, this example is hypothetical in all its details, but his reaction to it is deeply heart-felt.

A shipment, including a consignment of trinkets, lands at the port of Rome, which is actually some distance from the city proper. Each trinket sells for ten *sesterces*, a unit of Roman money. A merchant takes the time to travel to the port, selects the most attractive trinkets and brings them back to his conveniently located shop in Rome. He then polishes them, displays them to their best advantage and charges twelve *sesterces* per trinket.

To the modern mind, this is both reasonable and obvious. The merchant, by his labor, did a number of things to enhance the value of the trinkets by making them more attractive and more convenient to the buying public. Besides, if he sold the trinkets for the same price he had paid for them, going to all that trouble would make absolutely no sense.

However, to Cicero, a very smart and knowledgeable Roman, making the product more desirable and/or accessible did not warrant a change in the price. To him, such an increase was patently a form of theft to be despised, which likely accounts for why merchants were held in very low esteem by the "best people." He lacked, entirely, any notion that the merchant's labor increased the worth of the trinkets and justified an increase in the price. At no point does he ponder the question of why the merchant would go to all that trouble to buy the trinkets at ten *sesterces* and then sell them for the same price.

In part, this has to do with the fact that the workings of a market were not terribly interesting to him. He does observe that merchants who go very far afield and bring back grains or papyrus from Egypt, or other desirable goods from other distant sites, are entitled to some remuneration, because they are performing a useful public service. We are very far away from the world of capitalism here.

## Ancient Commerce

In ancient Egypt, with a traditional peasant base and a command structure at the top, trade at the lower ends was confined to barter, and at the upper ends to ceremonial or customary exchanges between temples or between temples and palaces. Trade between the courts of Egypt, Persia, Babylonia and Lydia were also ceremonial exchanges designed to impress the recipient with the wealth and generosity of the donor.

According to Herodotus, crude coins were first fashioned in Lydia, in Asia Minor, at a point that we date to 687 B.C. Then, sometime between 640 and 630 B.C., true coins were minted from electrum, a naturally occurring blend of silver and gold. The coins, themselves, could be part of a ceremonial offering both to cement a relationship and make a swank impression because they were made of precious metals. Alternatively, they could be used to purchase other luxuries for the ceremonial exchange.

Some Hellenes, notably the Athenians and Corinthians, both big on commerce, were quick to adopt the use of money. Those that did were more interested in the usefulness of a "money-commodity," a thing that had an agreed upon value and could be used interchangeably, regardless of what was being bought or sold. Although they would not talk about it in such sophisticated economic terms, the point is that Hellenes were mainly interested in the utility of coins as facilitating trade.

The Romans were still more relentlessly commercial and they invented and used a great many complex financial institutions, types of partnerships and convoluted monetary transactions. Some part of the complexity may be explained by a paradox. In the spirit of Cicero and his merchant bashing, men of the Senatorial class were actively forbidden to

engage in any form of commerce, and could lose their positions if caught. However, making it up the *cursus honorum**
was not cheap, so many of those who landed in the Senate were, and had been for years, very silent partners in some of the most lucrative commercial ventures of their day.

The involvement of Rome in so much trade and, indeed, in some serious manufacturing, has led some less-economically savvy modern historians to the myth of "Roman capitalism." A market in abstracted labor is essential to capitalism and it did not exist in the ancient world. Had such a market existed, the notion of labor adding value would have been obvious to Cicero. Capitalism devoid of wages and salaries, the monetary reward for providing abstracted labor, makes no sense. Slavery in the ancient world did not co-exist with capitalism, and this had enormous consequences as we shall see.

## Ancient Slavery

Without a market in labor, ancients bought three categories of goods. They bought the end products of labor, such as the farmers' apples, the masons' headstones or the restauranteurs' hot pies and other delicacies. As examples of the second category, they might commission something that would require labor, but which had not yet been made, like a custom fountain for the atrium.

However, if they wanted to commission a task that was too complex, too open-ended and too contingent on unknown

---

* The "way of honor" was a progression of political offices from senator to quaestor to praetor and, finally, to the highest position of consul.

variables, they bought a whole person. Therein lays the most dramatic and significant difference between ancient and American slavery. When Americans needed to commission complex, contingent tasks requiring decision-making skills, they *hired* a person. That was *not* an option for the ancients.

We must be very clear here. Ancient slavery did not come about because of the absence of a market in abstracted labor. That would be putting the cart before the horse. Buying and selling people is a very old practice. The point is that, in America, a plantation owner could hire all the necessary skilled workers to perform complex, contingent tasks. This, in turn, made it possible to relegate only the least-skilled, most menial tasks to slaves. Since the doctors, lawyers, accountants, bankers, etc. were all white, and the farm hands, servants, etc. were all black, racism had a fertile field in which to grow.

The situation in the ancient world was far more nuanced. A wealthy Roman land owner would buy a Greek doctor to minister to his household, including his slaves, and a Greek tutor for his children. He could not take the view that these men were inferior to him intellectually. Similarly, the manager of the largest bank in classical Athens was a slave simply because that was a very complex, open-ended and contingent job. Without the notion of abstracted labor, it was unthinkable to hire someone to do such a job. To let the bank managing slave get on with his work, he, too, would own slaves for his routine personal maintenance. This is very hard for the modern mind to grasp.

As we saw, Romans had a huge number of social clubs

based on some common interest where freemen, freedmen and slaves socialized together with no one batting an eyelash. Moreover, while race played a minor role in ancient slavery, it never led to racism of the sort so prevalent in America. It was more like specializing. Generally speaking, Greeks made good doctors and tutors while Germans were especially handy when it came to heavy lifting. Because slaves performed tasks from the most menial to the most complex, and because they were not limited to a single race or ethnic group, the nature of ancient slavery was radically different from the American slave experience.

In the various cities of ancient Rome, including Rome herself, the basic accounting and bookkeeping functions were done by slaves who were owned by the municipality. If they performed well, they were usually manumitted as a sort of retirement present. Any children they had while they were slaves continued to belong to the city and, usually, took on the same tasks and duties that their fathers had performed. Children born after manumission were free. These free men would often have brothers who were still slaves, while their father was, himself, a freedman.

In the ancient world, there were three basic ways to become a slave. A person could be born to it, as in the example above. Alternatively, "barbarians" sometimes sold what McEvedy has called "surplus progeny" into slavery. We think this may have happened to the Scythian slaves who formed the Athenian police force under Peisistratus.

Finally, a free person could be captured, either as part of a losing army or as an individual traveller who was kidnapped, and sold into slavery. In each of these cases, becoming a slave was an accident, of birth, of selection or of being in the wrong place at the wrong time. The chance nature of becoming a slave meant that there was no particular stigma attached to the status. The renowned Roman comic playwright, Terrence, was born in North Africa and probably started his life as a slave.

The brilliant Roman satirist, Horace, was the son of a freedman whom he idolized. Horace is best known to modern readers for adapting Aesop's fable of the city mouse and the country mouse. He is also noted for his satires. In "Book One Satire Five," Horace recounted a journey he took with Maecenas* to a summit conference that put off the final showdown between Octavian and Mark Anthony for a further six years. Horace had no apparent interest in the critically important politics of the moment. Instead, he comments, quite humorously, on elements of the journey itself, such as the "blasted mosquitoes and marsh frogs" that rendered sleep impossible.

He does mention Maecenas joining the journey, and notes that he and his companions "were envoys on a mission of immense importance; both were adept at reconciling friends ..." who had quarreled. They were also joined by Fonteius Capito, "a man of consummate charm and tact, who held a unique place in Anthony's affections."

That the son of a freedman could be hobnobbing with

---

* Maecenas was the best friend of Octavian who would, as you may recall, change his name to Augustus later. The Penguin Classics *Horace: Satires and Epistles*, translated and annotated by Niall Rudd, is a wonderful source.

the political elites of his day speaks volumes about the fluidity of the lines between slave, freed and free. Indeed, it would appear that, in multicultural Rome, there was no obvious way to distinguish between the free and the enslaved. This difficulty is evidenced by a little vignette played out in the Senate in the first century of our era.

A Senator put forth a proposal that slaves should be compelled to wear some manner of identifying symbol. This strongly suggests that they were indistinguishable from free people in ordinary, everyday life. Seneca, a well known Roman writer, reeled in horror at the suggestion because then "they" – the slaves – would be able to see quite plainly how many more of "them" there were than of "us." This, in his view, was to court disaster.

The changeable nature of status from free to slave or from slave to freed is also mirrored by the complexity of each status. A free Roman in a trade might apprentice his sons to learn the trade, but also one or more slaves to do the same. The master might keep the slaves and sell the products of their labor for his own benefit. He might also sell the trained slaves to a household in need of a carpenter, a butcher, a mason and so forth.

In the great households, made up of a number of estates as well as a mansion in town, it was usual to keep a comprehensive variety of specialized slaves. Carpenters might replace worn furniture or provide for a bride's dowry with a starter kit of household needs, appropriate to her status. Interestingly, such artisans, in their spare time, could make things to sell to the general public, paying a cut to their owner and keeping some for themselves. In a world in which you cannot hire a worker because there is no market in abstracted labor, economic relations can be extremely complex.

## Common Ground

While ancient slavery and slavery in America were two significantly different systems, they do have some common features. For instance, in both the ancient world and the American South the slave experience could vary depending on the tasks assigned to each slave. However, the discrepancies between jobs were much more pronounced in antiquity than they were in America. The ancients, as we have seen, had no concept of hiring a worker who is otherwise free. This meant that slaves might be doctors, tutors, bankers and the like. Nothing like this existed in the South.

For any point in history, including the ancient world, the worst kind of slavery for women was sexual slavery. Prostitute in Greek is *pornoi*, from which we get the word pornography, with its strongly negative connotations. These women should never be confused with the famous Athenian courtesans who were free and used wit, charm and intelligence to make their way in life. The *pornoi*, by contrast, were forced to appear naked in public. Herodotus expressed the most common Greek attitude to women and clothing. "A woman takes off her claim to respect along with her garments." For the slave *pornoi*, being forced into public nudity was a considerable humiliation. Worse, any man who paid her master's fee had a license to rape her.

For the master to have free sexual access to a slave of

either gender is one of the most universal qualities of slavery anywhere at any time. Instances of male slave owners in the American South having sex with female slaves have been extensively documented. Instances of male slave owners having sex with male slaves must also have occurred in the South, but who would have documented it? Certainly the owner would not, as he lived in a highly homophobic world. There does not appear to have been a practice in the South of organizing female slaves into brothels. This was most likely caused by a racism that condoned having sex with a black woman in private, but not paying for it in the more public setting of a house of ill repute.

Another factor critical to the slave experience, in both the ancient and the southern world, was the character of the master and the quality of the master-slave relationship. Cruel and sadistic masters existed in both worlds, of course, as ownership of another human being can bring out the very worst in anyone's nature.

However, because there was no racial component to ancient slavery, there was no sense of an inherent superiority of the master or inferiority of the slave. The quite famous relationship between Cicero and Tiro, his educated and literate slave, was one of close personal friendship. Cicero's favorite person, after his beloved daughter, was Tiro. The relationship was also professional in that Cicero submitted all of his writing for Tiro's approval. After Cicero's death, Tiro used his own money, earned in Cicero's service, to publish Cicero's as yet unpublished works.

No comparable relationship is imaginable in the American South, where it was frequently unlawful to teach a slave to read. However, strong friendships *did* arise between masters and slaves, particularly when they grew up together. In wealthy families, each child was assigned a personal slave, only slightly older, and they played together, talked together and knew each other, in all likelihood, better than either knew anyone else.

Eugene Genovese wrote a complex, subtle, and comprehensive book about slavery in the American South called *Roll, Jordan, Roll: The World the Slaves Made.* He relates a story that took place during the Civil War. A master calls in a slave who has been with him since childhood and asks, if the Yankees come, would the slave kill him. Oh, no, the slave reassures the master, "I would never kill *you.*" But, adds the slave, he would certainly go down the road and kill the master next door.

This brings us to another feature of slavery in the American South. It was all kinds of dreadful but it was not segregated. Almost forty years after abolition, an intriguing story about the kind relationships that could develop between masters and slaves emerged in some recently rediscovered newspaper articles. These were found in steamer trunks left untouched since 1917, when they were first put into a vault in the basement of a bank. They belonged to Mary Custis Lee, the oldest daughter of Robert E. Lee and a descendent, on her mother's side, of Martha Washington.

The trunks contained letters from her father with great historic value and others with small personal touches, like his consoling her on the loss of their Arlington plantation to

Union soldiers on Christmas Day in 1861. Mary also preserved a letter written to her mother by a former Lee slave. She wrote that she and other former Lee slaves had settled on the Arlington property, and that she was in a "comfortable home" of her own. Evidently, she felt that Mrs. Lee would be interested in this news. That Mrs. Lee saved the letter suggests that this was the case.*

There were also several newspaper clippings from June of 1902 that recounted the arrest of Mary Custis Lee for violating the segregation laws and sitting in the black section of a public transit vehicle. She did not show up for her court date and her bail money was forfeited. The judge did allow the conductor who had caused her arrest to explain how she refused to leave the black only compartment. Clearly, she was guilty as charged.

While this incident might seem baffling but, if you understand American slavery at a deeper level, it is not baffling at all. Most likely, one of the segregated passengers was a former Lee slave, perhaps even the writer of the letter Mrs. Lee had saved, and one with whom Mary had a bond of affection and loyalty. Lee accepted arrest instead of dishonoring that bond. Indeed, she was not alone in so defying the law. One report called her action, "Another fool exhibition of the asinine prejudice of 'chivalrous' Southerners."

It has frequently been contended that the object of segregation was to prevent poor white sharecroppers and tenant

---

* Details of the Freedmen's Village, which grew up on the Lee estate, can be found in an article mainly chronicling the estate's transition to the Arlington National Cemetery. "The Battle for Arlington," *Smithsonian*, November 2009, pp. 50-57.

farmers from making common cause with their poor black counterparts. It would also have had the effect of separating poor blacks from whites with political capital, like Mary's claim to an heroic and widely beloved father. That there was a group of people, these chivalrous Southerners, like Mary Custis Lee, speaks volumes about what American slavery was and what it wasn't. It was despicable and demeaning in a whole host of ways, but it was *not* segregated.

When people own people, however much they wish to objectify them, the fact of a shared humanity can, in the right circumstances, create richly nuanced relationships. This is the common thread running through slavery in ancient Greece, ancient Rome and the American South.

The similarities between ancient and American slavery are almost universal to all systems where one person works for another. There were kind, patient and generous slave owners, and mean, spiteful, vengeful slave owners. The same can be said of bosses and managers in the modern world. There are also, everywhere and at all times, better tasks and worse tasks. Both master and task shaped and defined the slave's lot in life.

## Structural Differences

Structurally, ancient and American slavery were quite different, largely because the latter shared the stage with capitalism and the former did not. Because the American South co-existed with capitalism, masters could employ people to perform complex, managerial or merely authoritative tasks, while keeping the slaves in menial jobs. This, in turn, helped to perpetuate the myths of slavery, which emphasized the inferior capacity of the slaves and their need for a master to ensure their survival in a tough world.

Concurrently, capitalism at the time* provided a grim example of how hard the world could be. Apologists for American slavery often compared the lives of slaves in favorable terms as against the lot of England's industrial workers. In the first half of the nineteenth century, British political, as well as charitable, institutions held hearings and made investigations into the mistreatment of workers. What they found was appalling. Children as young as five were employed to crawl through narrow tunnels and pull out heavy wagons of coal. The death rate was sickening. Workers lost limbs to machinery whose owners then found them useless and fired them with no compensation. The examples could, and did, fill volumes.

Life was, ordinarily, considerably better among the slaves in the American South, in part because owners preferred a self image of benevolent and paternal concern for "their" people. At the same time, capitalism had given rise to the scientific study of economics and there was a powerful economic logic behind not killing or maiming slaves. Buying a slave was an expensive investment from which you expected to receive an ongoing return for many productive years. Starving slaves, working them to death, killing them

---

* This would be the period before capitalism reaped the benefits of plenty that came with the maturity of the Industrial Revolution. These "benefits" are now drowning us in garbage and other industrial waste. This is not a defense of slavery, of course, but rather a comment on industrialization.

over some trivial but annoying misconduct was willfully to waste this investment. Southern states often passed statutes ostensibly protecting slaves, but also protecting the slave owners as a class from those stupid enough to engage in exactly such waste.

The situation in nascent English industrial capitalism was quite different. There was no initial fee to hire a worker. Potential workers outnumbered by far the available jobs, most of which involved no skills, and thus made workers entirely interchangeable. The dynamics of supply and demand dictated that the price of such labor would be extremely low. Moreover, these low wages were paid only after the worker had finished working. If they were insufficient to keep him alive, there were always many more where he came from.

Co-existing with capitalism allowed the slave-owning class to employ free white people to do the complex managerial and clerical jobs, and to fill the less-skilled but powerful job of overseer. This made possible a mythology of black inferiority that, in turn, could justify slavery as a protective force operating on behalf of these poor folks who could not take care of themselves. As we noted above, no such argument of inferiority could be made by a Roman landowner who bought one learned Greek to tutor his children and another to be the household physician.

Apologists for American slavery pointed to other ways in which their slaves were better off than English workers and their families. As we noted above, hard labor for small children was commonplace in England. This was not only uncommon but unlawful in the American South. Again, the slave-owning class liked to imagine themselves as "protectors" of their slaves, but enlightened self-interest was also in play.

A slave child was an investment in the future and should be allowed to grow up to be a strong and capable worker. As Eugene Genovese tells us:

> The courts and public opinion considered slaves children until about twelve and then tender adolescents until their late teens. Boys of twelve might already be plowing, but they remained boys at the beginning of a slow breaking-in process. On the recommendation of the Caroline County Court, Governor James Monroe of Virginia pardoned Scipio for his part in Gabriel's rebellion because he was a mere lad, no older than eighteen or nineteen.*

Generally speaking, children under eight had no chores beyond watching over any children younger than themselves. Sadly, there were individual exceptions all over the South, where "some masters worked the little ones unmercifully from the time they could toddle." But others, many others, waited until the child was somewhere between eight and twelve to increase their chores to

> cleaning up the yards, digging up potatoes, many of which they appropriated for their own illicit roasting parties,

---

* This and the following quotes come from Eugene Genovese in *Roll, Jordan, Roll: The World the Slaves Made*. 1974

shelling peas for the kitchen, or more laboriously, toting water for the field hands. Their hardest work came during the cotton picking season, when they were sometimes called upon to help. In the fields, with little expected of them and normal childish pride in doing the work of adults, they often enjoyed themselves.

In addition to caring for smaller siblings, young children could weed and water the family's garden to help out, while older boys learned to trap small animals to augment the family's food supply. As Genovese points out, the record indicates that the children were happy to be able to help the whole family.

An English observer was pleased to see these slave children "exempted from the cruel fate, which befalls poor children of their age in the mining and manufacturing districts in England." Genovese gives us an example of this cruel fate by noting that, in 1835, more than 220,000 worked in the cotton industry of the British Isles. Of these, roughly thirteen percent were twelve years old or younger.

> Their working conditions, exposed in parliamentary investigations ... produced a measure of drunkenness, debauchery, and moral degradation among the children that no amount of bourgeois apologetics about the glories of the industrial revolution will ever erase.

As we can see, the coexistence with capitalism supported the American slave system on two fronts. As noted above, the ability to hire white intellectual workers, such as lawyers, while keeping black slaves doing physical labor, helped support the myth of the good, the smart and the white caring for the dependent black slaves who needed their help. At the same time, the early stages of industrial capitalism were so outrageous and out of control that slavery looked benign by comparison.

The economic underpinnings of the two systems were less obvious. If you bought slaves, or if your existing slaves had baby slaves, wisdom argued for nurturing them in order to get a long lifetime of productive work. By contrast, if you pay for work only after it is performed, and there are many more seeking employment than there are jobs, working them to death is no problem from a purely economic standpoint. It was no accident that the people objecting to this were doing so on extra-economic grounds. Doctors, church folks, politicians and committees of concerned citizens were decrying the situation on moral grounds and an appeal to a common humanity.

## Old Age

Slaveholders who weighed in on the subject lauded the job their class was doing in caring for slaves in their old age. Certainly they did better than their capitalist counterparts, but it would have been nearly impossible to do any worse. One Mrs. Schoolcraft, argued that the respectable white community would put unbearable pressure on any slave owner who failed in his duty to care for "his" people in their old age. There is some evidence for this in both moral and practical terms.

Mrs. Schoolcraft may have been a romantic apologist for the regime, but she was neither stupid nor dishonest. She added that, the hostility of white neighbors aside, a slaveholder who mistreated his old slaves would arouse dangerous discontent from the younger ones.

Not everyone took her point. The most common way of avoiding responsibility for old slaves was to set them "free" and send them on their way. In Baltimore and other southern cities, there was a general outcry against this practice. The core objection was economic. This influx of newly free and thoroughly destitute old "country blacks ... could only become a public charge ..." Still, there is a faint whiff of an humanitarian subtext in the assumption that public institutions would not allow them starve.

Genovese makes several good points about this situation. As slavery came under increasing fire from abolitionists, the slave-owning class as a whole worried that some of its members might cave in to the moral arguments against owning other people. So, more and more southern states outlawed manumission under any circumstances. Ironically, this tightening down on slavery may have, indirectly, benefited some old slaves. We have to say "some" because the owners were all over the board on this.

The behavior of the slaveholders toward the superannuated ranged widely from full and kind concern through minimum attention to paternalistic responsibilities to indifference and sheer barbarism.

Here we can go back to a point made earlier. The slave experience in any society is deeply dependent on the character, moral values and compassion of the owner.

Another important point has to do with life expectancy. Despite the numbers of poor whites scratching out a living, slaves had a measurably shorter average life span.

> These statistics discredit one of the traditions about slavery: that a substantial number of aged "aunties" and "uncles" spent their declining years as pensioners living leisurely and comfortably off their masters' bounty. A few did, of course, but not enough reached retirement age to be more than a negligible expense to the average owner.

Genovese argues that those masters who gloried in the tradition of "pensioners living ... off their masters' bounty" were not so much lying as vainglorious. It was not their bounty that made those few slaves who reached "retirement" notable for their general cheerfulness. It was the treatment they received from the younger slaves.

Veneration of the aged is an African tradition. So all of the slaves, including the children, treated the aged with deference, dignity and honor. In addition, they were valuable practical contributors to the community. With parents in the fields, they could keep a benevolent but disciplined eye on the children.

> They taught the little ones how to pray and how to fish; how to show courtesy and how to feed the chickens ....
> With vegetable gardens requiring attention ... the old folks

helped out and contributed something to the comfort of their neighbors and kin.

They were also the ones most likely to know a good deal about herbal medicine and old ways of doctoring.

So, all of the credit that slaveholders gave themselves for the quality of life for their old slaves, Genovese contends, was actually an unjustified conceit. It was really the important role that they played in their own community and the reciprocal love and respect that they enjoyed in full measure.

> When freedom came, the old slaves faced the withdrawal of their masters serenely, confident that they would be taken care of by family, friends, and the black community at large, as they always had been.

In and of itself, this confidence makes it clear that security in old age was usually provided by other slaves and not by the benevolence of the Big House.

## A Brief Summary

If we approach an understanding of slavery in the ancient world as very much like slavery in the American South, we will be making a serious mistake. The primary element underwriting the vast differences between them is that capitalism did not exist in the ancient world and, for that reason, neither did the concept of abstracted labor. The absence of this all to familiar feature of capitalism cannot be emphasized enough. Without that emphasis, it is easy to miss the whole point, which is why it bears repeating.

Moreover, for the ancients, slavery did not involve a practical economic analysis. Absent this, the ancients often wasted what we would think of as an investment in a slave. For example, Brutus' mother doted on him to the point of obsession. One day, she surprised a young slave girl who was holding the baby, and in her fright she dropped him. Brutus wasn't hurt, but the slave girl was punished for endangering him. She died by crucifixion, a common Roman punishment.

Despite their many differences, ancient and American slavery share certain common features. The slave experience depended on the temperament of the master and also on the job. A Roman comic genius named Plautus wrote wonderful plays. One ironic joke that recurs in his work concerns a male slave who has returned from working in the mines. The irony lies in the fact that working in the mines inevitably resulted in certain death. By contrast, a favored slave, particularly one well-loved by a benevolent master, might expect a long and very pleasant life.

Such extremes were quite uncommon in the American South. Nevertheless, field slaves worked very much harder than house slaves, and under considerably worse conditions, while a good master versus a bad one could make all the difference in the slaves' quality of life.

Another issue, apparently more prominent in America than in the ancient world, is the notion that slaves can be logically treated like any other form of property. Alas for the theory, people, unlike clocks or cows, can think for themselves and form willful intentions. This can become extremely tricky when theory is put into practice, as we see quite often in the American South. If a slave owner's cow trampled a neighbor's field, the owner was legally liable to pay for the damage. If a slave murdered a neighbor's child, should the owner hang for it? Clearly the answer of the slave-owning class was a resounding "no," but it was an emotional answer. The search for a coherent theoretical basis for the difference is a fascinating story, which Eugene Genovese tells quite well in *Roll, Jordan, Roll*. It is a long read but a truly rewarding one.

### Slavery and Command

In the chapter called "Survival," we looked at three common solutions to the economic problems of acquiring, producing and distributing both goods and services. These are tradition, command and capitalism. The concept of tradition is not very useful for understanding slavery because there was absolutely no guarantee that people born into slavery would do the same job as their parents and grandparents. They might well do so, but the final decision was their master's to make.

By the same token, being a slave did not guarantee that your children would also be slaves. As we noted before, the great Roman writer, Horace, was the son of a slave who was later freed. Horace, himself, was born free and grew up to be on close terms with a very influential crowd. Ancient slavery was thus too fluid to guarantee traditional continuity.

American slavery was much less fluid and most children of field slaves ended up field slaves as well. However, it should be noted that this did not so much reflect a veneration of tradition as it did the convenience of the master. At his whim, a child of field slaves could become a companion to the one of the master's children. Conversely, the child of a house slave could be relegated to the hard labor of the fields, usually as a punishment.

Sometimes, though rarely, the child of a slave could undergo an even more radical transformation. In New Orleans, for example, the children of an affluent white father and a black mother, usually a slave but sometimes free, might be educated in Europe, taught classical music and the like. When the segregating Jim Crow laws were passed, to which Mary Custis Lee objected, these children and their children were "black" and were pushed in with the former slaves. This meeting of European melodies and African rhythms is widely thought to be the origin of jazz. But I digress.

In the American South, even when slave children did exactly the same work as their parents and grandparents, tradition was always subject to the master's will. He or she had the power to allow for continuity, or to insist upon change. In that sense, we can say that tradition was often aligned with command, but when change was desired by the master, command always trumped tradition.

The situation in the ancient world was far more complicated in terms of the whole idea of command. For example, the Athenian bank manager, himself a slave, routinely issued orders needed to run the bank. In his private capacity, he would also own slaves to tend to the needs of his household, to tutor his children, cook his meals, entertain his guests and do whatever else he needed done. He was, thus, both a slave to the bank owners and a man vested with considerable authority to command others. The whole idea of this duality is desperately foreign to us.

## Freedom

Musing about what it means to be free may seem like an odd way to end a chapter about slavery, but a quirk in Roman law got this musing started. It was strictly unlawful to enslave Roman citizens, thus making Roman citizenship a highly desired commodity. A Roman head of household, a *paterfamilias*, could kill his children. He could *not* sell them into slavery. However, the fact that your *paterfamilias* could kill you or have you killed raises the question of who, in ancient Rome, was truly free.

# Intermission

**I**N the beginning, we offered a brief introduction to hunter-gatherers who, as a rule, embodied a traditional economy, as well as a traditional society, in which children emulated their parents, grandparents and other members of their group. That said, we moved on to several societies whose economic base was settled farmers.\* These farmers also carried on the traditions of their forbearers, often while being governed by a structurally stable system of command at the top.

We now briefly return to hunters and gatherers, who typically move from place to place at a rate estimated at about five miles per day, in a pattern that is cyclical rather than migratory. That is to say, they returned to the same or nearby places during roughly the same phase of each cycle. The reason for the cyclical travel patterns can be found in the changing conditions of their habitats, such that one area was fruitful at one time while other areas presented new gathering opportunities at other times. These variations are

---

\* These farmers traditionally also kept animals for milk, cheese and traction. Only rarely did they slaughter their animals for meat. Jared Diamond does a marvelous job elaborating on these matters in *Guns ,Germs and Steel*.

unique to each habitat and govern the patterns of the peoples' cyclical movements.

Because hunter-gatherers walked significant distances virtually every day, and because they depended, in most cases, more heavily on gathering than hunting, they had relatively low levels of body fat. This fact, together with a general tendency to nurse babies for several years, kept populations low quite naturally. For the women, having low body fat postponed menstruation, resulted in longer gaps between having each child and an earlier onset of menopause. Having a population lower than the habitat can sustain contributes to the sustainability of that habitat. That is probably why humans lived as gatherer-hunters* over a much longer span of time than they have lived any other way.

## Nomadic Pastoralists

Pastoralists have, as their most central, vital and irreplaceable economic assets, animals. For continued success, these animals, like human animals, should not be allowed to deplete entirely the resources of any one place in their habitat. Animals must, therefore, be herded to a new source of food while there are still seeds and shoots aplenty left for the next round of grazing. This way of life is called nomadic pastoralism.

We are then left with a vibrant and intriguing contrast between the imperatives of farming and the imperatives of pastoralism. Farming makes settling in one place and tend-

* We noted in an earlier chapter that "hunter-gatherers" is the common usage but, for most of them, gathering is the more productive of the two activities.

ing that specific land carefully by far and away the most sensible choice. Pastoralism makes motion a *sine qua non*, a thing upon which all else depends. Nomadic pastoralists, when faced with a challenge to their territories by a stronger group, are well equipped to choose migration over a territorial fight. Farmers suffer much more dramatic losses when forced out of their homes and onto new lands. These relative calculations of retreat and/or defense will play out quite clearly in the struggles between these two ways of life down through the centuries.

Ancient nomadic pastoralists moved with their animals on foot as do some nomadic pastoralists in the twenty-first century. With the domestication of the horse, a new form of transport became possible. We examine how this change took place in the next chapter, "Horses and Humans."

## A Small Aside

For some reason, unknown to me, some of my students had a terrible time with the whole idea of nomadic pastoralism. What I have learned over the years is that it is critically important to find square one. At what point do they have an understanding that matches mine from which we can then build outward to a larger understanding? It turned out that the movie "City Slickers" was just such a shared base point for moving forward.

This is a movie about a group of urbanized men signing on to work a cattle drive from pasture to market. All it has in common with nomadic pastoralism is humans moving animals from one place to another. One then has to strip away all that is modern from technology to shops. The nomadic pastoralists, either on foot or on horseback, had to sustain themselves with the products of their herds, milk and cheese, or, more sparingly, with the sacrifice of some animals for meat. Augmenting their diets could be achieved by gathering, hunting, trading or raiding.

Moreover, in the film, the cattle drive went from one place to another and then ended, quite tragically, for the cattle. By contrast, nomadic pastoralists move their herds around and around with the changing seasons, always avoiding too long a stay in one place. This also, as noted, prevents an area from being eaten to death. The cattle drive ends; the cyclical nomadic movement, with any luck, does not.

For all the absence of congruence between nomadic pastoralists and "City Slickers," the image of humans moving animals seems to have been the key element in breaking the barriers to a better understanding, at some level, of a way of life otherwise foreign to the students. After many attempts, recourse to a modern movie worked to teach them about the past. A good teacher must be flexible and inventive.

### Crossroads

As noted above, "Horses and Humans" begins with nomadic pastoralists on foot. From there it presents a discussion of what we know, and don't know, about how and when humans tamed horses as a complement to their transient way of life. What is very clear, however, are the profound consequences of making that transition.

In the second part of that chapter we find the elites of

medieval Europe astride their horses, while basing their economy primarily on agriculture. In the case of mounted nomadic pastoralists, horses are relatively inexpensive because they are like the other grazing animals that people are moving from one naturally occurring pasture to another. Moreover, the horse is a labor saving device in that it is easier to ride along with the herds than to walk beside them.

By contrast, in an agricultural economy, a horse is a luxury item, which is why their ownership was confined to the ruling elites. Indeed, the economic organization of medieval Europe did an excellent job of providing the elites with horses. These horsemen were broken down into two broad categories, the secular and the clerical. The clash between them would be the defining internal struggle of the European Middle Ages. We will review this conflict in some detail in the chapter called "Church and State."

### Commerce

We will see that nomadic pastoralists can supplement their diets by raiding and/or trading with their neighbors. The same can be said for the next group of folks we will be taking up, the "Merchant Seamen." In that chapter, we will focus on what would become Venice in the richness of time. As a collection of islands, it had so little arable land that the people were forced to trade the products of the ocean, most notably fish and salt, for the important grains and vegetables that are part of a viable diet. We will, however, also take note of sailors such as the Vikings, who were considerably more adept at raiding than trading, and were thus more seamen than merchants.

The final chapter, "Venice and the Birth of Modern Europe," continues with the Venetians, with more emphasis on their politics, both internally and externally. It finds them at a point when the world they understood was about to be expanded to include what was, for them, an entirely new world. That the natives of this "new" world took a very different view is the subject for another book.

# Horses and Humans

When the first horsemen galloped onto the pages of ancient history, they were at the height of their powers. They were expert riders, with each warrior able to control his horse with his knees while using a bow and arrows to fire forward, to the side, or even backward over the rump of his mount.* They were history's first cavalry, and they had mastered a set of tactics so deadly and disorienting to their enemies as to be essentially unstoppable. These "Scythian tactics," as they came to be called, began with a ferocious charge, raining their lethal triple-tipped arrows down on their foot-bound foe. Then, just at the moment of engagement, they would wheel their horses about and retreat, still firing backwards at their dazed and disoriented enemy, choking on their dust.

Their homeland, at the time, was a place we now call the Ukraine, and there they had to confront the mighty army of Darius the Persian, also called "the Great." With just such tactics of advance and retreat, they led this army further and further from its base. As they went, they drove their herds

* There is some evidence that women also rode into battle on occasion. We will see more on this below.

before them, for they were nomadic pastoralists, and they burned the grass behind them and poisoned the wells. In such a way they evaded and exhausted the greatest army ever yet assembled.

How and why they got the idea to do any of this, most especially to ride a horse, we do not know and will probably never know. They kept no records as they were an illiterate people. Nor did the literate societies that encountered them learn their history from some oral tradition, if, indeed, such a tradition existed. Herodotus is our main source for these people and, while writing nearly a whole book about them, he never discovered what they called themselves. Had he known, he would certainly have mentioned it because his style was inclusive and exhaustive.

Greeks called the area where these horsemen lived Scythia and thus named them Scythians, which is sometimes shortened to Scyths. A related tribe living further afield was dubbed the Sarmatians. It seems likely that horsemen were spread across the great plains of grass that ranged from "Scythia" to the hinterlands of ancient China. When the Chinese encountered these mounted nomadic pastoralists, they called them the Yueh-Chi and the Hsiung-nu.* All the evidence indicates that Scyths, Sarmatians, Yueh-Chi and Hsiung-nu shared a number of common qualities, enough, perhaps, to think of them as a single nation divided into tribes.

We are then left with a set of burning questions. Where,

---

* They are thought to be ancestral to both Huns and Turks.

when, how and why did humans decide to tame and ride horses? What could possibly have given them to believe that riding horses was even feasible? The natural instinct of a wild horse when something lands on its back is to assume it is a predator and do everything in its power to shake it off. If you have ever been to a rodeo, you will have seen this phenomenon first hand in the bronco busting competitions. While the horses first tamed and ridden were smaller than modern horses, they could still kick or bite a man to death. Those were powerful disincentives to mounting a horse once, let alone repeatedly until it accepted the rider.

As to the where and when, Jared Diamond, in *Guns, Germs and Steel*, writes that the horse was domesticated circa 4000 B.C. in the Ukraine. We are here presuming that domestication was a prerequisite for riding a horse. In *The New Penguin Atlas of Ancient History*, Colin McEvedy specifically rejects this claim. In a narrative devoted to 4000 B.C., he says that:

> Despite claims to the contrary there is no evidence that the Dneiper-Don group, the Sredni Stog folk, had domesticated the horse which remained an animal to be hunted and eaten, rather than corralled and ridden, until well into the third millennium.

So, the most we can say about where and when the horse was domesticated is that there is strong scholarly disagreement right now. More evidence may emerge as time goes by.

As to how horses were domesticated, Diamond makes

an excellent point. In reviewing the characteristics that favor or discourage domestication, he writes about the importance of social structure.

> Almost all species of domesticated large mammals prove to be ones whose wild ancestors share three social characteristics: they live in herds; they maintain a well-developed dominance hierarchy among herd members; and the herds occupy overlapping home ranges rather than mutually exclusive territories.

He then uses the horse as an example of a wild animal having such a social structure. A typical herd of wild horses has only one stallion accompanied by as many as a half dozen mares and their foals. Among the mares, a dominance hierarchy determines the order in which the herd moves from one grazing area to another. In the lead is the dominant mare followed by her foals from the youngest (closest to her) to the oldest. Next is the mare in second order of dominance followed by her foals, again in order of age, and so it goes to the third, fourth, etc. dominant mare. The stallion brings up the rear.

Diamond argues that the advantage of this social organization for domestication is that humans can take over the lead position. So the dominant mare, under conditions of domestication, imprints on humans from an early age and will follow the humans while the other mares and the stallion will follow her. We must note here that the definition of a domesticated animal is one whose reproduction is governed by humans. The Scyths, for example, castrated all but a few stallions, which they kept to breed. They had large herds on the open steppe, and had they not done so, each stallion would cut himself a group of mares and run away.

Precisely how the horse was domesticated, whether by nomadic pastoralists with other herds as well, or by settled people, or by both at various times and places, we do not know. We also do not know exactly how people got the idea of riding horses, nor yet how they induced the horse to accept the rider. We are only sure that somewhere, somehow, ordinary men transformed themselves by forging a partnership with horses.

If their motive for undertaking such an extraordinary endeavor was somehow economic, it cannot be explained by either tradition or command. Whether the innovators were foot-bound pastoralists or settled farmers, their solutions to the economic problems of sustaining life would certainly have been traditional and not radically innovative.

The agent of change is supposed to be command. Yet, it is nearly impossible to imagine a leader telling the people, "Go out there and figure out how to ride a horse! I have never seen it done but you must do it! Die if you must! Just keep trying!"

Obviously, there were no market forces at play. Whatever created this novel partnership of humans and horses must have been extra-economic. It might have been a game, trying to ride a horse, or a popular dare. Perhaps a tired mother, walking with the horses from pasture to pasture, put a small child on a horse's back to ease her burden for a while. Its familiar smell and small size might have failed to trigger fear and reaction in the animal. We shall never know for sure.

What we can and do know is that the partnership, once forged, had enormous economic, political and military consequences. We also know that the Scythians had horses in historical times and we can, through archeological records and linguistic deductions, trace them back in history. Having done that, we can move forward again, and from this we will derive a very interesting picture.

There is a general consensus that the Scythian birth-place as a people was in the Altai* Mountains. By 2250 B.C., they covered a territory stretching from north of Lake Balkash in the east to the Volga River in the west. Linguists classify their language as a subset of the Indo-European family of languages called Aryan. This has nothing to do with vulgar Nazi racialism. The Germans at this point were confined to Scandinavia at the other end of Eurasia.

Modern scholars believe that the area that is today Iran was experiencing a general influx of these Aryans sometime around 1800 B.C. In what is unlikely to be a coincidence, horses first appeared in that region at about the same time. We know these particular Aryans were ancestral to modern Persians by the use of linguistic analysis.

Sometime around 1575 B.C., Aryans from Central Asia took off in several different directions. In two waves, they invaded the Indian sub-continent and essentially obliter-

---

* People native to this region are called Altaian or Altaic.

ated the local culture of the Indus Valley. As we know, a bit earlier the Hyksos had invaded Egypt. This foreign domination of Egypt, and a contemporaneous foreign rule in Mesopotamia, left intact the structures of these ancient civilizations, including their powerful command economies. Indeed, the invaders soon copied the conquered culture in almost every particular. That the reverse happened in the Indus Valley suggests that this was a much less robust civilization, and one lacking a command economy.

The main sacred texts of Hinduism are the four Vedas. The first of these, the Rig Veda, was composed around 1500 B.C., and provides a very good picture of these Aryan invaders. They were warriors using the very latest in military technology, the horse-drawn chariot. It is no stretch to assume that the Aryans invented it.

As McEvedy writes: "Aryans had the horses, and lots of flat, hard, open space needed to get people thinking about how to go faster." The spoked wheel was essential to the innovation and made the chariot a central element in the conquest of the Indus Valley, and other places, as well.

Meanwhile, another group of Aryans pushed further south of their beachhead in what is now Iran. There is some evidence that they provided the leadership and the chariots for a Kassite* invasion and takeover of Babylon. Another Aryan clan, the Mitanni, organized some local Caucasian folk into conquering a part of Mesopotamia. All in all, these first charioteers were a colossal pain to anybody in their

---

* These were probably an Elamite people.

way. Local rulers copied the chariot's design and adopted it for their own use, and so this technology radiated outward in an ancient arms race.

The chariot shows up in Chinese royal tombs in the thirteenth century B.C., and is strong evidence for Aryans probing the far eastern corner of the steppe. Not too very long after that, the archeological record suggests that Aryan tribes ranged across the entire steppe right up to China's northernmost province. It is not impossible that this eastward movement started at the same general time as the Aryan invasion of the Indus Valley and their wreaking havoc in Mesopotamia.

When humans move into an ecosphere very different from the one they left, their language changes. They lack words for its new natural features, such as birds, plants, animals, weather conditions and the like. There were also customs of the native peoples for which the Aryan speakers had no words. They might borrow such words or invent their own, but in either case the language changes and becomes more differentiated from other languages that had once been much closer. In this case, Aryan gradually sorts itself out into an "Indic" variation in the Indus Valley, an Iranian variation used by Medes and Persians, and a northern variation called Scytho-Cimmerian.*

What is especially interesting here is the reminder that the great Iranian empires of the Medes, the Persians and

---

* The Cimmerians were also Aryans, who had moved to the area of present day Ukraine before the Scyths arrived and, who were, presumably, displaced by them. They are thought to have given their name to the Crimea.

finally the Parthians were all cousins to the Scyths, and yet, when Darius came to fight them, he found their "Scythian tactics" completely incomprehensible. A millennium had passed since the split between their forbearers had taken the ancestral Iranians south of the Caspian and into Mesopotamia, the heartland of several ancient civilizations. By the time of Darius, Persian leaders were afflicted with the "civilized disease of valor." This phrase comes from *The First Horsemen*, written by the award-winning writer Frank Trippett. It is meant to suggest that civilization brings on a set of mannerly rules, including the notion that an honorable warrior stands his ground and does not retreat by choice.

An alternate explanation has to do with the economic basis for different social formations. Societies based on agriculture have a very strong stake in a particular patch of land. To abandon that patch is to give up their collective livelihood and with it the necessary sustenance with which to fight on. It is quite otherwise with nomadic pastoralists. They subsist primarily on their animals, and their various herds are entirely mobile and can be, as we saw with the Scyths, driven ahead of the warriors creating an ever-changing line of battle. These differences recur throughout history. The Scythians continued, to the bewilderment of Darius, to run away. In so doing, they also won.

## Horsemanship

In roughly the ninth century B.C., a momentous and extremely rapid change happened on the Eurasian steppe.

It was so rapid that the archeological record shows nothing of its process, only its result. Humans had mastered horsemanship. What came before and what came after were wildly different. Some tribes died out while others merged into larger units. Settled peoples took to the open spaces and produced many more weapons, which left their archeological mark. Such changes can be found from what is now the Ukraine, to areas as far away as the Yenisei River in Siberia.

Wherever it had first been practiced, the art of riding horses spread like wildfire across the vast expanse of the grasslands and changed everything in its path. Mastering the horse gave man extraordinary and novel powers as a hunter, a pastoralist and a soldier. On horseback, a man could fell such large and swift game as bison and elk. On horseback, a tribe could gather and manage much larger herds of cattle, sheep, goats and the all-important horses. To do so, however, required much more grazing land, something made possible by their new mobility. Thus they could find pastures farther and farther afield from their original homelands.

For the settled farmers living along the edges of the forests that defined the upper boundary of the steppe, and those living in the river valleys as well, this was not a change for the better. The archeological evidence has them living in small hamlets of eight to ten families. Completely at the mercy of the horsemen, they might escape ruthless plunder by cooperating with the demands for grains and other agricultural products. By the time the Scyths appear in written history, these settled people had long been accustomed to providing the horsemen with whatever they demanded.

Then new players entered into the equation. In the sixth century B.C., Greek colonies, *poleis*, began to spring up on the northern coast of the Black Sea. Nearby was the steppe that had become the home territory of some nomadic pastoralists. The Greeks called that region Scythia and its inhabitants Scythians. All of my sources on the Scyths say that they got olive oil, honey and wine from the Greeks. Archeological digs have turned up huge caches of Greek amphorae in the tombs of Scythian elites. Amphorae were the sort of pots that typically contained olive oil and wine in the ancient world. Because Athens was organized to export olive oil, honey and wine, it seems extremely likely that she was a principal source for these luxury commodities.

We know that Pesistratus, while in exile before his final triumph in Athens, had established valuable mining concessions in Thrace, which he used to buy himself a private army of Scythian slaves. This does not prove he visited Scythia, though it leaves open the possibility. It is absolutely proof that he had some trading connections with the region. Moreover, as a *tyranoi*, he organized and supervised the commercialization of Athenian agriculture specifically to trade luxury items for grains.

We also know from the Scythian side about their importing olive oil, wine and honey from Greeks, and their export of grains in return. We know they had wagons to carry grain from the hinterlands to Greek settlements on the Black Sea. Finally, we know that both sides had strong contacts with merchants in the Greek *poleis* on the north shore of the Black Sea. All this gives us what scientists call a "strong inference" that the Scyths and Athenians were trading partners.

In *The Shape of European History*, William H. McNeill assumes that Athens imported grain from agrarian elites, able to extract sufficient grains from peasants for export. Let us briefly recap that argument as it was presented in the earlier chapter, "Hellas." These local magnates extracted a "surplus" of grains from peasants over whom they exercised some dominion. However, they were limited in the intensity of this exploitation by the fact that they lived among the people being exploited and were vastly outnumbered by them. Athens, by contrast, was exploiting them as a collective (a *polis*), far enough away not to have to consider the possibility of revolt, and thus able to exploit them more thoroughly.

This argument is perfectly logical and might apply to some settled people that McNeill has in mind. However, he does not tell us what specific group he had in mind to produce the grains traded with Athens for luxury items such as wine, olive oil and honey. Conversely, he might have had no specific people in mind and was, instead, arguing from the apparent logic of the situation. If Athens was trading luxury goods for staple grains, they must have been trading with farmers.

The *actual* logic of the situation does not require direct trade with farmers. If Athenians were trading luxury goods for staple grains, they must have been trading with people who had access to "surplus" grains. The Scyths fit that bill quite well. The formidable power of horsemen could easily facilitate the extraction of grain from settled peasants living in small hamlets by the rivers or in the forests on the boundaries of the grasslands. Some of that grain would augment the Scythian diet and the rest could be traded with the Athenians.

It makes perfect sense for McNeill not even to consider the possibility that Athens acquired grains from nomadic pastoralists.* The very definition of this way of life is that they do not settle and they do not grow food. So, his missing this connection between Scyths and the Athenians is no grave mistake. Indeed, ironically, the finding of this connection simply emphasizes the fundamental strength of McNeill's core argument.

He contends that change happens when disparate peoples bump into one another and begin to interact. Certainly, the cultured, literate Athenian, with a penchant for abstract philosophizing, was thoroughly unlike the hard living, illiterate nomad. The Scyths eschewed the Greek custom of watering their wine and drank it neat. They were also quite fond of an intoxicating beverage made from fermented mare's milk, which is still drunk by Mongolian pastoralists today. Athens existed on settled agriculture while, as noted, the Scyths neither settled nor farmed.

If, as seems very likely, the Scythians provided at least some of the grain that brought the Athenian hill farmers a measure of economic security and military and political power, then they helped facilitate a major event in the history of Hellas. It further means that whoever the first horse-

---

* I did not go looking for this connection either. It found me when I began exploring the origin of horsemanship.

men were, they too played a role in setting the stage for Athenian democracy. That is exciting to think about.

## Scythian Gold

A key feature of being a nomad is that one cannot have too many possessions. So, the Scyths decided to carry their great wealth in very small packages. Turning to Greek artisans and, over time, possibly, to Scythian craftsmen as well, they held a good deal of their wealth in small objects of enormous value. These objects have made a significant contribution to the archeological record on which much of our knowledge about the Scyths is based. One example is a four-inch-high, solid-gold comb.* On top, with amazing detail for the scale, are three Scythian warriors to whom some Greek elements have been added by the artist. It could be worn to keep the horseman's long hair out of his face, and simultaneously as a lavish decoration.

These gold objects and other precious gems and metals worked into scenes of Scythian life, tell us a great deal about the people. One elegant five-inch-high vase provides clues for a different view of the Scyths. To the Medes, Persians and Assyrians, they were fierce and terrible warriors. Yet the scenes on the vase show them expressing tender concern for one another. One warrior appears to be trying to extract another's tooth with great gentleness. Another shows a warrior bandaging a comrade's wounds. Naturally, scenes of men interacting with horses abound.

* They traded for gold with people in the Caucasus region, in the Ural Mountains, and also in the Altaic ranges of Central Asia.

A spectacular golden pectoral, a mere twelve inches across, displays forty-four richly detailed animals, including a horse scratching himself and a mare suckling her foal. Some of the animals are mythic rather than real. The whole thing is exquisitely beautiful, hugely valuable, and it can be worn rather than carried, which works very well for a nomadic pastoralist.

In Anthropology, there is a school of thought called "Cultural Materialism," which argues that the material conditions under which a people exist both limit some cultural expressions and encourage others. Here is a very good example. If you are a nomad, you cannot have a large wardrobe, you cannot have a house of any size, and your culture cannot include monumental buildings such as the Parthenon or the Colosseum.

Jumping ahead in time, it may be that this explains the appeal of Islam to nomadic pastoralists such as the Arabs, the Mongols and the Turks. In the end, Muslims do not need a Mosque. All they need is to cleanse themselves five times daily, face toward Mecca, and pray. This requires a very good sense of direction, which is common among nomadic pastoralists.

Returning to the Scyths, they, like the people of many other cultures, poured a great deal of wealth into the tombs of their elites. It is in such tombs that archeologists have found the Scythian gold and other precious items. Some things, such as clothing, have not stood the test of time. Yet if we have a depiction of a person wearing a richly decorated garment, the placement of the decorations can be matched to the placement of their bones. The material may have vanished, but its form can be reconstructed from the combined sources.

There is a beautiful and very thoughtful book called *Scythian Gold*. Edited by Ellen D. Reeder, it was prepared to accompany an exhibit called *Gold of the Nomads: Scythian Treasures from Ancient Ukraine*. The graves of their elite were called kurhany. Here is a summary from *Scythian Gold*:

> From the sixth century B.C. onward, when trade with the Greek colonies was well underway, there is an increase in the quantity and lavishness of grave goods found in the kurhany, reaching a high point in the fifth and forth centuries B.C. To this period belong thousands of kurhany in Ukraine.

Not surprisingly, male burials included all manner of weaponry. The odd bit is that female burials sometimes did, as well. According to *Scythian Gold*, the Greeks believed the women of Scythia were the Amazons of ancient lore, as they sometimes rode into battle with the men.

By the second century B.C., the Scythians had grown opulent and many had abandoned nomadic pastoralism for the settled life, with all the amenities it could provide. When some distant cousins, the Sarmatians, swooped down on them, they were driven into the Crimea. There, they built a fortified city with monumental architecture and all the trimmings of civilization, including private homes with murals on the walls.

This new Crimean kingdom worried Mithradates the Great, King of Pontus in Asia Minor. He sent an army against them and won a victory sufficient to drive them, as a people, off the pages of history. Nevertheless, they will always have the distinction of being the first fierce warriors that nomadic pastoralism produced. They would be followed in time by the Huns and the Avars, the Mongols and the Turks, much to the dismay of the settled peoples living in their paths.

## China

Speaking of such folks, the Chinese at the other end of the steppe were also having trouble with horsemen at about the same time that the Scythians were flourishing in the west. The denser peasant populations were no better at standing up to the horsemen than dwellers in the tiny hamlets of the western steppe. The Yueh Chi and Hsiung-nu, as the Chinese called them, were just as disruptive to settled life as the Scythians. In particular, the Hsiung-nu employed very similar tactics as the Scyths. They would attack and then retreat when outnumbered, firing backwards as they went. This has led some scholars to call them "cousins" to the Scyths, but others stay cautious.

The Hsiung-nu were causing so much loss of life and grains that the Chinese organs of governance recognized the need to take preventive measures. As in ancient Egypt, there was an Emperor, thought to be divine, at the head of a very stable command economy. Beginning in the fourth century B.C., the Emperor had his agents enlist an army of peasants to build large walls at strategic spots to keep the intruders out. Some of these walls were as wide at their base as twenty-five feet and as tall as thirty.

These walls were ineffective for two reasons. First, the horsemen could go around them and, also, as the population of Chinese peasants expanded, their farming spread to the other side of the walls. To solve the first problem, the walls were finally conjoined in 214 B.C., creating the Great Wall of China that is over two thousand miles long. That left unprotected Chinese on the outside of the wall and, as they were decimated, the Emperor commanded a repopulation of the affected areas with yet more peasants. This may have been intended not only to retain China's claim on the land, but also to solve the recurrent problem of "surplus progeny." In either case, it served to perpetuate the problem of Chinese dying at the hands of barbarians.

In the end, the death toll was unbearable, and the Emperor and his agents decided to deal with the Hsiung-nu at the highest levels. They agreed to pay what was essentially protection money to the ruling nomad elite in amounts estimated at seven percent of annual imperial revenues. In the mid nineteen-seventies, the cash value of this annual amount was estimated at forty million dollars in modern American money, paid out to the Hsiung-nu in pure gold. That's a wow!

While the Chinese were trying to keep horsemen at bay with walls and money, the West was evolving a peasant agricultural economy, able to support a cavalry class. This unique combination was not intentionally created to counter the threat from nomadic horsemen. Instead it evolved

228 · HOW THE WORLD WORKED

organically from the melding of Gallo-Romans with the Germans on their border. This is a fascinating story.

## The West

When a horde made up of Arabs and Berbers,* both Muslims, arrived in what is now Spain in 711, they conquered all before them with lightning speed. Their advantage over the conquered people derived from their augmenting infantry with cavalry. One of their raiding parties crossed the Pyrenees and was having some success when it was stopped by a Frankish army brilliantly led by a chap named Charles. The Franks had only infantry, but they were doughty fighters and their choice of terrain was highly advantageous. Nevertheless, a victory by infantry alone against infantry augmented by cavalry is extraordinarily rare, making their success that much sweeter. Their leader came to be called "Charles the Hammer," which translates as Charles Martel.

Ironically, this victory of infantry over combined forces led to the creation of the only social formation, funded primarily by peasant agrarian labor, ever to have produced a cavalry class. These were the famous knights in shinning armor who loom so large in romantic lore. The social formation is medieval feudalism and, as noted, change comes about when very different peoples collide. In this case, the two groups were the Gallo-Romans on the one hand and the Germans on the other.

* These were the indigenous peoples of the north western coast of Africa, on the Mediterranean Sea.

The change began in the heart of the Roman Empire with some important innovations by Diocletian, which had the most profound effects in the Roman province of Gaul. It was then into that province that marauding Germans began the contact between the two. Let us, then, begin at the beginning with a very thorough emperor and the changes that he wrought.

When Diocletian came to power at the end of the third century A.D, the empire's finances were in a free fall. At the time of Augustus, there was a balance between the revenue stream and the expenditures of the government. This collapsed during the civil wars of the early third century, and the "solution" was to debase the coinage. This led to inflation, and made the problem much worse. Diocletian attempted to solve this by fixing prices. With his usual energy and attention to detail, he had his assistants prepare lists of the prices of everything, right down to bobby pins. He was, in short, attempting to create a command economy that could banish inflation. Sadly, he had no understanding of the economic forces underlying the problem. The only tool in his arsenal was to make violating his economic commands a capital offense.

So, a cobbler forced to sell shoes at a price that did not cover his costs, his taxes and the bare subsistence of himself and his family, faced a slow death obeying the law and quicker death if caught violating it. One last option was to seek a new way of life, for example leave town and try to find a niche in the countryside where food was cheaper. This option was nullified by an additional law, which fixed everyone in their jobs and extended that restriction to their children and their children's children. Life was bad, and looked to be getting worse.

When Diocletian divided the Roman Empire into Western and Eastern halves, he created two radically unequal entities. The East had been urbanized long before Rome was born, with towns in Egypt and Mesopotamia dating back before 2250 B.C., and towns in the Levant starting before 1300 B.C. Commerce was pandemic in the East and of long standing. Artisans were highly specialized and produced quality goods for a market that included a class of wealthy patrons who expected and paid highly for the luxury they demanded. All the cultural amenities associated with civilization had long been present. By contrast, outside Italy, urbanity was unknown in the West until the arrival of the Romans, and building cities was not among the first things they did when they got there. What few cities the Romans founded were administrative centers first and foremost. To spruce them up and make them habitable for Roman officials and Roman merchants, they were given a forum, baths, a theater and the like. Agriculture in the West was the foundation of all economic activities and the primary source of taxation.

Even when the same person ruled both East and West, their finances and administration were kept strictly separated. On the whole, the East benefited from the split. Taxes and tribute that had once flowed to Rome stayed in the East, and the building of Constantinople by Diocletian's successor added another booming metropolis to the mix, encouraging even more trade. The Egyptian grain "surplus," which had once gone to Rome, was now sent to Constantinople, further boosting growth and trade. Tax revenues were plentiful there, and life was generally good.

For Rome, all this was a disaster. To make matters worse, a new central army headquarters grew up in Milan, as it was closer to the action in the Western provinces. Rome, itself, was no longer the center of government in the West. Meanwhile, the cities created for Roman administration had always run on subsidies. Now, they were expected to be the source of additional revenue. Not surprisingly, they collapsed.

Furthermore, the goods and services associated with specialized artisans and the civilized life were newly acquired tastes in the West. It was easier and cheaper to go back to cutting your family's hair, making your own candles, and such. Urban life and trade, never strong in the West, very nearly vanished. That left agriculture as the last source of the ever increasing demands for funding the army.

There were essentially three classes of agrarian people. At the top were the landlords, holders of many estates that, when contiguous, formed huge entities called *latifundia*. Their owners had the political clout to avoid any sort of tax obligation on their land. At the other end of the spectrum was servile agricultural labor, treated as a part of the property. In between were those who were free and owned their own land. They were subject to taxation, and when Diocletian raised the tax rate to increase support for the army, they were very badly squeezed.

What many of them did in response, not as individuals, we suppose, but rather as villages and hamlets, was to offer a deal to the local landlord, himself immune from taxation. They would give over their land ownership to him in return for protection from taxation, and the right to keep a portion of their produce for themselves. This portion must logically have been greater than what they would have retained after taxes. Piecemeal, with different deals in different locations, serfdom was born. In the words of Colin McEvedy:

> In the Orwellian twilight of the West, citizenship had become slavery and the paradox was completed when serfdom became a free man's aspiration. To protect himself from the summary requisitions of the tax-gather the small farmer bought the protection of the local magnate with the gift of his freehold .... Caught in the spiral of dwindling revenue and increasingly rapacious exactions, the West was doomed.[*]

No one living through this process could possibly have imagined that anything good could have come of it. In fact, it was the first step in a process that would form the economic basis for medieval feudalism, with its mounted knights, and it was these knights, these horsemen, who would defend the West against invading horsemen from the steppes.

---

[*] *The Penguin Atlas of Ancient History*

## The Bigger Picture

In *The New Penguin Atlas of Medieval History*, McEvedy argues that the "demographic center of gravity" had been moving steadily westward from the Near East to Hellas to Italy, and that it only rested in Rome for a few centuries. Then, it began to move west again toward parts of the empire that were only superficially urbanized and Romanized. When the German horsemen began to move into the Western Empire, the Gallo-Romans were just Roman enough to influence these newcomers, yet also vulnerable to being changed themselves.

This stands in sharp contrast with the Chinese, whose cultural homogeneity was so intense that it overwhelmed and converted conquering horsemen, notably the Mongols, to the Chinese way. The new leaders wanted the life enjoyed by Chinese elites. They were thus drawn into the command economy, which directed the agricultural base and collected its "surplus" to support their new luxurious lifestyles. Moreover, they had to take over the economic machinery, because they suddenly had many more mouths to feed. So, some of these nomadic horsemen settled down.

However, as sometimes happens, the very weakness of the West provided a fertile field for a whole new social formation based on a fusion of settled agriculture and a horse riding culture. The result was to create an economy, a power structure and a legal system that could facilitate a thriving cavalry class, supported by a peasant base. Sadly, much of the building of this "feudal system" took place during the Dark Ages, when writing had largely vanished in the West.

This means that we know a lot less about the process than we would like. Here is how the story starts.

Overpopulation seems to have driven some Germans from Scandinavia to the south beginning in the second century B.C. By the end of the reign of Augustus, in the year 14 of our era, the Germans had resolved themselves into tribes, which archeologists have sorted into distinguishable groups. To the north, these include the Goths, the Gepids and the Burgundians. On Rome's western frontier, were the Hermanduri, the Quadi and the Marcomanni.

Beyond archeology, all that we know of the early Germans we have from the Roman writer Tacitus, who was born somewhere in the first century and died in 117.* He believed that the Germans were indigenous to the north, as no one would want to *go* there, it being very cold, with a harsh terrain and dense forests. He knew they were divided into clans or tribes, but argued that they were a single nationality in their shared physical characteristics. They had, in one translation, "stern blue eyes, ruddy hair," and they were typically very large folks.

The land produced grains and supported abundant herds of cattle that were diminutive in size. This, Tacitus attributes to the climate, but others propose inadequate food and protection from the weather to be the problem. The suggestion seems to be that they were less competent at animal husbandry than other groups. Tacitus does assert that they were adverse to labor and the heat, while cold and

---

* From here on, all dates will be assumed to be in our era unless otherwise indicated.

hunger were so much a part of their lives that these they bore well.

Tacitus wrote that they had no silver or gold. He argued that they did not place the same value on these metals as Romans, although the Germans living directly on the border did know something about Roman coins. He noted that they generally preferred the smaller ones, which were more useful for their everyday purchases. He then went on to point out that barter was the common form of exchange amongst themselves.

With an intriguing echo of the Scythians, the Germans had no reluctance to fall back, drawing the enemy deeper into unfamiliar territory, and then regrouping to attack once more. Tacitus, himself bitten by the civilized bug of valor, noted that they regarded so doing as a sensible strategy involving no element of cowardice.

Their kings were determined by birth, but their real rulers were military men chosen for leadership by their performance as warriors. Tribal assemblies were made up entirely of military men. A young man could not take up arms without the general consent of the assembly. He might receive his sword and his shield from his father or another male relative, or even one of the prominent warriors unrelated to him. This ritual initiated him into the company of warriors, to full citizenship in the tribe.

The best and clearest description of the blending of German and Gallo-Roman social formations was written by the historian Carl Stephenson and first published by Cornell University in 1942. *Mediaeval Feudalism*, with its odd spelling of Medieval, was on the required reading list for a course on English History that I took as a college sophomore in 1966. After becoming a teacher, many students said that my explanation of feudalism was the first one they had ever understood. Full credit for this goes to Professor Stephenson and his small, lucid, brilliant book. To avoid the tedious business of writing "he said" or the like before each fact, I will simply say that, unless otherwise noted, all that follows about feudalism derives from that book. But first, I will quote him:

> The typical German is a warrior. Leaving the management of his home and the tillage of his fields to slaves and womenfolk, he devotes himself to war or, in default of such excitement, to loafing, drinking and gambling ... Except when armed, they perform no business, either private or public.

A key element in the German social formation involved a distinguished chieftain with a group of companions who had reciprocal obligations to one another. In battle, the chieftain must not be outdone in bravery by his companions, who were obliged, in turn, to be equally brave. The companion who survived his chief in battle suffered great disgrace as protecting his chief was his primary and sacred obligation. A companion must also glorify his leader by his own selfless heroism on the battlefield. What the companions got in return was military equipment, food and a share in the spoils of war, not to mention a leader as committed to them as they were to him.

What matters here is that these Germans overran much of Western Europe during the five centuries after Tacitus described them, bringing with them a political economy based firmly on the chieftain-companion system. This same system was

> heard again and again in later centuries – among the Goths, the Franks, the Lombards, the Anglo-Saxons, and even the Vikings of Scandinavia. The brave *comes* who fights and dies for his *princeps* unquestionably reappears in the heroic gesith or thegn of the Anglo-Saxon epics.

What also matters is that this relationship was completely honorable for both parties. There was no hint of inequality or subservience on the part of the companions. Nor was the tie unbreakable between chief and companion. It could be severed by mutual consent. Thus, a young warrior starting his career as a companion could hope that one day his fame and wealth would draw young companions to himself as the new *princeps* or chieftain.

No comparable social formation existed among the Romans. A free citizen could attach himself to a wealthy patron, and as a client could expect some help. However, the role of clients for a rich Roman was a sort of conspicuous consumption. His clients swelled the crowds following their patron on public occasions, and fawned on his every word.

> Clientage, involving no military service and implying anything but social equality, was utterly unlike the

Germanic *comitatus*. And the dissimilarity remained even after the Roman institution had spread among the Frankish conquerors of Gaul.

Stephenson turns next to a Roman institution that the barbarian rulers of the western provinces adopted for their own. The *precarium* or *precaria* consisted of land granted to someone for as long as it pleased the donor. "Under Roman law such a 'precarious' tenure could be terminated at any time." Frankish usage evolved into a legal right to hold land for a fixed period of time, or even for life, in return for some stipulated compensation to the donor.

The term *precaria* implied that the land had been obtained through the prayer (*preces*) of the recipient; but the grant might also be styled a *benefice*, because it was a boon (*beneficium*) on the part of the grantor.

The choice of words mattered very little. What was vital was that these grants were not of empty land, but rather of land with everything necessary for the holder to skim his share off the top. In other words, the land was already organized for production, with tools, seeds and domesticated animals, used for traction and also for food. Of the utmost importance, the owner also had access to labor, either free or servile or both. Such a self contained economic unit was often called a manor.

We noted earlier that in the decline of the West, commerce had all but vanished and life was overwhelmingly agrarian. We also noted that there was a sharp division between the aristocratic landlords and the economically dependent peasants, some of whom had chosen to give up their free-hold to the local lord to avoid ruinous taxation. The holder of either a *precaria* or a *benefice* would be the aristocratic landlord.

When Charles Martel gained the sovereignty of the Frankish kingdom, he and his descendents, Pepin and Charlemagne, showed great creativity and good sense, harnessing established customs to the service of their rule. It was during these successive reigns that Roman and German usages were melded and put to the service of the Frankish state. One of these was linguistic.

> In the early Middle Ages we find numerous words for "boy" that might be used to designate either a slave, a free servant, or a military retainer: the Latin *puer*; the Germanic *degan* (Anglo-Saxon *thegn* ..., later knight ... and the French *vassal* ...). And it is a remarkable fact that in three cases – *thegn, knight,* and *vassal* – the honorable implications became exclusive.

The vassals of the Frankish kings were sent on important diplomatic missions, but their prime function was to serve as a military elite, a heavily armed cavalry class often leading their own vassals into battle. To support their deployment, they were routinely granted *benefices* – manors belonging to the king's private domain, or manors that had once belonged to the Church.

Vassalage, an honorable relationship between warriors, was Germanic in origin. The Frankish kingdom that had been created by Charles Martel and strengthened by his son, Pepin, and grandson, Charlemagne, is often labeled by modern historians as the "Carolingian" kingdom or dynasty. The fundamental basis of their power and authority was the loyalty of their personal military retainers, increasingly called vassals. Over time, anyone who served in a powerful position had to be a royal vassal.

The term fief was derived from a Germanic word signifying property or cattle. In practice, it was a fully functioning economic unit comprising one or more manors. The usual explanation for its development was to expand the size and viability of Carolingian cavalry by providing a means of funding their military expenses. In this way, the manorial system was economic. However, the fief holder also performed a variety of political functions, such as enforcing the law, rendering justice in disputes, and, at the highest level, joining in counsels that advised the king in matters of policy.

"It has become accepted usage to speak of 'feudalism,' rather than 'vassalage,' from that point in history when, with rare exceptions, there were actually no vassals without fiefs."* By "feudalism," in other words, we properly refer to the peculiar association of vassalage with fief-holding that was developed in the Carolingian Empire and thence spread to other parts of Europe.

* Here Stephenson is quoting another expert, one Ferdinand Lot.

Insofar as this association was effected for governmental purposes, feudalism was essentially political. It should not be thought of as a necessary, or even a usual, stage in economic history.

Of course, it only worked because it could rest on the manorial system. This system, in turn resting on the institution of serfdom, existed in England for centuries without producing feudalism. Serfdom was, of course, initially the result of Diocletian's avarice in the matter of taxation. So, we have a blending or melding of German and Gallo-Roman social formations to create something that was entirely new.

It was something, as we saw, that China never achieved: a political system able to produce and reproduce a cavalry class, funded by an economy heavily dependent on peasants. As Colin McEvedy writes with absolute truth, "Peasant societies don't readily produce armies of mounted men." This appears in his introduction to *The New Penguin Atlas of Medieval History* and rightly so. This accidental achievement of a Frankish kingdom was importantly determinative of the course of medieval history.

## Feudalism

The manor itself was a command economy sitting on top of a traditional economy. The tradition was reflected in the day-to-day activities of the peasants in cultivating the soil and caring for the domestic animals, as well as other skilled tasks ordinarily passed from parent to child. However, the fief-holder had fixed rights to the serfs' labor and could raise a levy for building a road, repairing a bridge, or digging ditches at his command or that of his representative.

One other general point should be made here. Feudalism was a system of governance and therefore political. Fiefholders had political power within a hierarchy, which we will examine in more detail later. At the same time, the fiefholder derived real economic benefits that were, in part, channeled into his ability to project military power. So, feudalism integrated the three sources of power that we discussed in an earlier chapter. In this sense it was a force for stability. It is frequently thought, instead, to be a force for anarchy, probably because the rise of feudalism corresponded with the fall of the Carolingians, but the one had nothing to do with the other.

When last we visited the Roman Empire, it had been divided into two distinct administrative and financial units, a Latin-speaking West and a Greek-speaking East, each with their own emperor. Moreover, in what were, literally, Constantine's last moments, both halves of the empire became officially Christian. When the Franks first invaded the Western Roman Empire, there was only one emperor, Julian, and he was adamantly pagan. He was also an able general and he defeated the barbarians with ease.

However, in 358, he did allow some of the Franks to settle in what is now Belgium. They could retain their tribal customs and tribal organization provided they swore allegiance to Rome. This arrangement would be used again and again because it served the dual purposes of blunting the destructiveness of the invaders and of increasing the population, and thus the tax base. Later, the term *foederatti*, from which our word "federation" is derived, would be applied to such tribes.

By the end of Julian's rule, the Ostrogoths had expanded their territory to the east and were abutting both the Alans, descended from the Scythians, and the Huns, a Turkic people originally from the Altai Mountains. In 372, the Huns expressed their displeasure with the encroachment by exploding westward. They delivered a humiliating series of defeats to the Ostrogothic cavalry, crushed the Visigoths and made slaves of the Gepids, who, most unfortunately, had occupied the fertile steppe much coveted by the Huns. There, the latter came to rest with their flocks and pretty much ceased to be any real trouble for a time.

Entire tribes of Germans, running from the Huns, moved westward along the Roman frontier, accompanied by some Alans displaced from their home in the Caucasus Mountains. They were headed toward the virtually defenseless Roman province of Gaul. "On the last day of 406, the leading elements of this host crossed the frozen Rhine at Mainz."* There was no army to oppose them "as they completed their leisurely pillage of Gaul," or to abate the further incursions by the Franks.

Meanwhile, the Huns had been quietly (for the most part) enjoying their pastures. Then, all that changed when Attila became their king. He unified the tribes (433-444) and then "instituted a policy of annual plundering expeditions." The

*For this and the next several quotations, the source is McEvedy's *The New Penguin Atlas of Medieval History*.

Eastern Empire was rich enough to buy him off with "a tribute which eventually rose to 2,100 lbs of gold a year."

The bad news was that the Western Roman Empire had nothing like those resources to assuage the ravening Hun. At the same time, their army was insufficient alone to oppose him. In the end, a Western general put together a coalition of Visigoths, Franks, Burgundians – all Germans – that was able to stop the Huns at Orleans, "the western most point reached by any Altaian conquerors." As we will see later, this setback did not deter Attila from invading northern Italy the following year.

All in all, the Western Roman Empire's borders were shrinking, as the earlier invaders had carved out chunks for themselves. The Visigoths had a kingdom in western Gaul. The Suevi had a kingdom comprising most of Spain and, worst news of all, the Vandals had taken over a rebuilt and Romanized Carthage, the second most important city in the west. It was also at the heart of a grain growing operation that shipped food to Rome, and had been vital to her survival ever since Egyptian grain was rerouted to Constantinople. So, the Vandals had the Romans under their thumb, hence the unsavory connotation of their name.*

By 476, German incursions had rendered the Western Empire as good as null and void. The Franks had established themselves in the north, right on the border of a large, personally held *latifundia*, which represented roughly half of

---

* Before embarking on their journey to North Africa, the Vandal king had a census taken of every man, woman and child. The total was 80,000, which McEvedy thinks is probably a "representative figure for a migrating tribe of the period."

what was left of the Western Empire. Clovis of Tournai was a master of "let's you and him fight." He conspired to assassinate several of his rivals and then executed a number of his co-conspirators for their part in the evil deeds. In so doing, he made himself the sole king of the Franks, while simultaneously expanding the territory under his sway. Specifically, he took over the neighboring *latifundia* and defeated the Visigoths, taking most of their share of Gaul.

Clovis died in 511 and, in typical Frankish form, left his kingdom to his four sons. This would appear to weaken the Franks vis-à-vis the Goths, but it was not so. There was no political unity between the Ostrogoths and the Visigoths, and neither had done much to integrate with the local people. By contrast, the Franks were successfully melding into Gallo-Roman society, laying a foundation for the feudal mix of Roman and German laws and customs. The Frankish kingdom was seen as one unified state endowed with four kings. We will see later how the smooth sharing of overlapping power was an essential feature of feudalism.

Meanwhile, the Germans were acquiring Christianity, at a time when there were two conflicting theories about the Trinity. Purely by accident, the Goths embraced the teachings of Arius, who argued that the Father and the Son had two distinct natures such that Christ was not God's equal. The Pope and the Trinitarian bishops saw Arianism as heresy, believing that the Son must be universally acknowledged as co-substantial with the Father. The Franks, as well as the Gallo-Romans, were converted in this belief. This congruence of religious doctrine may have helped Clovis boot the Visigoths out of Gaul.* He could then clothe a grab for power as the liberation of the people and their priests from heretical rule.

The four sons of Clovis actually expanded the Frankish kingdom south to the Pyrenees, and east to include part of the Alps. In 558, the last surviving son of Clovis reunited the kingdom. Then, when he died in 561, he left it to his four sons and they proved entirely unable to coordinate further Frankish expansion.

## Transitions

In 527, Justinian became Emperor in the East, and determined that he would reconquer the West. Belisarius, his best general, so demoralized the Ostrogothic king that he gave up Italy for a Roman pension. The collapse of his kingdom brought the Bavarians and the Lombards, two other German tribes, into the provinces just south of the Danube. The Bavarians accepted the nominal suzerainty of the Franks.

Around this time, a horde of Mongols and White Huns were roundly defeated by some Turks, and they reeled into Europe, where they came to be known as the Avars. They ejected the Lombards from the pastures they coveted, and made the Bavarians seek the protection of the Frankish kingdom, thus enlarging it further. The Avars also threatened the Balkans, and the Eastern Empire had to pay them off with bribes not unlike the ones Attila had

* Clovis was a pagan who married a Christian and was converted by her.

commanded a century and a half earlier.

Running from the Avars, the Lombards found them-selves right in between the Kingdom of the Franks and the Papacy in Rome. This would turn out to be a hugely impor-tant fact of history and geography, which no one at the time could possibly predict. Be patient. It will come.

For now, the big deal was an army revolt against, and subsequent murder of, the Eastern Emperor, Maurice. Not surprisingly, the Avar Khan used the disarray to pillage and plunder the central Balkans. Into the vacuum this created, there poured an avalanche of Slavic peoples who settled in the Balkan Peninsula. At the same time, also hoping to take advantage of dynastic strife, a Persian king dreamed of rec-reating the realms of Cyrus and Darius as they had been at their highest points. Now, they were ruled by the East Romans.* A new and more competent emperor called Hera-clius was largely able to hold the Persians at bay, such that East Rome's eastern frontier was secured by 629.

Heraclius then engaged in a major restructuring of the imperial organization, which included the explicit recogni-tion of its Greek character. Nevertheless, they did not change their name and called themselves Romans to the bitter end. Western peoples accepted the imperial appellation (hence Romania), but called the people Greeks.

Things were quieter in the west. The Frankish kingdom was reunited in 613, and divided again in 623. Only this time the division made geographic sense. Neustria meant

* Modern historians do not, at this date, change the name from East Roman to Byzantine.

the new land and was used for the southwestern portion, while Austrasia meant homeland and was applied to the northeastern part. These boundaries do not correspond with the present borders of France and Germany, but they were a start in that direction.

## Islam

At about the same time, Arabia was being transformed from the backwater it had always been, of little trouble to any of its neighbors, into a major power player. The key cause for the change lay in the revolutionary ideas of the Prophet Muhammad. He maintained the monotheism of the Jewish and Christian elements in the patchwork that had been the Arabic religion. His one God was Allah, his faith was Islam, and only by submitting to the will of Allah as outlined in his teaching could a soul be saved.

Muhammad was forced to leave Mecca in 622, allowed back in 630, and died in 632. By that time, all of Arabia had converted to Islam. By 651, not quite twenty years after he had died, the Arab Caliphate included all of what had been the old Persian empire, as well as all of inhabitable North Africa, save for the bit that had once been Carthage and a tiny tip near Spain. That is an amazing expansion for so short a time.

At this point, the Islamic revolution took a breather. Then, in the years just before and after 700, it expanded dramatically again, adding new territories in both east and west. For our story, the westward movement was more critical. In 698, the Arabs captured Carthage, and then, more importantly, conquered and converted the Berbers, a native North African people. With these new recruits, they swept westward until there was nowhere further to go.

So, they turned north and crossed to the Iberian Peninsula. There, they found an impressive mountain (*jebel* in Arabic), and they named it for their leader, Tariq. *Jebel-al-Tariq* is known to us, of course, as Gibraltar. The coalition of Arabs and Berbers defeated the Visigoths so soundly that nearly the entire peninsula fell into their hands. They were on a roll.

## The West Revisited

Meanwhile, the Frankish kings that descended from Clovis came to be called the Merovingians, and they ruled France for an impressive three centuries, besting both the much later Valois and Bourbon dynasties for longevity in power. The great vassals of the Merovingian kings were not only Franks, but included wealthy Gallo-Roman landowners who were particularly likely to be bishops.

Their rule was brutal, despite the bishops, and they were notorious for their debauchery. One Dagobert experienced so much conjugal bliss with his small army of wives that he famously died "of old age" when he was merely thirty-four. To make matters worse, they customarily left the kingdom of a dead monarch to all of his sons. In the words of Andre Maurois, this practice "turned every succession into a national catastrophe, followed by fratricidal wars." Over time, they became mere puppet-kings to be manipulated by the real power figure, the Mayor of the Palace.

Once the Mayor's job had been to mediate and communicate between the king and his companions, but as the Merovingians became weaker and weaker, the Mayors took over. In Austrasia, they led an increasingly independent aristocracy, able to ignore the king. For a hundred years, the job was dominated by a family named Pepin, who supplied the most powerful soldiers of their day. Charles Martel was a prime example. He battled to the top in Austrasia in 717, and then repeated that feat in Neustria in 719.

In 732, as we recall, he earned the nickname "Charles the Hammer" by crushing an Arab army that had invaded western France. This stunning victory also presented Charles with an opportunity he was astute enough to understand and to seize. Having saved Christendom, he was able to insist that the Church give up some of its vast holdings, organized along the manorial lines described above. These, he would then grant to his followers, so as to fund a Frankish cavalry class. This not only gave the Frankish Kingdom a larger and better-organized army with which to fight its enemies, but also strengthened the elite vis-à-vis the peasants.

Charles' son, Pepin the Short, inherited the title of Mayor of the Palace, and with it the Kingdom's most powerful position. As it happened, both he and the pope had something the other wanted. Pepin wanted permission to depose the last of the puppet kings and be crowned in his stead. The pope wanted Pepin to use his military might to crush their mutual neighbor, the Lombards, who were threatening to invade Rome. This would have been purely for the prestige of controlling it, as the great imperial city had suffered from neglect and the passage of time. Pepin defeated the Lombards and won himself a crown in the process. In Andre Maurois' words, Pepin the Short

> locked up Childeric III, the last of the Merovingians, in a monastery, and had himself crowned, together with his wife, Bertha Broadfoot, by Saint Boniface – a skilful maneuver since the sons born of their union were thus doubly hallowed.

His son Charles the Great* inherited the throne with his brother, who died in 771. This made Charlemagne sole king of the Franks, a position he enjoyed for forty-three years. Since his kingdom was ancestral to both France and Germany, he is a major historical figure. However, we are going to suspend the historical discussion and return to feudalism as a background for a richer discussion of both Pepin and Charlemagne.

## Feudalism Revisited

At the very heart of the system were vassalage and fief-holding. On the one hand, it was possible for a man to be a vassal without having a fief. On the other, however, it was impossible to have a fief without a vassal holding it. Land, or even a manor, could be let out for rent, but it was not a fief, and it was not subject to feudal law. To be a fief, vassalage must be involved.

This created a big problem for Pepin and the pope. They

---

* This was *Carolus Magnus* in Latin and, ultimately, Charlemagne.

were both willing to have some of the Lombard land that Pepin "liberated" go to the Holy Father, but not in a way that might even *imply* that the pope was a vassal of the king. So, Pepin donated the land to an ephemeral entity named "Saint Peter and Saint Paul." Thus began the temporal element of the Papacy, the Papal States, which, very much later, would become serious impediments to Italian unity.

Even as fiefs came to be understood as hereditary, the death of a fief holder did not cause the fief to come immediately into the legal possession of his heir. The heir had first to become the vassal of the lord who had granted the fief to his father. To become a vassal involved participating in a public ritual in which the would-be vassal (V) knelt before his future lord (L) and placed his hands, prayer-like, between those of L. V then pledged "entire faith as a vassal to his lord against all men who might live or die."* In equally formulaic terms, L accepted V's homage, helped him to his feet and, as a rule, kissed him on the cheek.

The next part of the ceremony was the oath of fealty. Homage rituals were common among the Franks as early as the eighth century and they were probably much older than that. The earliest homage rituals were likely German and heathen, and part of the process of becoming a companion. Andre Maurois wrote this about their origins:

> At its outset, the ceremonies of chivalry principally consisted of the investiture of new warriors. All primitive

---

* Quotations in this section will be from Stephenson unless otherwise indicated.

societies have had and still have such initiations. The Church was able to impose upon them a moral character.

An element in this moral character was the oath of fealty, which was a sworn statement recommitting the vassal to his homage promise taken on the Gospels or a holy relic. Homage always preceded fealty for vassals. The general public could also be asked to swear fealty (general loyalty) to the King, with no implication of their becoming vassals.

Lord and vassal were both making a commitment for life, with known exceptions. An edict of Charlemagne's delineates the circumstances that could justify a vassal breaking with his lord. All bets were off

> if the lord seeks to reduce him to servitude, if the lord plots against his life, if the lord commits adultery with his wife, if the lord attacks him with drawn sword, or if the lord fails to protect him when able to do so.

A faithless lord was called a "felon," as was a faithless vassal, with all the venality that implies.

A vassal was, as a rule, a gentleman and a warrior who had sworn to fight with and for his lord in battle and provide other services of more peaceful sorts. These include "suit to court," which meant presenting himself before the Lord and offering advice and counsel on various matters. Stephenson explains:

> Law was the unwritten custom of the country. To change or even to define it was the function, not of the lord, but of

his court. It was the vassals themselves who declared the law under which they lived; and when one of them was accused of a misdeed, he was entitled to the judgment of his peers, i.e., his fellow vassals.

On certain occasions, it became customary for a vassal to provide a contribution called "aid." In Norman England, three occasions were specified: when his oldest son was knighted, his oldest daughter married, or when the lord was taken hostage, requiring the payment of ransom.[*] Elsewhere, aid might be expected at the knighting of any sons, or the marriage of any daughters, or some other special event like a crusade. Finally, the vassal owed his lord hospitality, which we will consider in more detail below.

In medieval western law, there were at least two types of property. One was called allodial property and it was owned outright. It could be inherited, sold or given away by the owner. The second, of course, was the fief, which was held "of" another in return for specified services. It could not, as we noted above, be inherited without the heir becoming, actually and by ritual, the vassal of the original lord. Conversely, when a lord died, his son had to go through the investiture rituals with his late father's vassals. They could refuse, of course, but then they would lose their fief.

By late in the eighth century, fiefs were routinely passed

---

[*] On the Continent, feudalism evolved organically, with many small variations depending on local customs and conditions. By contrast, the Norman conquest of England in 1066 imported the feudalism of a particular region in France and imposed it wholesale so that it was far more uniform and thus easier to explain.

from father to son, and later they were described as "heredi-tary." However, that simply reflected the universal knowl-edge that a ritual in which both the lord and vassal agreed to renew their relationship would take place. Legally, the need for this ritual was quite clear. "When a vassal died, his fief reverted to the lord and really ceased to be a fief at all until another vassal had been invested in it."

If the vassal had no heir, the lord could do with the estate whatever he pleased. If there was an heir, the lord was legally obligated to grant him the fief but still a ceremonial investi-ture was required.

Another important element in feudal tenure was primo-geniture, a rule that gave the whole inheritance to the eldest son, or if there were no son, to the oldest of the nearest male relatives. As the system functioned to provide continuity in a cavalry class whose members could supply themselves with horses and gear, subdivision had the potential of disas-ter. With estates divided into ever-smaller plots to share with several sons, they could be reduced to the point where they could no longer support a horseman.

Ironically, at the top of the system, the Carolingians rou-tinely split up their kingdoms between several sons. Per-haps, the primogeniture rule was to prevent lesser folk, with smaller holdings, from doing the same. Moreover, the fief holder was a political and juridical officer of the state, and that power was, and had to be, indivisible if it were to be wielded effectively. There was one exception to the rule. A fief holder was permitted to divide it among his own vassals, but if they failed to show up and fight, his was the liability.

We will have more on this later.

In the matter of inheritance, there were two other important trouble spots.* If a vassal died with an infant son, the lord had the right of wardship. He took over the fief, enjoyed its revenues and saw to it that the boy was raised through the stages leading to knighthood. At that point, the son would be invested as a vassal and receive his father's fief. This insured that the fief was passed from one adult, trained knight to another. In the case of one or more daughters as the only heir, the fief would go to the husband of the oldest daughter. Because of this, the lord had a say in who the girl could marry, even while her father was still alive. This, again, guarantees that vassalage passed from one soldier to another, and that the other was trusted by the lord.

Dating back to the Carolingians, vassalage "had implied a personal obligation to fight for the lord as a heavy-armed cavalryman or knight." Every vassal whose fief came directly from the king was expected to turn up himself, with a group of his own vassals. The same would also hold true for those holding fiefs from dukes, counts and other major magnates. We are not sure what the exact obligation was before the twelfth century, but after that it was codified and written down. Ideally, the vassal brought the exact number of additional horsemen as required by the conditions of the fief. He was legally bound to do so at his own expense for no more than forty days out of any given year.

Stephenson then provides a wonderful example of how

---

* These could also be seen as two manifestations of the absence of an adult male heir.

this could work based on records derived from the conquest of England by William of Normandy (the Conqueror) in 1066. While the manorial system was in full flower in England, feudalism was unknown, and William brought it with him wholesale from the continent. While lifting many of the ideas directly from Stephenson, I will paraphrase him, and integrate some information from other sources, but still give him credit for the clarity of his example.

Let us say that William granted a fief consisting of twenty-five manors to Lord Arthur in return for the service of ten knights. Arthur would, of course, show up for any fight that William got into.* What Arthur then needed was nine more knights, and there were two basic ways he could enlist them. He could find knights without fiefs and invite them to join his household. Since it was much easier to move people to food than food to people, Arthur and his entourage, including but not limited to the nine knights, would move from manor to manor to munch. These knights were his vassals and had sworn homage and fealty, but they were not granted a fief of their own.

The other solution to finding nine more knights was to grant some of the lord's vassals one or more manors as fiefs of their own. Arthur granted eight manors to his cousin Bertram in return for the service of four knights. At this point, it is quite easy to pose a trick question. Once Arthur has granted eight manors to Bertram, how many manors are left in Arthur's fief? The easy answer is seventeen, but the cor-

---

* As we saw, there were fixed limits on the number of days per year that a vassal was obliged to fight and they had to be consulted and won over if more were needed.

rect answer is twenty-five. Arthur's fief remains untouched in that it contains twenty-five manors granted from the king in return for the service of ten knights.

What makes this possible was that feudal tenure, feudal "ownership," was not exclusive. One approach, though not Stephenson's, is to talk about overlapping use values. The king could show up at any one of Arthur's manors and expect hospitality, which would include the consumption of Arthur's produce, the hunting of Arthur's game, etc., because Arthur does not own the fief outright, but rather "holds" it "of" the king. Arthur, as Bertram's lord, has the same rights of hospitality on the manors granted to Bertram as part of his fief.

In modern civil law, we have something superficially like it called a usufruct. *Black's Law Dictionary* defines usufruct as:

> The right of enjoying a thing, the property of which is vested in another, and to draw from the same all the profit, utility, and advantage which it may produce, provided it be without altering the substance of the thing.

The most usual example of this would be renting a house. The renters may live in the house, furnish it to their taste and enjoy apples off the tree in the back yard. They would need permission by the owner to alter anything substantial about the house or to cut down the apple tree. So it is a tempting analogy but fatally flawed. The landlord has no right to show up, expect a meal and a place to sleep for the night. After military service, hospitality was a major obligation of a vassal to his lord.

Returning to the hypothetical Arthur, he could expect Bertram to join him with three other knights. Bertram faced the same two decisions Arthur had. He could recruit three knights to join his household, or he could grant one, two or all three a fief of their own. Let us assume that he took the second course. Meanwhile, "five landless adventurers" have agreed to become Arthur's vassals in return for one good manor each. Arthur has one lord, William, and six vassals, Bertram and the landless knights.* Bertram has three vassals, each with one manor as fief. Arthur and his six vassals make seven, including Bertram, whose three vassals complete the requirement for the service of ten knights.

Modern scholars use the term "subinfeudation" to describe the process of vassals creating their own vassals who might then create their own vassals and so on. During the early development of feudalism, clerical vassals were commonplace, and they did the actual fighting. As the Church became strong enough to insist that clergy could not take human lives, subinfeudation solved the problem. Important churchmen were almost invariably royal vassals. By granting fiefs to their own vassals, they could meet the military service requirements without going into battle themselves.

A critically important point is that no matter how many layers of subinfeudation existed, it was only possible for Wil-

* Not a bad name for a rock band.

liam to import feudalism to England because there was a manorial system already in place. A vassal consumes, for military purposes as well as for hospitality, the "surplus" off a fully self-enclosed productive unit based on agriculture and domesticated animals, and having all the labor and craftsmen needed to function effectively. Barren land has absolutely no value to a knight who requires a "surplus" to support his horses, feed himself, his family and his retainers, and support his sons as they become knights themselves.

A second important point is that in feudal societies, everyone except the king at the top and the lowliest baron at the bottom had dual roles. They were each both a lord and a vassal. Moreover, in mature feudalism, there was an absolute divide between that lowly baron and the agricultural laborers of the manor. He was a gentleman. They were peasants. It is possible that in the early years, a strapping peasant with brains, brawn and a heroic and valiant temperament might have crossed the line. However, as the technology of cavalry and the complexity of politics increased, the barrier grew to a prohibitive height.

Training to become a knight and vassal required the leisure provided by skimming off a "surplus" from the labor of others. It also meant the ability to afford several large and well-trained horses. Sons of a vassal might be sent to the lord's court as a page, to learn how to behave in aristocratic, but also martial, society. They would have to learn horsemanship not long after they learned to walk. Stephenson describes the whole process in fascinating detail, and, if you are interested in knights and chivalry, you could not find a better-written or more accurate source.

The important idea for the moment is that the manorial system, which organized the agricultural base, and the feudal system were intertwined, with the latter being economically dependent on the former. However, they are two separate and distinct elements in a single social formation. That social formation, manorial and feudal, would be the basis for economic, political and military power for centuries to come.

Because an elite caste dominated all three major sources of power and also married among themselves, the system was quite stable apart from clashes between these elites. In fact, there were three strong European feudal families still very much in evidence at the beginning of the twentieth century. These would be the Hapsburgs of the Austro-Hungarian Empire, the Hohenzollerns of the German Empire and the Romanovs of Russia. It took the chaos and devastation of the First World War to bring them down.

In 1848, amidst turmoil and revolution, the Hapsburg family forced the inept and vacillating Ferdinand to abdicate in favor of his nephew, Franz Joseph. This bright, wily and forceful ruler held the reigns of power until his death in 1916. That was quite a run.

His successor ruled a much-reduced territory for a scant two years before loosing the crown altogether. He retired to his private estates in Austria until the victorious Allies demanded his removal to neutral Switzerland. In 1920, he staged two failed attempts at seizing power in Hungary. After the second, even the Swiss didn't want him back. He died, in abject poverty, in Madeira, in 1921.

Tsar Nicholas II and his family were put under house arrest early in 1917 by bourgeois revolutionaries. Later, the Bolsheviks exiled them to a more remote part of Russia. When anti-Bolshevik forces seemed to be coming too close, a minor local official ordered the entire family shot.

The last emperor of the Hohenzollerns, Kaiser Wilhelm, did considerably better than the others. He remained comfortably alive in exile in Holland until he died, of natural causes, in 1941. He was eighty-two years old.*

---

* These stories are told in lavish detail in a wonderful, lush B.B.C. drama called *The Fall of Eagles*. It is long, but worth every moment.

# Church and State

IN the previous chapters, we have looked at the importance of a balance or an imbalance in three major sources of power: economic, political and military. In this chapter, we will add to that equation the power of faith, and of its earthly vehicle, organized religion. Specifically, we will consider the complex relationships that existed between the Roman Catholic Church and the various states that were emerging in Western Europe.

## The Carolingians and Beyond

In 773, Pope Adrian asked Charlemagne to come to his aid against the revived threat of the Lombards. The king brought a huge host, defeated the Lombards, and put their king's traditional iron crown on his own head. In 774, he arrived in Rome, and, despite the depredations of the centuries, it appeared to him as splendid, with its magnificent churches and their holy relics, beautiful music, grand ceremonies and even remnants of the glories of the old Roman Empire.

Charlemagne was enchanted and conceived the plan of making his kingdom into a centre of culture and beauty. The Pope consecrated him King of the Franks and King of the

Lombards and made him a Roman patrician. From that day, he looked upon himself as the protector of Christendom and styled himself "King by the grace of God," a new formula among the Franks.[*]

> Charlemagne was at war for his entire forty-three-year reign. Because his brother had died, leaving him the sole claimant to the Frankish throne, these wars were never familial. Instead, as Maurois tells us, he was following a "vast scheme" to recreate the power and greatness of ancient Rome. He began by conquering two provinces, Lombardy and Aquitaine, which had once been Roman.

He also attempted the reconquest of Spain in 778, but had to rush home to meet a Saxon invasion in the north. Along the way, his rear guard got separated from the main force. The stragglers were ambushed by Basques. Roland, nephew and vassal of Charlemagne, refused to sound an alarm that might have brought the main army back, needlessly risking the life of his uncle and liege lord. The gallant Roland and his companions perished, one and all, at the hands of the Basques.

> This episode of little military importance remains famous because it is the subject matter of the Song of Roland – thus demonstrating the superiority of poetry over history.[†]

[*] Andre Maurois, *A History of France.*
[†] Andre Maurois, *An Illustrated History of Germany.* This is also the source for the next two quotations.

The second phase of Charlemagne's "vast scheme" centered on

the struggle against the Barbarian invaders of the Empire: Saxons, Slavs, Avars, Saracens and, later, the Norse pirates who were establishing themselves along the coasts of the English Channel.

Another of his major projects was the conversion of the Saxons to Christianity. This would be no easy feat. Like most other Germanic peoples, they were nomads and so, having no homeland, their gods had no temples. These gods occupied an unearthly paradise called Valhalla, which would become a hero's home after his valiant death. The Saxons were the most recalcitrant of the lot. Their only concession was the inclusion of Christ in their pantheon. Their society was rigidly hierarchical, with nobles at its pinnacle, followed by freemen in a distant second place. At the very bottom were the peasants. It was inconceivable to the Saxons to suppose any kind of equality, including spiritual equality of the sort preached by the Church.

In Charlemagne's day, the Saxon leader, Witikind, was extremely hostile to the faith and quite prone to murdering the faithful.

Charlemagne then convoked a general assembly of the people ... in the heart of Saxony and there displayed full authority. A great many nobles and free men were forcibly baptized. Witikind, the very soul of resistance, proceeded to devastate Hesse and Thuringia, massacring priests and driving the monks from Fulda.

Finally, the two men and their armies met in battle in 782, and Charlemagne was victorious. Scholars long believed that he had a huge number of the Saxons beheaded (*decollati*) based on an eyewitness account. In those days, copying exactly and without attribution was not plagiarism, but rather a holy act of preservation. The notion that the Saxons were beheaded has been revised based on the discovery of an older document. This version of the story states that Charlemagne caused a large number of Saxons to be dispersed (*delocati*). From the point of view of the Saxons, there was all the difference in the world between being dispersed and being beheaded. From the point of view of some obscure monk copying out an eyewitness account of the battle, the difference amounts simply to switching a mere couple of letters in the tedious process of transcription.

In 800, on Christmas Day, Pope Leo III crowned Charlemagne "Emperor of the Romans." There are a variety of theories about why Leo did this. One suggests that his actions reflected a desire to deflate the power of the Eastern Emperor and his Patriarch. Indeed, the first reaction in Constantinople was annoyance that Leo was puffing up his own consequence and that of a country bumpkin to boot. A few years later, the parties made amends and agreed that, once more, there were two emperors, one of the East and the other of the West.

A second view is that Leo was setting a precedent for the future. Only a pope could anoint a western emperor, and thus the papacy was pre-eminent over whatever secular power Charlemagne and his descendents might amass. This seems a bit too elaborate and foreshadows the struggles between popes and German emperors that do not manifest themselves until several centuries into the future.

At that time, Leo need not have bothered. After Charlemagne's death in 814, his Frankish Empire was to go seriously on the skids. His son, Louis the Pious, revolted the hearty Frankish warriors with his mawkish sobbing over his real or imagined sins. At the same time, Louis' sons were plotting against one another for the spoils of his demise long before he quit this earthly plane. Because of this disunity, subsequent popes had nothing much to fear from Frankish power for quite some time.

My own more humble view is that Leo III wanted to lavish praise upon his military protector, and that the most august, impressive and all around spiffy title he could think of was "Emperor of the Romans." It did not cause a re-Romanization of Gaul. Charlemagne was certainly powerful, but the power was personal, in the sense of centered on his person via the loyalty of his followers. It was a stage in the development of what we call feudalism.

Charlemagne's power was not remotely imperial, as it did not create or stem from an established official position at the head of an imperial apparatus of government. Augustus forged an empire so well organized that it lasted unchanged through the tenure of many emperors, including some real dolts. Charlemagne's "empire" essentially collapsed when he died.

He did have a vision of a united Europe, and he did try to put in place an organization that could last. He divided the territory under his control into administrative units called Gaus, each having a "count" who was a military vassal to Charlemagne and who provided the usual local services of keeping the peace and settling disputes. The populations were so low, and personal rule so systemic, that someone losing a dispute could appeal over the head of the count to the crown directly.

Charlemagne did not make his headquarters in Rome, but rather in Aachen,* our best guess about where he was born, certainly his favorite residence after 768, and the site of his great palace. Yet, despite its magnificence, he lived simply as was appropriate to a great warrior. When needed, he could appear quite regal, in cloth of gold, but as a rule he wore serviceable Frankish garb. Instead of a great show of wealth, he lavished time and resources on learning. Sadly, however, despite his love for reading, he never learned to write. He assembled the greatest scholars of the day to his court, including his friend and biographer, Einhard. He founded a school, where he himself studied under these great masters, and where boys, selected by merit rather than by birth, were trained to be the future administrators of his

* Aachen was located at what would now be the Belgium border with Germany, about forty miles west-south-west of the city of Cologne.

domain. The boys were fed, clothed, housed and educated at the court's expense.

Charlemagne also encouraged his agents to find and buy not only works by the Church's greatest writers, but also the great Latin classics. In addition, aided by Einhard, he caused the ancient epics and stories passed down by the generations of Franks to be written down and cherished. Sadly, his sole surviving son had these "pagan" tribal memories deliberately obliterated to salve his overactive fear of sin.

Charlemagne had connections with heads of state as far ranging as King Alfonso of Asturias in Spain to the kings of the Scots. Francis Russell, in *A Concise History of Germany*, shares this wonderful story:

> His most singular and one of his most durable friendships was with the legendary Baghdad caliph, Harun al-Rashid, a ruler he never met [but] with whom he constantly corresponded. The caliph sent him magnificent gifts of perfumes, silk stuffs, and jewelry, and even an elephant that managed to live a number of years in the unlikely northern climate.

Finally, and this will have huge implications for the future, Charlemagne insisted on appointing all the bishops in his territory, although he kept the pope posted about his selections.* He also effected Church reform and presided

---

* The convention for capitalizing or not capitalizing "pope" or "emperor" is to capitalize the title of a particular incumbent, as in Pope Leo III, but not the office itself.

over meetings of churchmen to discuss and make decisions about ecclesiastical matters.

There is no question that Charlemagne was a great man and thus deserving of a great title, such as Emperor of the Romans. However, it would be a very grave mistake to think that something resembling the old Roman Empire, with an imperial bureaucracy and an imperial army, had been recreated by papal fiat. It is more sensible to think of it as an honorary title. Nevertheless, an honorary title, gracing the real power Charlemagne wielded, was nothing to sniff at because the title itself added prestige to the power.

## Devolution

Any number of factors contributed to the collapse of the Frankish Empire. Fratricidal wars weakened it until 844, when Charlemagne's three grandsons agreed on a division.

> Charles the Bald got what would become France west of the Rhone and the Saone rivers. Louis the German united Austrasia, Bavaria, Swabia and Saxony. Finally, Lothaire accepted a bizarre strip of land, very long and narrow, which ran from the North Sea to Calabria, extending along the valleys of the Meuse, the Rhine and the Rhone. It was to this prince that Lotharingia (hence Lorraine) owes its name.

These are the words of Andre Maurois, who believed that this division set the stage for further division by revealing cultural differences among the peoples of the former empire.* Indeed, he argued that as early as 888, "seven different kingdoms could be counted: France, Navarre, Provence, Burgundy, Lorraine, Germany and Italy," and that each of these had developed a national character. Although the idea of a nation-state was almost a millennium away, Maurois still thought that cultural differences contributed to these political divisions.

Carl Stephenson focused more heavily on certain features of feudalism as a political economy, most notably vassalage. Because the relationships between lords and vassals were personal relationships, they were limited by distances. It is self-evident that the only basis for these relationships was face-to-face contact. When that was possible, in a small state like Flanders, feudalism could form the basis for efficient government and viable self-defense.

In 954, another Carolingian Lothaire was defeated by Hugh the Great, who founded the Capetian dynasty in what would, much later, become France. They were poor as church mice and had effective control over only the Isle de Paris, an island in the middle of the Seine. The principle vassals of the king, in theory, ignored him completely in practice. Stephenson sums up the situation in these words:

> France, obviously, had ceased to be a state in any proper
> sense of the word. Rather, it had split into a number of

---

* A bilingual treaty between Charles the Bald and Louis the German has one column written in *lingua Romana rustica*. The rustic or less-sophisticated Latin would evolve into French. The other language was Germanic.

states whose rulers, no matter how they styled themselves, enjoyed the substance of regal power.

In the middle of the ninth century, Vikings began to raid the islands and coastline of Western Europe. They were so successful that, after a time, they started to set up camps to store all the loot they had amassed before they got around to taking it home. Later, many of these camps became more permanent settlements, and some, like Dublin, were the basis of future cities. In France, the Danes set up camp at the mouth of the Seine, and from there attacked up river as far as Paris. At this juncture, two very different stories have been told.

McEvedy says that, in 911 "the French king granted the Viking chieftain Rollo extensive lands at the mouth of the Seine, the condition being that he kept his countrymen within these bounds." My regard for his scholarship is boundless, but this cannot be right. The French king did not have enough military power to defend Paris, where he was based, against Viking plunder. He could not possibly control "extensive lands at the mouth of the Seine" under these conditions.

It seems much more likely that Rollo controlled the land, but that he wanted the elevated status of a royal vassal, which only the king could provide. Indeed, Rollo became the Count of Normandy.* It is likely that we have a document "granting" land as a fief to the newly minted count. McEvedy adds that Rollo must have kept his countrymen corralled because "the

---

* Normandy is where these Norsemen settled. Later, folk from Normandy would be called Normans.

grant was enlarged in 924." Given their relative military might, it seems virtually certain that Rollo did the enlarging and the king gave it his blessing. One of Rollo's descendents, increasingly French in character, became the Duke of Normandy, most likely by the same process.

In Flanders, a count came to the fore and became the hereditary head of both military and political affairs. He had, of course, vassals of his own who provided for defense and local governance in their own fiefs. As Stephenson explains:

> For both civil and military purposes the county was divided into *chatellenies* – districts constructed about castles, such as those of Ghent, Bruges, Ypres, Saint-Omer, Lille and Arras. Each of these districts was entrusted to a *chatelaine*, who in all respects acted as the count's deputy and for that reason was often styled vicomte (viscount).

The castle would be garrisoned by knights from the surrounding fiefs, so part of the vicomte's commission was to ensure that the castle was duly provisioned. In the event of war, he summoned all the other knights in the *chatellenie*, organized them, and acted as their commander. In peace, he collected the count's revenues from that district in the form of "manorial income, subsidies, tolls, and the like." The chatelaine was also responsible for holding a "court that met inside the castle to administer the count's justice." The *chatelaines* were recompensed for their services by large fiefs in close proximity to the castle. In general, the office became hereditary by the mid-twelfth century.

These *chatelaines* had enormous power on a feudal scale and they could, like the great vassals of the Capetian kings, have struck out on their own. That they did not was probably dependent on the character of the lord. The Counts of Flanders were usually highly able, brave and competent men who commanded the loyalty of nearly all their vassals, and a wariness on the part of would-be rebels. Flanders remained a player in European politics into the modern era.

## Germany

Among the German speakers in the east, the situation was essentially quite similar to that of France. It simply took a bit longer for the central authority of the king to be diminished and replaced by powerful smaller units of governance. Descended from Louis the German, Carolingians continued to claim the royal mantle in the east. They had their ups and downs, but in the long run, the battle for a centralized, authoritative king was a losing proposition. Maurois tells us why this was so.

> The nobility, whether religious or lay, counts or bishops, all had their fortified castles and vassals. Arrogating royal privileges to themselves they set about minting money, raising levies and administering justice. Authority abhors a vacuum; if it is not exercised by a monarch, feudalism intervenes, and peoples* prefer tyranny to insecurity.

---

* It is likely that Maurois uses the plural because he is actually talking about the people attached to the various nobles, so each group is a people preferring tyranny to insecurity and collectively they are peoples.

So, the ancient tribal divisions of the Germans reasserted themselves and duchies sprang up as Bavarians, Saxons, Franks, Swabians, Thuringians and the like. They were governed by dukes, and their frontiers were protected by vassals called margraves. Disunion ruled, but not entirely. They would sometimes band together against Viking raids from the north, or Hungarian raiders, mounted on their tiny horses, marauding from their recently settled home on the steppe between the Carpathian Mountains and the Danube River. As McEvedy tells us, their raiding was

> as rapidly conducted, wide-ranging and savage as that of any seaborne pirates. Germany and Italy bore the brunt, but France, Burgundy and Provence all suffered as Magyar bands roamed at will through Western Europe.[*]

Faced with worsening chaos, the powerful Archbishop of Mainz called together the nobles, ecclesiastical and lay, and proposed that they chose a king. Thus was reborn the custom of electing a king, which was reflective of ancient Germanic practices. They chose a Frank, but he was unable to rally the divided tribes into a viable fighting force. With time, their loyalty swung over to the Saxon duke, Henry, who was as fierce as a German could be. He also came with a good pedigree. He could claim Carolingian blood and was married to Matilda, herself descended from the Saxon hero Witikind, who had so staunchly resisted Frankish/Christian rule.

* Magyar is what they called themselves, and is today the name of their language. Magyar is pronounced ma jar as in "I caught a butterfly and put it in ma jar."

In 926, Henry signed a nine-year truce with the Hungarians wherein they agreed to stop their endless assaults in return for an annual tribute. This was a ploy to buy time to build a series of strong defensive forts. These would serve as staging points for gathering armies and launching assaults, and also as strongholds into which the people could retreat and be safe. Taking advantage of the truce, he honed his cavalry into a fine fighting force by attacking the Slavs. Crossing the Elbe, he forced the Bohemian Duke Wenceslas to acknowledge him as his lord.

In 933, the truce ran out. Henry declared war on the Magyars and cut off their tribute payments. The Hungarians threw everything they had against Saxony; only this time the outcome was different. They were repelled and forced to withdraw, at least for the time being. They would be back.

Henry died not long after declaring Otto, his oldest son by Matilda, Duke of Saxony and king of the Germans. Continuing the German custom of electing the chief, the other Dukes affirmed his kingship and actually took positions in his court. This voluntary unity did not last. When it dawned on the Dukes that Otto sought to reduce them to the status of vassals instead of independent princes, they rebelled. Otto won and gave some of the defeated Duchies to his relatives to govern.

Otto liked to bestow clerical positions on his allies, which was a brilliant political strategy. The upper echelon of the Church, protected by their spiritual immunity and invested with considerable powers over wide areas, became a great political and financial force in Germany. A feudal distribution of property to them by Otto made them his vassals.

That cemented his ability to govern with or without the cooperation of the nobility. Here we see the apparatus of the state being staffed by the church in such a way as to promote unity and a powerful, independent monarchy.

Otto's largesse also resulted in the building of monasteries and schools. The first Germanic chronicles began in his reign. He was bringing to the Germans a level of cultural awareness they had never known before. When Otto celebrated Easter at Aix-en-Chapelle in 949, he was surrounded by ambassadors from all over, even as far off as Constantinople. His tall figure, long beard and air of authority were reminiscent of the great Frankish Emperor Charlemagne, and commanded respect.

He took his first trip to Italy in 951. The region was in complete disarray. Anarchy was the order of the day. His arrival aroused in many dreams of another Charlemagne, who could bring peace and stability out of the chaos.

> Adelaide, widow of Lothair II, king of Italy, had complained to the German king when she was being held captive by the margrave Berengar II. Otto hastened to her rescue, married her and assumed the title *Rex Francorum et Lungobardorum*\* which Charlemagne had born.

Yet another revolt by German nobles, as well as trouble on the eastern border, called him home. He left his son-in-law, Duke Conrad of Lorraine, at the head of his army in

---

\* King of the Franks and the Lombards. The source is Maurois, *An Illustrated History of Germany.*

Italy, which turned out to be a mistake.

Conrad and Berengar agreed on terms that gave the latter a free hand in Italy. At the same time, Conrad teamed up with Otto's son Liudolf, Duke of Swabia, to encourage and assist an Hungarian invasion of Otto's realm. Otto quelled the revolt, repulsed the Hungarians and confiscated the Duchies of Conrad and Liudolf, giving them, instead, to loyal friends and supporters.

In 955, Otto led his cavalry to a massive victory over the Hungarian nomads at Lechfield. He was then able to force them to settle down in the fertile plain of the Danube, where Hungary can be found today. These successes gave him the title of Otto the Great. He created a buffer zone between the many Duchies that comprised Germany, and their potential enemies, the Magyars. This zone came to be called Oesterreich, which meant "East of the Empire" Its creation freed Otto to return to Italy.

Pope John XII paid homage to Otto for his temporal holdings and invested him with the title "Holy Roman Emperor;" "Holy" because Otto had saved Christendom from the still pagan Hungarians, and "Roman Emperor" because it was a really terrific title that evoked the likes of Augustus and Charlemagne. The key problem here is that Augustus had centralized power over a state made up of many constituent nations. So did Charlemagne. Otto did not.*

---

* There is some controversy over whether Otto was crowned "Holy Roman Emperor" or just "Roman Emperor." Indeed, in *The Encyclopedia of World Biography* the abbreviated caption calls Otto "Holy Roman Emperor," but the main text has him crowned merely as "Roman Emperor."

However, he did do something that Pepin the Short had been very careful not to do. When Pepin donated Lombard land to the papacy there was no implication that the pope thus became Pepin's vassal. By contrast, Otto insisted that Pope John XII pay homage to him, thereby accepting Otto as his Lord, and confirming that he had become a vassal to the newly created emperor. To further weaken ecclesiastical power, John was forced to affirm Otto's absolute right to select and invest his own bishops. This would create huge problems in future quarrels between emperors and popes.

Otto's final adventure was an effort to relieve Constantinople of some holdings in southern Italy. The military results were mixed, but the diplomatic payoff was huge. As a result of negotiations, the Eastern emperor agreed to recognize Otto as the Western emperor, and proposed to seal the deal with the hand of the Greek princess, Theophano, for Otto's son, another Otto. After their marriage in Rome, Otto senior returned home where he died in the next year.

His accomplishments were epic. He had restored a stable government, last seen in the reign of Charlemagne more than a century before. This, in turn, fostered commerce and the spread of civilization. As Francis Russell tells us:

> He had brought into existence the Romano-Germanic Empire of the West which would later be known as the Holy Roman Empire. From his time on only German kings would wear the imperial crown. During his reign Germans

had become conscious of themselves as members of a nation rather than members of a tribe.[*]

Once the word "German" had meant only a language. In Otto's time it had become both a geographic reference and the common culture embodied by those who lived there. For this, alone, he deserves his title of Otto the Great.

Otto had also reinforced the links between Germany and northern Italy that had atrophied after Charlemagne's death. The advantages of this connection were several. Northern Italy embodied what remained of a very high civilization, and some of this rubbed off on the Germans. More importantly, Italy connected Germany to vital trade routes in the Mediterranean and beyond.

The downside was equally significant. Generations of Germans would spill blood and treasure attempting to dominate both the politics of northern Italian cities and the secular, ecclesiastical and doctrinal aspects of the papacy itself. Meanwhile, the task of pulling the Germans together into a modern state would be utterly neglected. As was true for Hellas, there was not a state called Germany until the nineteenth century.

## But First More Ottos

A mere eighteen when his father died, Otto II faced the same unrest among the nobles as they tested his measure and asserted their own independence. His native Saxony was

[*] *A Concise History of Germany.*

invaded by Harold Bluetooth, the king of Denmark. In all, it took him five years to secure his borders and assert his rule. Once these two goals were accomplished, he was drawn into Italian affairs by his Italian mother, Adelaide, while his wife, daughter of the Eastern Emperor, set him on the defense of her father's interests in southern Italy against Muslim assaults. He died without succeeding in either endeavor.

His son, Otto III, was a very interesting character. He became emperor at the age of three, so the question of who would be regent was vital. Two powerful churchmen won the political battle, while his grandmother and mother won over his heart and his mind. The Archbishops of Mainz and Rheims then combined to compel all the variously titled German rulers to accept the authority of this child, so that they might rule through him.

> Government was now in the hands of prelates and women. Otto personally assumed power at the age of fifteen. A child prodigy, he could speak Greek, Latin, German and Italian. The son of a Western emperor and, at the same time, a relative of an Eastern emperor, he would surely have cherished limitless ambitions had he not been of a religious, mystical turn of mind.*

We will see this side of Otto III again and in more detail later.

A year after his accession, Otto traveled to Italy, and in

* Maurois.

996 caused his cousin and chaplain, Bruno, to be crowned Pope Gregory V, (the first German to be pope.) Thus they held the two most powerful positions in all of Europe. Bruno was all of twenty-four while Otto was just sixteen. This would have seemed less remarkable to their contemporaries than it does to us because of their typically short life spans.

As part of his vision of Germany as "the right arm of Christ," Otto staffed all the administrative positions in Rome with Germans. This spurred the rebellious Romans to install an anti-pope as rival popes were called in those days. Otto marched down across the Alps, threw out the anti-pope, and reconfirmed Gregory.

Times were difficult for the empire. In the east, Slavic tribes first threatened and then destroyed the achievements of Otto the Great, while Hungarians and Bohemians deserted the empire. To the north and west, the Frisians opted out of imperial rule and the Normans were wreaking havoc again. Meanwhile, with almost Nero-esque disdain for the troubles of his realm, Otto lived lavishly in Rome. When Gregory V died, he anointed his tutor as the first French pope, Sylvester II. Maurois writes, "This was a strange association – the most highly educated of popes, a mathematician as much as a theologian, and the most fanciful of emperors."

Among the Germans, however, a rebellion against being "ruled" from Rome simmered, boiled and then erupted against, as they called him, "the Roman Saxon." With delicious symmetry, the Romans rose up against "the Saxon Roman." The combined insurgency drove Otto and Sylvester out of Rome, barely escaping with their lives. Both died in exile shortly thereafter.

## Church and State Promote Reform as Partners

As we have noted, there was a strong German tradition for electing a chief. So, each succession from Henry I to his son Otto the Great to Otto II and III had been confirmed by election. The last in this line was a Duke of Bavaria, who won the crown by election and ruled as Henry II. His goal was no less ambitious than to recreate the strong and supple empires of Charlemagne and Otto the Great.

He was in luck. The abbot of the Benedictine monastery of Cluny in Burgundy, Odilio, was leading an ambitious program of church reform. The Cluniac* movement sought to limit the reach of secular power in favor of increased authority for the church. Henry II and Odilio were friends. What happened next might have been a stroke of genius or merely a willingness to go with the flow. Henry agreed to give the church considerably more political power. Indeed, he would govern through ecclesiastical assemblies rather than through the German nobility over whom he had yet to achieve feudal allegiance, let alone feudal mastery. Henry reserved to himself the right to appoint (technically to "invest") bishops and to depose them if they did not serve him well.

Whether by clever design or happenstance, the arrangement put the emperor in the driver's seat. Henry stood with

---

* Cluniac refers to the monastery in the town of Cluny.

the reformers seeking greater political power for the church, while retaining the right to hire or fire these ecclesiastical authorities. He strongly supported the Cluniac ideas about reforming German monasteries, and also undertook a number of campaigns in Italy, which resulted in consolidating his empire. The husband of a saint, Cunegonda, Henry died in 1024.

With no male heirs to the Saxon line, nobles and churchmen assembled to discuss the available candidates and to vote for the next emperor. Their choice was Conrad of Franconia, in part because his great grandmother was a daughter of Otto the Great, and in part because of his energy and military prowess. Most unusually, the succession was not immediately challenged by a rival contender and he was crowned amid festivities as Conrad II.

By this time, there was no longer the possibility for the German Empire, or as it was called the "Holy Roman Empire," to be the sole great power in the west. France, Denmark and England were very much in contention. Conrad recognized this and made an alliance for his clan by marrying his son to the daughter of King Canute of Denmark and England. He consolidated imperial power in Germany and made alliance with the Cluniac cause.

The reformers particularly abhorred clerical marriage and the practice of simony, which was the word for the buying and selling of ecclesiastical positions. This was rampant. On occasion, even the papacy was put up for sale. Maurois has this to say on the subject:

In these times of violence and corruption, when one pope would excommunicate another, when the pope chose his emperor and the emperor his pope, when the peasant was reduced to a state of utmost misery by the quarrels of the great, it was vital that, if the Church was to save civilization, she should begin by making herself worthy of her mission. Such was the mission of the monks of Cluny. They achieved a notable success.

Conrad II was crowned in Rome in 1027, in the presence of throngs of German and Italian aristocrats, but there was rioting in the streets between Romans and these German outsiders. Since his policy was to fill vacancies in Italian bishoprics* with Germans, this is not a bit surprising.

Interestingly enough, however, in a bitter dispute between feudal great lords and their vassals, both sides asked Conrad to mediate. At issue was the fact that, in Italy, vassalage had not yet become hereditary as it had elsewhere. In 1037, Conrad gave his judgment that vassalage ought to be hereditary, and that vassals holding imperial or ecclesiastical fiefs could not have them taken away except by the judgment of their peers.

By the same token, he sought to replace the German tradition of electing an emperor with a strong presumption of hereditary right. His results were mixed. He appointed his son, Henry, as his successor when the boy was only nine. However, he did bow to the elective principle by having this

---

* A bishopric is the office held by a bishop. Similarly, the office occupied by an archbishop is called an archbishopric.

choice ratified by the German nobles.

Henry III had been carefully groomed for his job by his father, and is widely held to have brought the empire to new heights. He accepted the Cluniac notion of a "fast from war" lasting from every Wednesday evening to the following Monday morning. It was known as the "Truce of God." That such a small weekly respite from chaos should have been welcomed speaks volumes for the place of fighting in medieval life.

Maurois goes on to note that Henry "renounced all simoniacal practices and castigated those bishops who had been guilty of 'buying and selling Divine Grace.'" Famously, in 1046, he deposed all three prelates claiming to be the rightful occupant of the chair of St. Peter, as the papacy is sometimes called. In their stead, he appointed "a wise and active pontiff, Leo IX, who made the Cluniac Rule a powerful force for good."

Leo IX began the attempt to make the papacy an international institution with claims above those of any secular rulers, including emperors and kings. He started to travel all over Christian Europe, selecting men of many nations for appointment as cardinals. Leo had been appointed to the papacy by an emperor, Henry III, and then went on to insist that papal power transcended, and, indeed, trumped imperial power and all other forms of secular rule. "The relationship between pope and emperor had become the great issue of the eleventh century."

Before taking up this great issue, another important series of events in the eleventh century must be added to the mix: the very famous Norman conquest of England and a much less famous Norman conquest as well. A minor Norman knight named Tancred d'Hauteville had ten sons who saw few opportunities to advance at home. William and Drogo d'Hauteville, with a party of knights, rode into southern Italy in search of adventure, land and wealth. They had doubtless heard that the ongoing struggles between Lombards and the Byzantine emperors were fertile fields for mercenaries.

Though their numbers were not impressive, they were superb horsemen and they used the stirrup, which was apparently unknown to Italians. By 1040, they had captured a castle in a no man's land between the combatants. By 1060, the sixth son, called Robert the Cunning, or Robert Guiscard, had started eating away at the Byzantine province in southern Italy. By 1071, he had control of the area that would come to be called the Duchy of Apulia. Here, as in England, Norman conquest brought feudalism in its wake.

Robert managed to land in Sicily, but was stopped before he could conquer the island. That task was left to the youngest d'Hauteville, Roger, who concluded its conquest in 1091. The previous rulers had been Zirid Muslims based in the North African Emirate of Madhya. In general, in the middle ages, Christians referred to all Muslims as "Saracens," a word with no apparent reference to anything Muslims called themselves.

Whereas northern Italy was dotted with urban centers, feudalism kept the south rural, and with the passage of time, increasingly backward as compared to the north. Still today, the north is modern, densely populated, commercial and wealthy while the south is backward, less densely populated, more rural and generally poorer as well. True, some of that is changing. Still, that an invasion in the eleventh century should have left its mark well into the twenty-first shows how heavy the weight of the past can be.

This brief but important digression into Norman affairs in southern Italy might call for a recapitulation before we move on. Otto the Great had compelled the pope, John XII, to swear homage and fealty to him as a vassal and to allow the Emperor to select and invest his own bishops. This meant, or at least strongly implied, that secular power trumped ecclesiastical power when the two disagreed.

When his grandson, Otto III, became Emperor, he made his cousin, Bruno, who was also his personal chaplain, the first German Pope as Gregory V. He then staffed all the important clerical posts in Rome with Germans, and when Gregory died, Otto III replaced him with his personal tutor as Pope Sylvester II. All this sparked rebellion in the Romans and they threw the bums out.

After this affair, close ties again grew up between an Emperor, Henry II, and a powerful cleric, Odilio, abbot of the Benedictine monastery at Cluny and guiding light behind major church reform. Henry III also allied himself with the Cluniac reforms while exercising the power to dethrone claimants to the papacy. His ability, indeed his right, to appoint the next pope, Leo IX, was part and parcel of business as usual. In the reign of his son, Henry IV, all that was going to become quite problematic.

## A Clash of Titans

Henry IV was six when his father died. His mother, Agnes of Poitou, "a woman of great culture and real goodness," became the regent and bungled the job quite badly. Bishops Hanno of Cologne and Adalbert of Bremen sent her off to a convent and forced Henry into a distasteful marriage. When Henry was nine, a Cluniac pope, Nicholas II, decreed that, henceforth, the cardinals alone would choose the pope. This was a huge blow to imperial power. Moreover, as was becoming true for other European monarchs, the emperor was losing his right to appoint bishops, even in his own territory.

This was a particularly vexing problem for German rule because of the integral role churchmen had played in imperial governance for a long time. For example, when Otto II invaded Italy, seventy percent of his soldiers were provided by ecclesiastical vassals. Clerics staffed the less-marshal elements of the government as well. When the cardinals, not Henry IV, chose the next pope, a Benedictine monk called Hildebrand, a struggle for power between the Emperor and the Pope of epic proportions was about to begin.

In 1073, Hildebrand ascended to St. Peter's throne as Gregory VII. In his elevation, Cluniac reform found its most vital and vigorous voice. Maurois describes this son of a Tuscan peasant, as "a great man with a clear mind and an inflexible will." Others before him had advocated ecclesiastical supremacy, but they did not bring to the table his fearless conviction that he was right, and for that he would win. One of his most famous doctrines was this:

"The Catholic, Apostolic and Roman Church has never been mistaken and will never be mistaken. The Roman Pontiff has the right to depose unworthy emperors. He can release subjects from their allegiance to iniquitous princes ... "

These are not the words of a man who knows the meaning of compromise.

When Henry IV achieved his majority at sixteen, he took over as king, but without any real experience, training or guidance, and already weakened by ambitious Germans, like the usually disloyal Saxons or Godfrey of Lorraine who had taken upon himself the royal authority in Italy. Gregory VII, by contrast, was backed by some of the strongest of his neighboring powers, including the indomitable Matilda of Tuscany.

Despite the obvious foolhardiness of the gesture, Henry gathered those of his nobles and bishops who were still in his camp and denounced "Hildebrand, henceforth not pope, but a false monk." He then demanded that Hildebrand stand down from the papacy, pretty much just because Henry had so ordered. Do not put money on a gamble of that magnitude.

Gregory VII, as might have been expected, excommunicated Henry and absolved all Christians from any oaths they might have taken to support him. To some, this may have tried their consciences, but the German nobles saw it as a splendid opportunity to break with their king and look out for themselves. Gregory further announced his plans to visit Germany, and there stage a major church council (a synod). Literally, to head him off at the pass, Henry hightailed it over the Alps in the snow to find Gregory visiting Countess Matilda in her castle at Canossa.

Gregory refused to receive him and probably would have preferred to crown Rudolf of Swabia, recently elected by the German nobles to replace Henry. However, a pope is also a priest, and he could not ignore Henry's repentance. For three days in the cold and snow of January, Henry stood barefoot and fasting, in the shift of a penitent, before he was forgiven and allowed to take shelter.

Having been absolved of his sins, Henry had just cause against the German plotters who had brought him to this humbling experience. He ignored his promise to the pope not to retaliate and civil war engulfed the Germans. Gregory excommunicated him again. Henry replied by setting up an anti-pope, Clement III. Gregory backed an anti-king, Hermann of Luxemburg. Henry won, marched on Rome and was crowned emperor by Clement III.

Romans typically back a winner, so Gregory had to go into hiding. He called on the Norman leader, Robert Guiscard, Duke of Apulia, Calabria and Sicily for help. There is much irony in this as Robert himself had quite recently been under papal ban. Despite their prior falling out, and only after he had quelled a rebellion in the south, Robert "flew to the pope's assistance with a weird and brutal army of Norman and Saracen hordes who devastated Rome. Thousands of Romans were sold into slavery." Pope Gregory VII, who had invited this catastrophe, could not remain in Rome, but had to follow Robert back to Sicily where he died in 1085. He claimed to the end that he had always "loved justice and hated wickedness, which is why I am dying in exile ..."

Maurois argues that he fell prey to his own rigidity. "Excommunication is a weapon which must not be abused. The first time it inspires terror; when used a second time its edge is blunted." So while the pope overplayed his hand, Henry failed to curb the autonomy of the nobles, whose independence was a constant obstacle to German unity.

The "investiture struggle," as this tug-of-war between pope and emperor over ecclesiastical appointments is usually called, continued for some time. In 1123, compromise brought it to an end. The emperor's right to have a significant say in clerical appointment or elections, especially in Germany, was recognized and accepted. The pope, however, retained the right of investiture with ring and staff in perpetuity. Sadly, the jockeying of power between pope and emperor did not end here, but we shall leave it in all its convoluted detail to look at another conflict involving Germans.

### German v. German

Meanwhile, a new feud was growing up between two powerful families, the Welfs and the Hohenstaufens. These were relative newcomers to the nobility, as most of the old families had been wiped out in the incessant civil wars of the time. Ironically, Henry IV had contributed to the elevation of each one. He had given the Duchy of Bavaria to Welf IV and the Duchy of Swabia to Frederick I of Staufen. Later, an emperor, Conrad III, tried to use his imperial power to blunt the conflict between the Welfs and Hohenstaufens, which was wrenching Germany apart. He failed entirely.

Then, on his deathbed, Conrad pulled off a coup. Instead of his son, he named his nephew, Frederick of Swabia, to succeed him, and gave over the royal insignia to him. Frederick was the head of the Hohenstaufen family (his father was Frederick the One-Eyed), but his mother's brother was Henry the Proud, once leader of the Welfs. So he was, in his very biology, the bridge between the two. When the nobles gathered in Frankfurt to elect him, he was their unanimous choice. He then became, simultaneously, both King of the Germans and Holy Roman Emperor, as the two positions had been unified for a long time. However, he would not be formally crowned in the latter position for three years.

Francis Russell writes, "Not in generations had a king been so welcomed .... Not since Charlemagne and Otto the Great had any emperor been so successful, so admired, and honored." Extending the comparison to Charlemagne, Russell notes that Frederick had

> his great predecessor's energy, decisiveness, judgment, and qualities of leadership. Though not a scholar, he admired scholarship. Though he could not speak Latin, he understood it. In his own tongue he was eloquent. He was interested in history and in his ancestral past. A friend of Roman lawyers, he became a great lawgiver. Deeply

pious, he led a blameless life. Better than anyone else he came to express the imperial ideal.[*]

He even looked imperial, of middling height but extremely handsome. Frederick was a man who was

> vigorous in mind and body, with a face always ready to break out in a smile. A man who loved hunting, riding, and swimming, a courageous fighter who exalted in combat, he seemed the very embodiment of medieval chivalry. His most striking physical characteristic was his red beard, for which he would go down in history as Barbarossa; in generations to come he would be as legendary a figure as Charlemagne, whom he so much resembled.

He was able to win the loyalty of most of the German Dukes, Counts, Margraves, etc., by compromise, by appealing to rules of honor between a royal vassal and the king, while also recognizing their legitimate interests in governing their own territories. He would not easily bring the same spirit of compromise to his dealings with the north Italian cities or the papacy. He wished to have harmonious relations with the papacy, but with the understanding that he must have control over general policy in Italy, with the Holy See restricting itself to questions of ecclesiastical administration.

He set off for Italy for the first time in 1158, accompa-

---

[*] Unless otherwise noted, all the quotation in this section are from Russell's *A Concise History of Germany*.

nied by a small retinue, which reflected the reluctance of his noble vassals to support an Italian military campaign. During the journey, he learned that the pope had died and been replaced by an English cardinal called Nicholas Breakspear, who would take the name Adrian IV. He would be the pope to crown Frederick as Holy Roman Emperor. Many of the north Italian cities did not accept his authority, but for the time being Frederick was content to go home.

There, he placated his rivals, consolidated his power and made an advantageous marriage to the heiress of Burgundy. He also made strong alliances with non-Germanic neighbors such as the king of Hungary, and put some fractious Poles on notice to behave. "North of Alps peace and order reigned in his empire."*

Frederick intended, when the time came, to subdue Lombardy, "then Tuscany, the Papal States, and Rome in preparation for a final attack upon Sicily." Since he made no secret of his intentions, a very alarmed Adrian IV signed a treaty with Sicily's king. This enraged Barbarossa, who began putting his plan into action. He succeeded so well that the only thing that saved him from excommunication was Adrian's death. Frederick appointed a friendly replacement, but the College of Cardinals rejected that appointment. Instead, they chose a strongly anti-German cleric who would serve as Alexander III. It is usual for historians of this period to describe the College's choices as "popes" and the emperor's choices as "anti-popes."

* This and some of the following quotes are used because it would be too wordy to do anything else.

Pope Alexander III was "an astute, gifted priest-politician who saw himself as the champion of the Church's liberties." He promptly excommunicated Barbarossa. Unable to win the victories he sought, Frederick returned to Germany where, at his home in Aachen, he had Charlemagne disinterred and canonized by his own papal appointee.

After a time, he returned to Italy with a substantial army and fought his way to Rome. He appointed Pascal III as the Vicar of Christ, as popes are sometimes called, and Pascal returned the favor by re-crowning Frederick emperor. It appeared that he was on the verge of realizing his dream of Italian unification under his rule. Fate, or as an ancient Roman might say, "the forces" stepped in.

Shortly after his coronation in August, 1167, torrential storms flooded Rome. The sewers overflowed, and in the fetid heat that followed, pestilence swept through the German army, forcing Barbarossa to lead the dispirited remnants of his soldiery to the cleaner air of upper Italy.

Frederick's retreat emboldened the Lombard cities and ,with Venetian financing, they joined together and formed the Lombard League. He had dreamed and labored for a unified Italy that accepted his authority. All he had been able to unify were his Lombard enemies. He had, of course, no way of knowing that Italian unification would have to wait until 1861. So his dreams were way ahead of the curve.

In 1174, Frederick rode over the Alps for a fifth time,

bringing with him a small army of mercenaries and the intention to crush the Lombard League. Instead, with the wealth of Venice at its backs, the Lombard League fielded an army that held Frederick in check. A truce ensued.

By 1176, the imperial army was much depleted, largely because Barbarossa was running out of money to pay his mercenaries. This shell of an army met the Lombard League at Legnano, about eleven miles from Milan. The League's well-financed and thus numerous and well-armed infantry first swarmed and then broke the German ranks. Infantry not only beat cavalry, it actually went on to deliver a crushing defeat.

In the face of so great a loss, Frederick reacted diplomatically. In Venice, at St. Marks Basilica, he agreed to recognize Alexander III as the legitimate pope, while Alexander removed the ban of excommunication and recognized Frederick as emperor. Barbarossa also signed a six-year truce with the cities of the Lombard League. He made a separate peace with Sicily, which had thrown in with the League. As a sweetener, he arranged a marriage for his son to Constance, heiress to the Sicilian king. When he left Italy in 1178, his imperial legitimacy was acknowledged by all. Of course, his announced intention to leave might have made that recognition easier to give.

Frederick had inherited a Germany torn by factional strife and used his blood ties to both sides, plus considerable diplomatic skills, to end the conflict. As noted, he had also dealt with the factionalized and feudal nature of German governance to give royal vassals real power on their own turf. What would have happened had he applied the same compromise and diplomacy to his Italian subjects is anyone's guess. Still, he came to it in the end of his almost forty-year reign. By then, he was the very embodiment of Christian Europe.

Probably for that reason, he took the Cross and headed off to the Crusades. He was felled on the way by a freak accident. This is probably a blessing for his place in history. If it took him nearly forty years to become tolerant toward Christian Italians, we cannot have expected him to deal fairly and justly with Jews and Muslims.

> Frederick Barbarossa the legend engulfed the man. As emperor he was in fact the most illustrious of Germany's medieval rulers. Never had the empire been so honored and so feared as at his death. Yet he had built his strength in Germany on the foundation of his princes.

In other words, his power rested on a feudal hierarchy in which, theoretically, these nobles held their fiefs from him. Since the vassals provided all the elements of governance in their fiefs, they separated the emperor from his subjects. This was fine so long as they stayed loyal. As their independence grew with time, they would become a force for disunity. In the end, Germans did not come together as a nation-state until 1871, when Bismarck engineered a spectacle at the Palace of Versailles, with German princes hailing King William of Prussia as their liege lord. Almost comically, it took a feudal ceremony to create a modern state.

## Between a Rock and a Hard Place

There would be many instances in the future where the interests of the emperor and those of the pope were incompatible, or worse. One classic case involved Charles V. In 1519, at the age of nineteen, Charles of Hapsburg became Holy Roman Emperor. There were, by tradition, seven electors who chose the emperor, and they were heavily bribed by Henry VIII of England and Francis I of France, who both wanted the prestige that went with the job. They were also paid a handsome sum by rich German bankers, the Fuggers, to back Charles. Pope Leo X favored Francis. Despite all this pressure, their first choice was a Saxon prince, Frederick the Wise. He turned them down. Charles was first runner-up.

To understand what happens next, it is necessary to understand "indulgences." One of the benefits offered to truly repentant sinners by the Catholic Church was God's forgiveness. The sincerity of the repentance could be demonstrated by acts of self-sacrifice, and even of doing bodily harm to oneself. To this day, in the Azores, for example, you can see – mostly older – people crawling around the Church on their hands and knees, which have become quite bloodied.

The Church also recognized sincerity when the sinner went on pilgrimages ... or paid for other people to go on pilgrimages. One can see where this is headed. Donations of stained glass windows were proof of sincerity. Donating the money to commission the installation of stained glass windows also proved sincere repentance. In time, funding the ecclesiastical coffers became a much-traveled road to salvation.

This proved to be a very slippery slope. By the fifteenth century, the Church was increasingly penurious* and needed ways to increase its cash flow. It began to develop an increasing dependency on the sale of "indulgences." Here is McEvedy's explanation:

> These spiritual pardons could be obtained (at a price) for any sin committed by any person, living or dead ... In its economic aspect credulity is like any other demand and has its level of satisfaction: to maintain the value of a currency equivalent like indulgences requires a sober hand on the printing press.

By the early sixteenth century, such a sober hand was entirely lacking. A Dominican friar called Tetzel had a smashing success in selling indulgences to Germans on behalf of the Archbishop of Mainz. With his tongue very firmly in his cheek, Colin McEvedy comments on the degree to which money sometimes trumped piety in clerical circles.

> For example, in 1514 a shrewd operator bought the Archbishopric of Mainz (which carried one of the seven votes cast at the election of a German Emperor) although the revenues were already entirely absorbed in paying the interest on the public debt. For the Archbishopric and for the right to sell indulgences he paid the Pope forty

---

* Penury is the noun form from the Latin *penuria*, meaning extreme poverty or destitution, which is not quite an accurate description of the Church. It was more the case that its expenses were far exceeding its income.

thousand ducats, which he almost entirely recovered from the sale of the indulgences. At the next Imperial election, that of Charles V four years later, he sold his vote for ninety thousand ducats.

Martin Luther was notable for his objections to the sale of indulgences, but his main contribution to theological change was the idea that faith and not deeds would lead to salvation. The Reformation is a very large topic and we will have to leave it for another time. For now, it is enough to say that Luther attempted to win the young and idealistic Charles V to unite the Germans around a reformed theology.

As a practical matter, it was quite impossible for Charles to do any such thing. His father's father was the Emperor Maximillian, whose patrimony was Austria. His father's mother had inherited Burgundy. If that were the whole of the story, Charles might have reflected the general geographic pattern of the Reformation. The farther north a place was from Rome, the more likely it was to be Protestant.

However, Charles' maternal grandparents were Ferdinand and Isabella of Spain, and two more Catholic monarchs one could not find. Through them, Charles inherited the Spanish Kingdoms, which included all the islands in the western and central Mediterranean and Italy up to the Papal States. There were also all the Spanish claims in the "New World."* Leaving aside the fact that Charles was quite passionately Catholic, it would have been madness to alienate

---

* Charles had a son called Philip who lent his name to the Philippines.

all those Catholic subjects. Charles V was also very influential in Northern Italy. So, he had the pope surrounded.

When Henry VIII of England asked the pope to annul his marriage to Catherine of Aragon, Charles stepped in to prevent the pope from complying with that wish. Quite often people imagine that Henry wanted and eventually got a divorce, but this is not so. There was no such thing as civil divorce in those days. The only way out of a marriage was to have it annulled, and that meant, as a practical matter, that the parties were never legally married.

For Catherine, this would mean that she had had sex with a man who was not her spouse over a fairly long space of time. For their daughter, Mary, an annulment would make her illegitimate. Catherine was the aunt of Charles V and Mary was his first cousin. He made it very clear to the pope that he would strenuously object to making his aunt a juridical harlot and his cousin a bastard. This is why Henry had ultimately to name himself head of the Church in England and grant himself an annulment.

The power of the Holy Roman Empire, or as McEvedy calls it, the German Empire, with its tentacles into northern Italy, increased several fold when it fell to the heir of all that Spain owned. One comical manifestation of the ubiquity of Charles V was a young man at my gym who used to say, "Tell me another story about Chuck Five."

## Double Takes

A gathering of German nobles during the middle ages and into the Renaissance was called a "diet," much as the modern Japanese parliament is called a diet. Writers of German history rarely, if ever, stop to explain this particular usage of the word "diet." When they write about a particular diet, the D is capitalized and the name of the meeting place gives it some specificity. Where the lack of complete specificity comes in is with the tendency to meet in the same places repeatedly. For example, the town of Worms in the Rhine Valley has seen a number of Diets of Worms.

One of the most famous concerned Martin Luther. He was quite a popular topic for student papers and so, with no context provided by the author, the students would read that, somehow or other, the great Protestant reformer had to do with a Diet of Worms. Might a diet of worms be some medieval punishment for heretics? Might it be a protein supplement, and if so, how exactly was Martin Luther involved? While these results are comical, they illustrate a real problem because experts usually write for each other, leaving the amateurs to fend for themselves.

After a lecture that outlined the basic theological arguments first of Luther and then of Calvin, and pointing out how different they were, a student rushed up after class. "If they are so different, why are they both called Protestant?" he asked breathlessly. "Because they are both, in different ways, protesting against the Catholic Church," I replied. He sighed with relief, wiped his brow and said, "Good. I can sleep tonight." They are quite endearing, students. Their curiosity, when aroused, should never be fed an unexplained Diet of Worms.

# Merchant Seamen

A mong the world's most successful sailors were the Venetians. At the heart of that success was their geographic position and the topographic features of the lagoon that they made their home. That said, let us begin with the opening lines of a brilliant history of Venice written by the master, John Julius Norwich.*

> The origins of Venice encircle her still. No great city has managed to preserve, in its immediate surroundings, so much of the atmosphere and environment which gave it birth. The traveller approaching Venice, whether by sea as she should be approached, or by land across the causeway, or even by air, gazes out on the same flat, desolate expanse of water and reed and marsh that the first Venetians chose for their own; and is struck, more forcibly every time, not just by the improbability but by the sheer foolhardiness of their enterprise.

> What drove this enterprise in the first place? The answer

---

* As the son of a Viscount, and thus a noblemen, he is entitled to be referred to as Lord Norwich.

is simple: fear of something much worse. In the first instance, it was the invading Visigoths, who were passing by on their way to Rome, where, in 410, they put it to a fairly mild sacking, as sackings go. However, the mere fact that Rome could not protect herself from barbarians came as a frightful shock to everyone involved, pagan as well as Christian. Fortunately, the imperial court had earlier been moved to Ravenna, a coastal city made less vulnerable by the surrounding marshes and well positioned for reinforcement from Constantinople.

Along the way the Visigoths also severely sacked the wealthy city of Aquileia, the ninth-largest metropolis in the Roman Empire. Refugees from this attack appear to be the first to choose the Venetian lagoon for the safety it provided against land-based invaders. As Lord Norwich puts it, they fled to a place "unenviable and inaccessible," whence the Goths would have "neither the incentive nor the ability to follow them."

After the danger passed, some stayed but most went home completely unaware that the Visigoths were themselves fleeing an even more fearsome scourge, the Hun. Attila and his forces arrived in northern Italy in 452, and sent the locals scuttling back to the lagoon. In their absence, the Huns sacked Aquileia, leaving it completely devastated. Then they moved on. As for the refugees in the lagoon, some stayed but most went home. Those who stayed had in common their descent from citizens of the old Roman province of Venetia, and so we can call them Venetians. A single and unified community that became the city of Venice remained a long way off.

Nevertheless, great cities, as great nations, often have foundation stories that vary considerably in their probability. One story has it that three consuls from the Roman city of Padua, representing the imperial government in the West, came to found the city of Venice precisely at noon on March 25, 421. This story emerged at the height of Venetian power a full millennium later. It stressed the Venetian pedigree from Imperial Rome, and its status from the beginning as a free and independent city. Neither assertion was true and, as luck would have it, the story emerged soon after a fire in Padua, in 1420, destroyed most of the city's archives.

What we do know is far more prosaic. In 466, representatives of the various lagoon communities agreed to elect twelve tribunes annually from the "people" (however defined) to do their collective business. Among themselves, this probably involved keeping the peace and settling disputes. Externally, it likely meant trying to maintain cooperative, even cordial relationships, when possible, with the mainland.

A decade later, the tottering pretense of the Western Roman Empire in Italy was terminated by a German general named Odoacer. It had been customary for foreign generals to have puppet Roman emperors to legitimize their rule. Odoacer felt it was high time to acknowledge that he was the boss and that poor young Romulus Augustulus was no more than a pawn. Nevertheless, the Eastern Roman Empire had enough clout that Odoacer offered a nominal pledge of loyalty to Constantinople in return for permission to take the title "King of Italy."

Odoacer was a vigorously martial German. He annexed Dalmatia, a region of a bit less than five thousand square miles on the eastern Adriatic coast, which was the birthplace of Diocletian and the place where he built his retirement villa. Odoacer spent much of the remainder of his energy fighting off attempts by other Germans to penetrate his frontiers. Apparently this made him popular with Italian provincials, as they deeply feared another round of pillaging, looting and worse.

Quite another view was taken in Constantinople. Seeing the Kingdom of Odoacer expand and strengthen was thoroughly worrisome to the emperor and his advisors. At the same time, they knew they lacked the power and resources to stop his advances so they recruited the services of Theodoric the Ostrogoth, leader of a tribe that was also a problem for them inside the northwestern corner of their empire. Having Theodoric contend for Odoacer's kingdom was a winner all the way around. Regardless of which man triumphed, the East Romans lost one rival to their power. With luck, they might beat each other to the ground such that neither man remained a threat. As it happened, after vigorous fighting and some clever double crosses, Theodoric won himself a somewhat enlarged kingdom and gave the lagoon some new neighbors.

We get a picture of life in the Venetian lagoon from a letter, possibly a copy, written in 523 by one of Theodoric's

ministers, Cassiodorus,* and addressed to the twelve tribunes elected to do the peoples' business. He asked them to
provide help in transporting wine and oil from the port of
Istria to the imperial town of Ravenna, now a Gothic administrative center.

> The Istrian harvest of wine and oil ... have this year
> been particularly abundant .... Pray show your devotion,
> therefore by bringing them hither at all speed. For you
> possess many vessels in the region ... and you will be, in
> a sense, sailing your native country. Besides your other
> blessings, there is open to you a way which is ever free
> of danger; for when the winds rage and the sea is closed
> against you, you may sail up the pleasantest of rivers. Your
> ships need fear no angry gusts since they may continually
> hug the shore .... Be diligent, therefore, to repair your
> boats – which, like horses, you keep tied up at the doors
> of your dwellings – and make haste to depart ...

It was a very flattering letter, praising the Venetians for
making no distinctions between rich and poor. Instead, they
all shared in the bounties of the sea, most particularly the
fish and sea birds that provided plentiful food, and the salt
that could be traded for the things they could not produce

---

* Cassiodorus was a Roman statesmen and writer. After serving in the governments
of Theodoric and his successor, he retired. He founded monasteries where monks
were required to copy and translate Greek documents. His own writing, including
lofty tributes to Gothic kings and queens, was a compilation of government
documents that became an invaluable reference for the political life of the
Ostrogothic kingdom in Italy.

themselves. "For there may be men who have little need of gold, yet none live who desire not salt."

The letter attests to the nautical talents of the Venetians and implies that they had already created a niche for themselves in the northern Adriatic maritime trade. This niche was not limited to carrying goods from the mainland purveyors of wine and oil to the important administrative center at Ravenna. Clearly, the Venetians were also trading salt with their own trading partners for their own benefit. As Lord Norwich tells us, by "the middle of the sixth century, the flat-bottomed Venetian trading barge was a common sight on the rivers of north and central Italy."

This foreshadows the absolutely central role commerce would play in Venetian life. Waterfowl, fish and salt do not make a viable diet. The people of the lagoon, like nomadic pastoralists, had to augment their protein intake with grains, and, importantly, grains in sufficient quantity required arable land. This, of course, was missing in the lagoons, save for some small garden plots. The choice boiled down to trade or extinction. Happily, their nautical skills and their place in the world gave them access to markets for the exchange of their own goods and as middlemen between more distant trading partners. Wealth was to be made in each of these endeavors. As the reach of Venetian trade expanded exponentially, so did that wealth.

## Trade and Empire

In the early years of the sixth century, Constantinople was a key terminus in a trade network that included the famous overland silk route from China and the vitally important trade in spices by sea. McEvedy explains:

> These long distance routes carried only low-bulk, high-cost articles. Chinese silk is the perfect example, a luxurious material that shouted status, especially when worked up into designer fabrics.*

The East Romans, as they called themselves, or the Byzantines, as modern historians usually call them, were, by either name, ignorant about the origin of silk. They were thus forced to import it. Another example of low-bulk, high cost items were condiments, especially pepper from India and cloves and nutmeg from Indonesia.

> However, the spice trade also concerned itself with a whole host of other commodities, which changed hands in small amounts and at high prices: preservatives, perfumes, dyes and mordants, pigments and gums, incense, and an alarming list of substances that hope rather than experience suggested might be of medical value.

Some of it came from the Orient, but Arabia contributed frankincense and myrrh and dominated the shipping of spices from India westward. All of this trade was done strictly for profit.

Mediterranean trade was different. It usually involved

---

* This and the following quotations come from his *Atlas of Medieval History*.

high-bulk items such as wheat, oil, wine, timber or metals, and it was frequently requisitioned rather than bought. Egypt was particularly victimized in this regard. It produced flax in a quantity that supported a state-supervised linen industry.

> It had a monopoly on papyrus, the preferred writing material of the time, and, in the specialist glass manufactories of Alexandria, an industry that produced articles of international repute. Add the transit trade in spices and you have a very considerable volume of exports. However, much of the wheat and at least part of the linen and papyrus were extracted from the country by imperial authorities without payment of any sort, so the Egyptians weren't all that well off. Indeed, they probably found they had to work hard to pay for the timber, iron, wine and oil that they imported.

Remember that Egypt's wheat had been diverted from Rome to Constantinople, that Rome had had to manage on wheat from Sicily and Carthage, and that these sources disappeared with the success of the Vandals. By 528, Rome itself, Milan and Ravenna were the only former West Roman administrative centers left with fifteen thousand or more inhabitants. London and Paris did not make the cut.

So that was the situation when, in 527, Justinian became emperor in the East and committed his reign to the reconquest of the West, a project few in his government expected to succeed. The first step was to regain control of the western Mediterranean, which had been in the hands of the Germanic Vandals for several decades, ever since their king found a fleet in Carthage's harbor and figured out how to use it. Justinian's chief general, Belisarius, sailing from Sicily with aid from the Ostrogoths, completely surprised the Vandal army guarding Carthage and beat them handily. He and his troops entered that fabled city in 533. When the Vandal king returned from Sardinia with the other half of his army, the East Romans vanquished them, as well. Belisarius then took the king and his treasure, including a famous seven-branched candelabra, home to Constantinople to proclaim complete success.

Justinian then decided to move against his erstwhile allies, the Ostrogoths, but he could only spare an army of nine thousand men. He had other frontiers that also needed attention, notably his border with Persia, whose ruler was ambitious to recreate the empire of Darius the Great. Nine thousand was just a bit more than half the size of the army that beat the Vandals. Still, Belisarius easily re-took Sicily and moved on to occupy Rome. The Ostrogoths counterattacked, but their numerical superiority was no match for the East Roman's strategy of fighting a defensive war. Gothic numbers dwindled and when Belisarius went on the offense, the king threw in the towel in exchange for a Roman pension. Belisarius went home in triumph again.

Venetia, once a province of the now defunct West Roman Empire, willingly submitted to its new status as an East Roman subject. Locally this made no real difference as tribunes, elected by "the people," ran the day-to-day business of governance. Constantinople was far enough away to permit quite cordial ties.

Meanwhile, there were still some powerful Ostrogothic warlords on the other side of the Po River, and with the great general gone, they thought they might be able to translate their numbers into victories over the lieutenants he had left behind. They were right, but not decisively so. The fighting continued for ten years until Justinian was able to marshal the funds needed for adequate troops. These troops were commanded by Narses, a septuagenarian eunuch who had started his career as an archivist. Presumably as a result of reading accounts of successful battles, he had developed into a superb tactician. He marched his army through Dalmatia, where he picked up five thousand Lombard mercenaries. At one point, ships provided by the lagoon communities ferried these troops to Ravenna. In so doing, they helped Narses' army defeat the Goths permanently.

Italy was finally brought back into the fold of an empire that called itself East Roman. Legend claims that Narses expressed his gratitude to the lagoon by building two churches on the thinly populated islands of the *Riva Alto.** Paradoxically, with the rewards also came threats to the lagoon's self-governance. The Eastern capital, Constantinople, was still far away. Now, however, two of its representatives governed the province of Venetia from Ravenna.

After a very long campaign ended in victory, Narses embarked, in 553, "on a program of reorganization and reconstruction – on which he was still engaged, twelve years later

---

* This translates as "high bank." It will later be called the Rialto and become the core of the modern city of Venice.

at the age of eighty-seven," when he was dismissed from his post. Then, as Norwich explains, to add insult to injury

> the Empress Sophia sent him a golden distaff and invited him, since he was no true man, to go and spin in the apartments of her women. 'I will spin her such a skein,' Narses is said to have muttered, 'that she shall not find the end of it in her lifetime'; at once he sent off messengers, laden with all the fruits of the Mediterranean, to the Lombard King Alboin in what is now Hungary, inviting him to lead his people down to the land which brought forth such abundance.

Needless to say, Alboin took him up on the offer and invaded Italy in 568. Colin McEvedy tells the story wonderfully well, but remember, by Romans, he means East Romans, those based in Constantinople.

> The Romans had no army in Italy that could face the Lombards* in the field: all they could do was lock themselves up in the towns and hope that the invaders would run out of food before they did. On the whole this strategy worked reasonably well on the coast where the Romans could bring in supplies by ship, but the results in the interior were disastrous: the Lombards took over most of the Po Valley, all of Tuscany and much of the mountainous spine of the country.

*As a reminder, the Lombards were an ancient Germanic tribe.

The East Romans kept Rome, Ravenna and Genoa and their dependencies, as well as Naples, but the Lombards also got a good chunk of south central Italy. Because of a rivalry between two Lombard factions, the southerners were happy enough to leave the East Romans a corridor between them and their more powerful compatriots to the north. All this meant that Venetia still lay within the frontiers of the empire based in Constantinople.

Meanwhile, at the outset of the Lombard invasion, whole communities of frightened people had fled to the safety of the lagoon, led by their religious leaders and toting whatever sacred relics they chanced to possess. They had had enough of the turmoil and had no intention of returning home. These immigrants swelled the local population and also gave it definition. Groups coming from different places on the mainland gravitated to different islands, possibly because the existing inhabitants were from their hometowns.

The letter from Cassiodorus that we discussed above made much of the egalitarian nature of the lagoon communities. If this was true, and many scholars doubt it, the new immigrants did not reflect that spirit. A body of written records of various kinds, including wills and deeds, reflect the idea that some are nobles and some are not. As is usually the case, the nobles monopolized the best areas to fish and to harvest salt, as well as the best estates on the mainland.

But which came first? Some scholars believe that a landed nobility were able, through their pre-existing power, to command the best resources of the lagoon. Other scholars argue the earliest immigrants, regardless of their previous status, automatically took the best fishing spots and the best salt pans. Passing these down to their descendents conferred noble status on them.*

## Diocletian, Again?

When, in 286, Diocletian divided governance of the Empire in two, he appointed a trusted military genius of his own generation, Maximian, to serve as the emperor in the western provinces, while he retained control in the east. In so doing, he was responding to more than a century of civil war, in which victorious generals led their armies into conflicts with other victorious, or merely competent, generals, all of whom were trying to seize the imperial title and the power and wealth that went with it. Diocletian also set up a chain of command such that the emperor, of the West or the East, was the only general in his sphere.

A chain of command is a sort of pyramid. In Diocletian's scheme, the soldiers were divided into small units, each one incapable of insurrection. Their leaders answered to someone above them in the chain, who had no direct contact with the soldiers. That someone owed his power to the chain itself rather than to the boots on the ground, to borrow a modern phrase. A commander closest to the

---

* This theory mirrors the notion, explained on the chapter "Hellas," that the first settlers in Athens got the first crack at the best land and from this privilege derived their status as nobles.

emperor, called a *dux*,* was thus farthest away from the troops and therefore unable to use them to set himself up as an imperial replacement.

Going back to the parceling out of Italy between Lombards and East Romans, the latter, as we saw, claimed the province of Venetia. Imperial officers based in the old Roman administrative center of Ravenna had been nominally responsible for her governance, but not very well able to work their will. The new idea was to have the Venetian government answer directly to Constantinople, which would make its leader a *dux*. *Dux* in the Venetian dialect comes out as Doge.

Legend has it that the Patriarch of Grado called for a "general assembly of all the people" to meet at Heraclea in 697, and to reconsider their system of governance. He argued forcefully that their abject failure to come together, plus their endless wrangling, threatened the very existence of Venetia. He then suggested that they elect a single leader to replace the twelve tribunes. Finishing out the legend, the people chose Paoluccio Anafesto, who became their first Doge. His initial act in office was to enter into a "treaty of friendship with the Lombard King Liutprand."

Lord Norwich believes that this is just a legend. Although he wryly notes that, in every subsequent list of Doges, "there, sure enough, is Paoluccio's name at the head; we even have

---

* We do not know how Latin was pronounced, but *dux* does give rise to the modern English word duke. In deference to Diocletian, the term "East Romans" is used in the next paragraph, but is then dropped entirely in favor of the modern usage of Byzantines for the people, and Eastern Empire for the state apparatus.

an imaginary portrait of him .... Unfortunately, he never existed; at least not as a Doge, nor even as a Venetian."

Original sources, documents dating from the period in question, say that a certain *dux* Paulicius, with Marcellus, his *magister militum*, his magistrate in charge of matters military, was responsible for fixing the Venetian boundary line near Heraclea and that this line was later accepted by the Lombards.

> Venetia being as we now know a Byzantine province at that time, the obvious and indeed the only legitimate conclusion to be drawn from this is that the mysterious Paulicius was none other than Paul, Exarch of Ravenna from 723 until his murder ... in 727 – the very year, incidentally, to which John the Deacon[*] ascribes the death of Paoluccio.

Only an official of Constantinople, such as Paul, Exarch of Ravenna, would have had the power to set provincial boundaries and negotiate with the Lombards to accept them. Paul could have morphed into a Latin version as Paulicius, the *dux* of Venetia. Centuries of legend building could easily have changed his name to Paoluccio and transformed him from an imperial official to an elected Doge. This comports with the proud claim that Venice was always an independent republic, a place where the sovereign people elected their own leader.

---

[*] This is the writer of the eleventh century source for the Dogeship of Paoluccio.

Norwich completes his brilliant analysis by situating the *magister militum* in the same mythic context. Marcellus, "by a similar triumph of wishful thinking, has gone down in history as the city's second Doge." Bracketing this argument are two great sentences. Here they are, in tandem:

> One of the most infuriating aspects of early Venetian history is the regularity with which truth and legend pursue separate courses .... It is the historians of Venice, just as much as her architects, who have sunk their foundations into shifting sands.

## A Conflict over Icons

A powerful test of the ties between Venetia and Constantinople came in 726, in the reign of Eastern Emperor Leo III. To understand it in detail, we much first consider the background. Popes had long held that they, and they alone, were the ultimate authorities on matters doctrinal. Emperors were equally certain that true doctrinal purity lay in their capable hands. Initially, the emperors tended to get their way. It is for that reason that very early on, the popes had been "induced" to regard the patriarch in Constantinople as their number two man. What matters here is that the patriarch was also number two man to the emperor. In the Eastern Empire, secular power trumped clerical power, and we will see Venice following in this pattern later.

Direct command of the military also, initially, favored the emperor. Justinian had a pope summarily arrested and removed from office in the sixth century. Constans II followed suit a century later. McEvedy explains it quite succinctly:

> But by the end of the seventh century the imperial presence in Rome was too weak to sustain such high-handed acts. On one occasion an official sent to arrest the Pope ended up hiding under the Pontiff's bed. The Papacy found that without any very positive action of its own it had achieved political independence.

So this became a very tricky situation with neither popes nor emperors having the slightest power to compel obedience from the other.

It was into this vacuum that an argument about icons, that is religious paintings, mosaics, statues, and their value as aids to worship, flared up and threatened conflagration. Icons had been proliferating rapidly in the east and Emperor Leo III decided to ban them.* He may well have been motivated by the stark contrast between such religious imagery among Christians and the iconophobic Muslims who were also monotheistic.

We think of Christianity as monotheistic also, but these were the glory years of splitting doctrinal hairs. Were the Father, the Son and the Holy Spirit all one being, or independent entities, or some blend of the two? This question kept adherents to various factions thoroughly well occupied for a long time.

---

* Norwich tells us that "the cult of icons had reached such proportions that they frequently served as godparents at baptisms."

In any event, Leo III banned all icons. Western clerics, who were not guilty of the excesses of the east, appealed to the pope and he offered his protection to the lot. Pope Gregory II then excommunicated Leo and his patriarch. Leo struck back by removing all the territory under his control from papal to patriarchal authority. This included Sicily, southern Italy and parts of the Balkans. This split the Church in two. In the west, there was Catholic or Latin Christianity, and in the east, what has been variously called Eastern, Orthodox or Greek Christianity.

For Venetia, the significance was considerable. Gregory II ordered all imperial communities still existing in Italy to revolt against both Leo's edict and his Empire. The uprising was so vehement that Paul, Exarch of Ravenna, was assassinated in 727, as we saw above. Venetia and the remaining Byzantine communities in Italy became free and began selecting their own local leaders. Sometime between 727 and 730, the tribunes and clergy of the lagoons selected Orso (Ursus) as Doge. Impressively, he was to have 117 successors before the Republic fell to Napoleon's forces in 1797.

Once Pope Gregory II realized that the ban on icons could not and would not be enforced in the west, he encouraged tempers to cool and redirected his energies toward containing the heretic Lombards. Specifically, he suggested that the new democratic institutions in the various cities should acknowledge, at least in name, their continued status as part of the Eastern Empire. Lord Norwich explains:

Thus it comes as no surprise to learn that within a few years of the uprising Doge Orso was granted the imperial title of *Hypatos*, or Consul – a distinction of which he seems to have been so proud that his descendants came to surname themselves *Ipato*. Whatever developments might have occurred in the political sphere, Venice's institutional and emotional links with Constantinople clearly remained unbroken .... Many a Byzantine maiden was to be shipped off to the West, into the arms of a Venetian bridegroom; many a Venetian was to send his son eastward to finish his education in Constantinople.

After a brief interregnum,* Orso's son was elected Doge in 742. He immediately moved his seat of government from imperial Heraclea to Malamocca, a more central island with more republican leanings. Then, in 751, the Lombard king captured Ravenna, the main Byzantine administrative center in Italy. Suddenly, Teodato Ipato found himself a Doge without any local imperial authorities to constrain him.

In that same year, Pepin the Short, son of Charles Martel (the Hammer) and father of Charlemagne, took over the Frankish throne, as we saw previously. As we also saw, he followed this up by trouncing the Lombards and pleasing Pope Stephen III. The land thus amassed, Pepin donated to the papacy but not directly to the pope, avoiding any hint of papal vassalage. The Franks brought a new power to the Venetian neighborhood, and they were going to shake things up.

That shaking would be made easier by the fact that the

* An interregnum is a period between two rulers and comes, of course, from Latin.

people of the lagoon were deeply factionalized. There were fights between settlements, feuds between families, commercial rivalries and political infighting. As Norwich puts it, "Venice might have found a form of government that suited her; but she had not yet achieved internal stability or cohesion." The situation would get worse before it got better.

Orso's son became Doge by popular election, but also by a formal appointment from Constantinople. Possibly because he represented the twin sins of germinating dynasty and Byzantine subservience, he was deposed and blinded "by his successor who, scarcely a year later, suffered the same fate." Meanwhile, the powerful families had gotten together long enough to elect two tribunes per year, whose function was to guard against abuses of power by the Doge. After eight years in office, the fourth Doge manifested so much impatience with tribunal limitations that he, too, was thrown out of office.

This was the situation when, in 764, the tribunes and the clergy elected a nobleman who claimed the ancient Roman Emperor, Galba,* as an ancestor, hence the family name of Galbaio. Maurizio Galbaio's election signaled a wish to return to a more pro-Byzantine and less Republican position than had been fashionable for some time. He brought a measure of calm and stability to the job until, in 778, he associated his son Giovanni with himself as, in effect, a companion Doge. Earlier, Orso's son had succeeded him, but

---

* Galba was elevated to the purple by the Praetorian Guard following Nero's death. After a reign of about six months, he was killed by soldiers, making him a tenuous link to an illustrious past.

not right away, and not without popular election. This looked to be an outright hereditary grab at the succession, with no popular consultation at all.

For a new Republic, this spelled trouble. However, as long as the Doge had sons, the system did guarantee an orderly transfer of power from one generation to the next. Venetians, Norwich tells us, probably wanted "the minimum disruption of everyday life – and, of course, of trade." For awhile, it worked. Under Maurizio, prosperity increased as did the population. These additional people needed to settle in new areas of the lagoon. The Rialtine islands had been scarcely inhabited because they were muddy and subject to easy flooding. However, they were centrally located while still far enough away from the bickering, which made them attractive to new settlements. In the end, they would become the heart of modern Venice.

In 775, Maurizio died, and as expected Giovanni took over. Sadly, he had none of his father's talents for leadership. With Charlemagne at the helm, Frankish influence in Italy was growing apace. Giovanni appeared to have no idea how to deal with this power that was beginning to threaten Venetian independence. The pope relied completely on Frankish arms to protect and secure the territory Pepin had given him. So he, and most of the Italian clergy, were strongly pro-Frank.

What this meant for Venice was that its two traditional factions, one more or less pro-Byzantine and the other republican, were joined by a third, the pro-Frankish party, with a heavy clerical component. They thought that Venice and her interests would be best served by cozying up to the most proximate big power, a view that was strengthened in the year 800, when Pope Leo III crowned Charlemagne "Emperor of the Romans."

What we see here, in its embryonic stage, is what will be possible, not inevitable, but possible for Venice. She might secure her independent republican status by balancing the two great powers on her flanks. In so doing, she might also grow as a commercial power, as the maritime link between east and west.* First, however, she had to deal with political mayhem and murder.

The Patriarch of Grado (note the very eastern use of the term "Patriarch") had ecclesiastical jurisdiction over the lagoon. His pro-Frankish stance, together with his rebellious attitude toward the central government in Malamocca, was beginning to worry Giovanni. He had followed his father's tradition and associated his son with himself as Doge, and it was not only for himself, but for this son, called Maurizio after his grandfather, that he sought to save the ducal throne. In brief, he sent his son to Grado with enough military might to kill the Patriarch. This they did.

As Lord Norwich notes, "Political assassinations seldom achieve the purpose for which they are intended." In fact, this one backfired so completely that Giovanni and Maurizio had to flee the city, barely escaping with their lives. The hero of the uprising, Obelerio degli Antenori, became Doge, of

---

* We know, with twenty-twenty hindsight, that she eventually did both. However, these outcomes were not foreordained and the story of exactly how they happened is still to be told.

course, and elevated his brother to the ducal throne in another attempt at creating an hereditary claim to power. More chaos ensued. Then, the nephew of the murdered Patriarch, Fortunatus, showed up with an offer from Charlemagne. If Obelerio would acknowledge the Frankish candidate as patriarch, and the Franks as having sovereign power over the lagoon, "the Doge and his brother could rely on the protection of the Western Empire."

While Obelerio and his brother had dethroned the pro-Byzantine Giovanni and his son and heir, they were animated solely by personal ambition. They had no strong preference between Frank and Byzantine. However, faced with massive domestic opposition, they had no choice but to agree to the alliance that might shore up their power. So, they dashed off to Charlemagne's principle seat at Aachen where they swore homage to this "Emperor of the Romans." One brother, Obelerio, took a Frankish bride and brought her home to Venice where she became "the first *dogaressa* known to history."

Inevitably, Constantinople saw all this as rank treachery, sent a Byzantine fleet up the Dalmatian coast, and anchored it at the lagoon. The admiral found himself rebuffed at all turns and finally, driven by frustration, he decided to attack a Frankish flotilla about forty miles away. He and his ships were roundly defeated and he returned to his home base a beaten man. This gave Venice breathing room from the claims of Constantinople.

However, it also ignited a firestorm of factional conflict at home. Invoking their treaty, the brothers called on Charlemagne for help. His son, also called Pepin, was running the Carolingian's Italian holdings from Ravenna, and he responded by marching on Venice.

Nothing could have been more useful in uniting the people. They collectively deplored the brothers' treachery in inviting invaders to their shores, but agreed, *en group*, to let that issue alone until Venetian victory was assured. The citizens in their numbers removed all markers indicating shallow channels and other such impediments, and drove a welter of stakes into the ground forming a sort of palisade.

The Franks easily occupied the mainland settlements, but absolutely could not make any headway into the lagoon. After six months of this stalemate, three factors broke it. Disease and discontent were mounting among the Frankish soldiers. Indeed, Pepin's own health may have been an issue, as he died a few weeks after abandoning the siege. A Byzantine fleet was rumored to be on the way, and the people of the lagoon offered to pay the Franks an annual tribute.* So, Pepin and his army left the field. Unlike his grandfather, this Pepin has almost no place in any but the most specialized accounts of French history. This is made beautifully ironic by the fact that his attempt at conquest triggered deeply important changes in the history of Venice.

As the seat of government, Malamocco had proved woefully inadequate. The fact that its last three Doges had been catastrophic did not auger well. In addition, it was too closely associated with one faction to function as the capital

---

* Their most likely motive was to end a siege, which blocked them from importing needed grains and other foods, and from their profitable commercial enterprises.

of all Venetians. Finally, Pepin had captured it and thus proved its vulnerability.

The once sparsely populated Rialtine Islands looked an attractive alternative. They had become a haven for those who wished to avoid partisan strife and extremism. In this role, the people had cultivated tolerance, restraint and a practical outlook. Lord Norwich has a line marvelous in its eloquence and its analysis. "The inhabitants, being at once champions and refugees from practically all shades of political opinion, were collectively impartial." This is a fascinating concept, this idea of collective impartiality, and an important one.* These islands were also superbly located for defense. Anyone unfamiliar with the shoals and shallows around them would not be able to navigate, especially given the Venetian tactic of removing all the hazard markers when under attack.

Pepin's invasion, while unsuccessful (apart from the annual tribute), gave rise to fundamental changes in Venetia. Two sets of Doges in succession had demonstrated dynastic ambitions and the latter had actually invited a foreign army to invade the lagoon. Together these events created a strong victory for republicanism as a political philosophy and political goal. Wider power sharing would be a disincentive to dynastic impulses and treason for the sake of personal gain. Many people saw this more clearly after Pepin's assault.

---

* It goes to the very heart of the mechanism thought to produce the "fair and impartial" jury. One might be "tough on crime" while another might value civil liberties, but they have all committed to trying, very hard, to reach an agreement.

Moreover, eluding the invasion redistributed the populations of the various settlements. Families fled the more vulnerable coastal areas toward the more defensible center. At the heart of this defensive zone were the Rialtine islands, until then quite sparsely populated.* Their ancestors had not needed to flee to quite such a remote place. Now, in the face of Pepin's threat, the people of the Rialtine Islands had rallied around Agnello Participazio, one of the oldest local settlers, who would become Doge in 811.

Finally, Pepin's assault had solidified the once very disparate populations of the lagoons. Lord Norwich sums it up nicely: "Pepin had marched against a group of bickering communities; he had been defeated by a united people." Venice was born. Its midwife was the inappropriately gendered Pepin.

In 811, Venice got another civic boost from the resuscitation of a peace treaty between Charlemagne and the Byzantine Emperor Nicephoros called the *Pax Nicephori*. In the original version of this treaty, signed in 803, Charlemagne acknowledged that Venetia was a Duchy of the East Roman Empire without getting what he really wanted, a clear recognition from the East that he was the West Roman Emperor. His dissatisfaction with the situation, together with the other factors noted above, may have contributed to his unleashing his son Pepin on Venice.

When the treaty was revitalized after Pepin's failed invasion, the new Emperor of the East, Michael II, acknowl-

---

* These included the *Riva Alta*, an island that is, today, the most popular tourist attraction in Venice.

edged Charlemagne's title as West Roman Emperor. At the same time, Charlemagne relinquished any claim to Venetia, and acknowledged her as a Duchy within the Eastern Empire. In truth, Venice was autonomous and self-governing, and Constantinople accepted that fact. They cared primarily that Venice be independent from the West, so that her long cultivated nautical skills and the maritime power these gave her could never be used against the East. The importance of both positions, a laissez faire stance toward local Venetian self-government, and an absolute terror that Venice's naval power would fall into enemy hands, cannot be overblown.

Constantinople carried the imperial standard of the old Roman Empire, but the East Roman Empire was Roman in name only. Spiritually, culturally and linguistically, she was existentially Greek. This is why, as we noted, later scholars have, *ex post facto*, changed her name to the Byzantine Empire.* By the same token, the spiritual culture and language of Italy found its fullest expression in Rome, despite its dilapidated condition. However, the *Pax Romana* had been imposed by Charlemagne and it was his capital, Aachen, which reflected and projected political and military power. The *Pax Nicephori* established Venetian independence, *de jure*, from this western power and distance gave her *de facto* independence from the east.

As we know, Charlemagne's empire collapsed with his

---

* From here on, I will use Eastern Empire and Byzantium to refer to the same entity. Similarly, the adjectives imperial (when used for the East) and Byzantine are also interchangeable.

death, and the devolution discussed above set in with a vengeance. This had the effect of reducing almost to zero any threat of a western power grab in Venice, at least for quite some time. This is another instance of *de facto* independence.

Ironically, two processes were at work at the same time. On the one hand, there was the devolution to smaller units of governance, smaller states. On the other, two new nations were being formed. In one, the triumph of Gallo-Roman culture over Frankish conquest gave rise to a language that would evolve into French. We touched on this briefly in "Church and State." The victorious Franks lent their name to this new tongue, but the majority of its speakers gave it life.

Meanwhile, the Frankish dialect of the common German language came to be called High German, or the sort of German spoken by the elite. Naturally, Saxon, Bavarian and other German nobles would adopt High German as they sought to be more cultured, more worthy of their noble status and more accepted by their peers.

Around the same time, in the 860's, a Count of Flanders called Baldwin Iron-Arm built heavily fortified castles in what would become two of the leading northern European trading centers, Bruges and Ghent. The impetus for building fortresses was most likely a reaction to the most successful raiders of the time, the Vikings. In the words of the celebrated medieval historians, Joseph and Francis Gies, "these red-bearded roughnecks from the far north" had sacked every major burg in western Christendom including Paris, Rouen, Bordeaux, Tours, Poitiers, London, Nottingham,

York and Utrecht. It was a debacle and it further reduced the chance that any power in the west could threaten the independence of the lagoon.

Ironically, the Vikings were also seamen, but the aid they provided to Venetian independence by decimating Western Europe had that effect entirely by accident, as they were acting solely for their own benefit. What was not accidental was the Vikings' ability to reach and sack the places listed above. It was both common and sensible to settle by a river for easy access to fresh water. The down side occurred when fierce Viking seamen used that river to turn up, out of the blue, and create havoc. Thus the west had enough turmoil without trying to meddle in Venetian affairs, quite apart from Charlemagne's promise not to do so in the *Pax Nicephori*.

However, the *Pax Nicephori* had a vitally important role to play in Venetian independence. By underlining her status as a Byzantine province, she was able to stay out of the tug of war between popes and western emperors that tore apart other Italian, and especially northern Italian, cities. The faction in Italy that saw the popes as sovereign came to be called Guelf, while the opposing, pro-imperial faction, was called Ghibelline.* As a subject of Constantinople, she was able to keep out of mainland politics for several centuries.

While other northern Italian cities were torn asunder by these factions, Venice grew still richer and remained republican. "Thus, paradoxically, it was through her very submis-

---

* "Sovereign" means having the final right to rule. The easy way to remember the two sides is that Guelf and pope are the shorter words while Ghibelline and emperor are the longer two.

sion to the Empire of the East that her independence was achieved and her future greatness assured." Here Lord Norwich presents us with a beautiful example of the much-misunderstood concept of a dialectic, something that contains its apparent opposite. In this case, Venetian compliance gave rise to her independence.

Venetian prestige and power were at such an exceptional level that it seemed impossible for things to get any better, but they did. In 828, two Venetian merchants brought back from Alexandria an extraordinary holy relic, the remains of St. Mark the Evangelist. According to the legend, while on route to Rome, St. Mark stopped by the Rialtine islands. On the very spot where St. Mark's Basilica would one day stand, an angel appeared before him and said, "*Pax tibi Marce, evangelista meus. Hic requiescet corpus teum.*" The first part, which means "Peace to you Mark, my evangelist," can be found today all over Venice, inscribed on the open book held in the paws of Mark's very famous lions.

The second part goes to the very heart of the issue about Mark's bones, which is, of course, whether or not they are actually his. It translates as, "On this spot shall your body rest." In what can only be described as an entirely circular argument, the legend of the vision and its location was thought to support the fact that the chap they planned to bury in the legendary location must be St. Mark. What matters here is not the illogic, but rather the import. By the end of ninth century, nearly all of Christendom believed that St. Mark was buried in Venice. Since faith was one of the major currencies of the time, this gave Venice a lot of spiritual capital.

What also matters is that the Doge had St. Mark buried in his personal chapel, attached to his residence and the seat of government. This important symbolic gesture asserted that the spiritual authority of the two principle clerics in the region was subordinate to the Doge and his government. This replicated the arrangement in Constantinople, where clerical power was always subordinate to secular power. This situation was also common around the Byzantine Empire in areas practicing Eastern or Orthodox Christianity. It was unheard of elsewhere in the west, and was, yet again, symbolic of the many ways in which Venice was both different from, and independent of, her local neighbors.

### Further Expansion of Trade

In the sixth and seventh centuries, monastic expansion had put more land under cultivation, while individual monasteries became a draw for farmers, craftsmen and merchants. The old Greek colonial town of Marseille, with others, provided some trade in papyrus and spices as the Benedictines tried to drag themselves out of the Dark Ages. Less elevating was the fact that slaves were often the returning cargo.

The wild success of Muhammad in converting large numbers very quickly, and the military successes of his followers, altered the course of Mediterranean trade. The small quickening of western, Christian trade was engulfed by Muslim fleets as they moved into the central and western Mediterranean. Cities like Marseille were frequently raided and sacked.

Genoa, once a busy port, declined to a fishing village. New cities, flying the banner of the Prophet, blossomed along the shores of North Africa – Cairo, Mahdia, Tunis .... In the harbor of Alexandria ... new shipyards furnished the vessels for Moslem commerce and piracy, the products of which, in turn, made Alexandria's markets the largest in the Mediterranean.

Only one port was busier, and that was Constantinople, located at a key crossroad of major trade routes from east, west, north and south. Sailing close behind were the merchants of Venice.

As we saw with the letter written by Cassiodorus in 523, the people of the lagoon were already not only trading salt and salt-preserved fish locally, but were also being employed in the carrying trade as early as the sixth century. The rivers of northern Italy provided them with transport to inland markets where they could obtain wheat, wine and oil, as well as other products of farming and light industry. Also, from a very early date, their sailors were the mainstay of the Byzantine Empire in the North Adriatic.

This made Venice the most powerful link between Western and Central Europe, and the highly desirable spices and the manufactured goods, most notably silk, coming from the east. However, the actual transport of eastern luxury goods was usually in the hands of Greeks or Syrians. This began to change in the decades leading up to the "translation of St. Mark," as his voyage from Alexandria to Venice was called. The Byzantine Empire was being threatened on several fronts and this took resources away from the protection of shipping in the Adriatic. This, in turn, increased pirate activity and discouraged the Greeks and Syrians from entering those troubled waters. Venice sailed into the vacuum.

Having done so, she was then faced with pirate problems of her own. These problems are complex and fascinating, as were their solutions, but they are outside the scope of our story. By force or by bribery, Venice made sure that the pirate problem did not stand between her and prosperity.

At the same time as she was fending off pirates, Venice faced competition from several northern Italian cities, most notably from Genoa, and it was then that these rivalries begin to take shape. We will visit some of the consequences of these commercial conflicts at a later date but we can, for now, simply note them and move on.

One practice by Venetian merchants at this time was called the triangle trade. They sold salt and fish to Muslims for gold and silver. They used the precious metals to purchase luxury items in Constantinople, and then shipped these luxuries home to keep some as riches and to sell others to their western and northern neighbors.

To their traditional local commodities of salt and fish, the Venetians added three more. The first was light manufacturing. Most famously, some of their artisans were becoming adept at blowing glass and their glassware was finding ready markets around the eastern Mediterranean.*

---

* This, of course, is the origin of the marvelous Murano glass.

The second was timber. While most of the Mediterranean costal regions were completely or nearly completely deforested, northern Italy still had vast hardwood forests. Well within reach, the Alpine foothills had evergreens in such abundance that they could be harvested to fill market demand without any obvious limits. Wood, of course, could be used to build ships, siege engines, chariots and weapons, so popes and emperors, from east and west, became absolutely apoplectic at the very idea of trading these commodities to the "Infidel." The Venetians steadfastly ignored their flurry of bans, prohibitions and injunctions.

The third new element in Venetian commerce was the slave trade. Pagan people from the north, most notably Slavs, who were new to the area, accessible and well received by the markets, were frequent targets of the slavers who then traded them to Venetian merchants. The correspondence between the words "Slav" and "slave" was not accidental. When the Slavs converted to Christianity in the eleventh century, they should have become immune from enslavement. Such was not the case. It is possible that the rationale was that they, the Venetians, were Latin Christians. The Slavs by contrast were Greek Christians and thus little better than Infidels. Then again, the Venetians might just have considered the bottom line.

There was a lively demand for slaves in Italy but the really big markets were in the Islamic world. Since many Muslim states deployed slaves in their armies as fighters, papal authorities and Byzantine imperial governments both loudly condemned the sale of slaves as a clear violation of the standing military embargo. The Venetians shrugged and lined their pockets.

The increase in long distance trade augmented but did not replace their local commercial activities in the least. Indeed, they were expanding their contacts with, and control of, mainland trading communities, while increasing their naval capacity to wipe out pirates, as well as their Italian commercial rivals.

Venetian seamen brought a lot to the table. They had nautical skills in great abundance. They were willing and able to trade with Constantinople, with Europe and with the Muslim world. They were poised to be the fulcrum of trade and wealth between and among these forces. As we will discuss in detail later, sailors would change the world and Venetians would figure prominently in that process.

# Venice and the Birth of Modern Europe

O ne object of this chapter is obviously to explain Venice's very important influence over the course of early modern European history. Another is to show how many elements that we have already seen, both concepts and characters, turn up in the course of this story. There was a shipbuilding command economy and a balance in the distribution of political, economic and military power, in Venice's case, naval power. In the last chapter we saw how the Venetians became supremely successful merchant seamen. Here, we begin with their lives on the domestic front.

At home, political developments altered Venice in ways that would, in time, be very important for her commercial success. In 864, a new Doge was elected, one Orso Participazio. In an extraordinarily uncharacteristic move for a ruler, he set out at once to limit his own power. Venice was, theoretically, a democracy. There was an assembly consisting of all adult male citizens, which could be convened to vote on issues involving the security of the Republic. By 864, it had not actually been convened for quite a long time.

There was also a provision for the election of two tribunes whose function was to check any improper conduct or extralegal power grabbing by the Doge. However, over time, their importance had shrunk to the point of impotence. The governance of the Republic had shifted into the hands of the Doge and his clique of supporters.

> Orso now instituted a system of elected *giudici* or judges – high state officials, part ministers, part magistrates, who formed the nucleus from which the future ducal curia was to grow and provided an effective check on the arbitrary misuse of the supreme power. Meanwhile, changes in the structure of local government brought the outlying islands into closer dependence on the central administration.*

This would be one step in a series of steps that would lead Venice to become a curious mixture of democracy and oligarchy, in which the oligarchs decided, from among themselves, who would hold which public office in a democratic election that restricted the franchise to themselves.

How this all played out is very interesting, but the details of Venetian political history are outside the scope of this essay. The consequences are not. Staffed by members of a commercially based oligarchy, the government would never impose confiscatory taxation. In economics, a typical example of confiscatory taxation would be taxing the rich to redistribute goods or benefits to the poor, or even the not so well

---

* Unless otherwise noted, all the following quotations come from Lord Norwich.

off. Here, we have the mirror image of the economic notion that the top taking from the bottom involved gathering a "surplus." Economic jargon is rigged against the poor.

The class whose wealth was based on commerce also produced the officer corps in the navy, which embodied the Venetian military.* So, as we noted before, a balance between political power, military power and economic power tends to produce stability. Such a balance was present in Venice from the reign of this Doge Orso. This also assured a government that was always mercantile, which means making choices that favor commerce. The only issues that had yet to be resolved were ways to provide checks and balances within the oligarchy to prevent dominance by one family, clique or commercial alliance.

The flowering of local and long-distance trade over the ninth, tenth and early eleventh centuries brought great wealth to Venice, including dominance on the seas, and a land empire, as well. One very important fact about all this is that Venice was never feudal. As we know, feudal nobility derived its wealth from the land and the labor of the serfs. As time went by, some wealthy Venetians would buy themselves estates on the mainland and play at feudalism, but it was entirely false and merely an imitation of their northern neighbors. The wealth of Venice was existentially commercial.

By contrast, feudalism was a highly structured system of political and military power with wealth determined by the size and location of the fief. In Venice, the commercial basis

---

* If called upon to fight on land, Venice relied on her allies and/or hired mercenaries.

for society allowed wealth and power to be more competitive, and this could lead to ruthless infighting and vicious interfamilial feuding. After a particularly bad patch of this, in 991, the Venetians selected a new Doge, Pietro Orseolo.

> They could not have made a better choice. Statesman, warrior and diplomatist of genius, Pietro Orseolo II towers above the other Doges of his day like a giant among pygmies; and from the outset his subjects seemed to have recognized his greatness. With his accession, the feuding that had so long poisoned civilized life stopped as suddenly as if it had never happened. It was as though the Venetians had grown up once again into an adult, responsible and gifted people, and now stood ready to follow him on the road to glory.

For the Venetians, glory derived from commerce. During the chaos created by the constant feuding, relations had soured with both the east and the west. So the new Doge set out to restore amicable and mutually beneficial trade relations in both directions. During his first year in office, he negotiated a trade agreement with Basil II in Constantinople with more favorable terms for Venice than ever before. Foreign merchandise coming into the empire was subject to a tariff that made it more expensive than the same merchandise made at home. This agreement exempted goods that originated in Venice from the normal tariff and subjected them to a lower rate. This did not put Venetian products on a par with comparable Byzantine products, but it made them more competitive, and put them at an advantage to comparable products by any other producer.

The same document, called an imperial *chrysobul** and dated March 992, also gave the Venetian merchants in Constantinople an advantage in dealing with the notoriously convoluted, frustrating and obstructionist Byzantine bureaucracy. They were authorized to deal directly with a high ranking palace official roughly comparable to a Minister of Finance. With this authorization, they could bypass the bureaucracy, which virtually assured them access, when necessary, to the Emperor himself. Venice, in turn, promised to keep her fleet ready, at short notice, to transport imperial troops wherever they might be needed. It was an excellent bargain.

The young Emperor of the West, Otto III, a descendent of Otto the Great, became the Emperor at the age of three. He grew up with all of his namesake's ambitions blended with a mysticism acquired from his Greek mother. His grand vision was to create

a great Byzantinesque theocracy of Germans, Italians and Slavs alike, with God at its head and himself and the Pope – in that order – as His twin viceroys. The pursuit of this dream made him still more preoccupied with affairs in Italy than his father had been before him; a young man's

---

* *Chryso* is a combining word that means gold and is Greek in origin. Here the "*bul*" part is similar to a Papal Bull, which is a signed and sealed document not a version of the creature so desired by Minos' wife. So a *chrysobul* here is sometimes called a Golden Bull.

hero-worship for the ablest ruler west of Constantinople did the rest.

That extremely able ruler was Doge Pietro Orseolo II.

Otto III first crossed the Alps in 996 on a journey to Rome for his coronation as Holy Roman Emperor. Along the way, he expressed his admiration for the Doge by compelling two bishops to return to Venice land they had misappropriated for their own use. He then granted the Doge the authority to create and run Venetian trading stations and warehouses along the banks of the Piave and Sile, "simultaneously guaranteeing safe conduct and tax exemption to Venetians on imperial territory." On a more personal level, he had the Doge's third son brought to him in Verona, where he sponsored his confirmation, and gave the child his own name, Otto.

Doge Pietro Orseolo II had secured first class trading terms for Venetian merchants in the two great empires of Christendom, and he had only been in office for five years. The Republic had been expanding trade with Muslims but some, even in Venice, had qualms about a close association with the dreaded Infidel, as Christians were given to calling Muslims, who used the same slur in reverse. Pietro Orseolo would have none of it.

> Off went his ambassadors to every corner of the Mediterranean where the green banner of the Prophet flew – to Spain and Barbary, Sicily and the Levant; to the courts of Aleppo, Cairo and Damascus, to Cordova,

Kirouan and Palermo. Emir after Emir received them with courtesy and accepted their proposals. Agreement after agreement was brought back with pride and satisfaction to the Doge.

Otto III and Basil II may have had reservations about these decisions to trade with Muslims, but "for Pietro, true Venetian that he was, commerce was always preferable to bloodshed – and good deal more profitable as well."*

The importance of mercantilism to Venetian politics cannot be given too much emphasis. Mercantilism is a philosophy of governance, which argues that doing what is best for the economy should be the central principle of the state. We see it here in foreign policy. In its domestic political economy, the sharp distinction between nobles and merchants, prevailing in the rest of Europe in this period, was missing in Venetia. Instead, nobles presided over fortunes built on trade and wealthy merchants were elected Doge. In 1043, a wealthy silk merchant, Domenico Flabanico, was chosen as Doge for his well-known and very firm opposition to ducal dynasties. His reign, and that of his successor (1043-1071), are widely considered by historians as laying the foundation for the quasi-democratic oligarchy that would govern the Republic for the next seven centuries.

In the near term, however, trouble was brewing, and to understand it we have to remember the clash between

---

*The Piave is a river 137 miles long that rises in the Alps of southern Austria and drains into the Adriatic Sea about 22 miles east-northeast of Venice. The Sile, or Sil in the Venetian dialect, meets the Botteniga River at Treviso.

Emperor Henry IV and Pope Gregory. One of the players in this conflict was the Norman Robert Guiscard, who came to Rome to rescue the pope from Henry, and then stayed to sack the city. This so discredited Gregory that he had to flee with Robert back to Sicily.

Before Robert "saved" the pope, he was on his way to the conquest of Constantinople. To put it mildly, the new Byzantine Emperor, Alexius I Comnenos, was nervous. Not only did he have to confront rampaging Normans on his western frontier, but he was also fending off Turkish attacks from both the north and the east. He appealed to the Venetians to deal with the Normans at sea.

The Venetians eagerly agreed. They had their own worries about Norman expansion in the region. They sent a vast fleet, commanded directly by the Doge, and deployed some extremely creative tactics. For example, archers crouched in small rowboats, that were then hoisted up into the masts and spars of their ships. From there, the archers could rain arrows down on the Normans, their height providing them with a distinct advantage. They also used large blocks of wood, studded with nails, to ram holes in the Norman ships. In all, they won a great victory at sea. Sadly for their side, the Norman land army roundly defeated their Byzantine counterparts, and took an important city on the route to Constantinople as their own.

In the 992 *chrysobul*, the Byzantine Emperor had granted the Venetians a number of concessions in tariffs, and also a reduction of bureaucratic red tape. In 1082, in gratitude for the Venetian struggle to prevent a Norman takeover of the capital, another *chrysobul* was pronounced by Alexius I Comnenos. This one went considerably further. It allowed the Venetians to trade with no customs duties or other forms of taxation whatsoever. This gave them an extraordinary economic advantage over the taxpaying citizens of the empire. The Venetians were also granted the privilege of having their own commercial district in any Byzantine city. The Venetian colony in Constantinople got special anchorages on the Golden Horn,* and the right to their own warehouses. The subtext of these concessions was, of course, *please go on fighting the Normans!*

This they did with inconsistent results, and it looked as if Robert and his army were poised to take Constantinople, when Pope Gregory VII implored Robert for help against Henry IV. Robert rushed to Rome with the idea of a quick clean-up, and then a return to his main goal, control of the Byzantine Empire. Having started life as an impoverished adventurer, Robert Guiscard had beaten Henry IV, Holy Roman Emperor, had the Byzantine Emperor on the ropes and, "the greatest of all medieval popes" Gregory VII in his snare.

By the time Robert was able to return to the eastern campaign, Venice had made his position much worse. The Venetians beat him handily at sea, twice, and then decided to go home. Norwich has this to say about that choice:

Throughout his long career, people had tended to

---

* The Golden Horn is an inlet about five miles long that forms the harbor of what is today Istanbul, but was then Constantinople.

underestimate Robert Guiscard; invariably – if they lived at all – they lived to regret it. For the Venetians, it was an understandable mistake .... But ... Robert recognized his chance. Summoning every vessel he possessed that was still afloat, he flung the broken remnants of his fleet against the unsuspecting enemy galleys in a last desperate onslaught. He had calculated it perfectly.

The stunned Venetians had every one of the disadvantages associated with misplaced overconfidence. It was a humiliating defeat.

Nevertheless, Venice retained her commercial concessions in the Byzantine Empire and, with the death of Robert and most of his army from typhoid, the Norman threat "would vanish ... as suddenly as it had arisen."

Venice might be embarrassed, but she still had the trade concessions from the Eastern Empire. These resulted from the enormous gratitude the emperor felt toward the Venetians, and included "a special tribute to the treasury of St. Mark's" that was paid out of Byzantine taxes on the merchants of rival Amalfi. It was immensely satisfying. There came to be

finally, in 1082, the extension of former trading privileges [until] they amounted to full exemption from all taxes and customs duties for Venetian merchants throughout the empire. The importance of this last concession is almost impossible to exaggerate.

It was as if Venice had suddenly come into possession of all of the lands under Constantinople's control, and with it unlimited access to all of the Orient. From that day forward, Venice would become a formidable trading power across the known world.

This ebullient assessment of the Venetian future has a darker side. What happens if and when the emperor no longer controls the gates of the Orient? Without wanting to give away too much of the story, it must be said that, in the richness of time, the emperor does suffer such a loss. To flesh out the details of that eventuality, we have to deal with ...

### More Horsemen

New waves of nomadic pastoralists surged from the Eurasian steppes westward to collide with settled civilizations. One of the first and most successful of these waves involved a loose federation of related Turkic tribes led by the Seljuk clan. This description of them from Jason Goodwin's *Lords of the Horizons* is quite telling.

> They could fire arrows backwards from the saddle at a moving target ... and their archery was so accurate that as late as the nineteenth century, when the Turkish Sultan wore a frock coat and spoke passable French, it is said that he placed an arrow at 800 yards between the legs of a doubting American ambassador.

In time, the Seljuk Turks crossed paths with militant Arabs who were spreading the word and making conversions and conquests at an amazing rate of speed. "Within twenty years of the Prophet's death, the Arabs had created an empire to rival Rome's."*

Islam differed significantly from Judaism and Christianity in that it wholly lacked a priesthood. Goodwin describes one consequence with delightful prose.

> A nomad can vanish for weeks on end but the all-powerful, all-seeing God goes with him: five times a day he must clear his mind and wash his hands and call on God. Islam is a powerful weapon in the struggle against uncertainty ... and its rules are firm. There is no God but God, and Muhammad is his prophet. The five daily prayers must be said. Pork and wine are forbidden. Alms must be given. The believer must tirelessly combat unbelief, but peaceably, unless provoked.

To the Turkish nomads, these rules, their portability and their comfort against an insecure world held a very great appeal.

Returning to the period right after Muhammad's death, the empire created by these newly minted Muslims was initially a single Caliphate. The Caliph was the spiritual descendent of Muhammad, and thus the spiritual guide of the faithful. A Caliphate was a state in which governance emanated from the Caliph in his role as a temporal leader. The first Caliphs were selected from among the Prophet's inner

---

* McEvedy, *New Penguin Atlas of Medieval History*. The Prophet died in 632. The Seljuk Turks became major players on the world scene in the eleventh century.

circle. Since they were only mortal, the system had a limited lifespan. So the question arose: should the Caliph continue to be elected or should this become an hereditary office?

The third Caliph was a member of the noble Umayyad family, and he appointed his kin to a number of the important posts whose occupants comprised the electorate. Clearly this was a bid to make the Caliphate hereditary. However, a majority thought that an hereditary Caliphate should go to Ali, a cousin of the prophet, as well as his son in-law, and one of his earliest converts. Ali won the next election and served as the fourth Caliph under very stormy conditions. In the end, he could not outmaneuver the entrenched Umayyads. They retook the Caliphate and held it for the next century.

In Persia, descendents of Caliph Ali served as the nucleus of a group of supporters who called themselves Shiites. Those who favored the Umayyad dynasty came to be called Orthodox or Sunni. What started out as a simple and understandable difference became layered over time, as each group had their own heroes, martyrs, victories, honored historical events, etc. It is these layers that make the distinction important today, when, as Colin McEvedy remarks, the Umayyads are no more than a strain on one's spelling.

The Umayyad dynasty was followed by the Abbasid Caliphate, whose leaders showed a keen appreciation of the martial talents of the Seljuk Turks, most especially their skill as archers on horseback, and began integrating them into its army as an elite slave fighting force eligible for promotion. In time, many positions in the officer corps and in the political administration were held by Muslim Turks.

Meanwhile, in the middle of the eleventh century, Turks were on the move in two directions. Some headed toward Russia, where they were generally confined to the steppes and thus had little effect on history. Others headed toward what is today Iran, and then fanned out across the region creating the Seljuk Sultanate, the first in a series of empires established by nomads that would include the famed Empire of the Mongols.

The Seljuk Sultanate* abandoned nomadic pastoralism and settled down to become a respectable, civilized and ably governed state. There were, however, still horsemen who wanted nothing to do with statecraft, the settled life and its burdens of taxation. They took their herds and their faith and kept on moving. Not surprisingly, their government hastened their departure as best it could. Nomads threaten farmers, who pay the bulk of all taxes. For that precise reason, as they entered other settled areas, they were again pushed west.

A bit earlier, the Byzantines had their last great burst of expansion. In Europe, they eliminated a large entity known at the time as the West Bulgarian Empire (1018), and successfully claimed mastery of the Serbs. In Asia, they con-

---

*A Sultanate differs importantly from a Caliphate. In the latter, as noted above, the Caliph has both spiritual and secular authority. Sultan is a term used by Sunni Muslims to denote a purely political leader and to emphasize that the Caliph's power is limited to spiritual matters.

quered the Armenian Kingdom of Vaspurakan (1022). "All in all," remarks McEvedy, "a pretty good performance from a state whose arteries were a good deal harder than those of it rivals."

In the era of the Norman conquests of England, southern Italy and Sicily, the Seljuk Turks were wildly more successful in their expansion. By 1071, the Seljuk Empire reached east to the Oxus River (today called the Amu Darya) and the Aral Sea, and west to the Red Sea. Its northwestern border corresponded with the eastern frontier of Byzantium, while its southwestern border ran along the Levantine frontier of the Fatimid Caliphate of Egypt. This second-largest Islamic empire to date shared borders with two powerful neighbors, a situation which would lay the foundation for a highly consequential misunderstanding.

The Seljuk Sultan, Alp Arslan, sent a force into Armenia, in all probability to protect his flank in the east, while he moved full force against the Fatimids. It seems to historians thoroughly unlikely that he had any designs on Christian Armenia, which had absolutely no strategic value to his overall empire.

However, the Byzantine emperor, Romanus IV Diogenes, did not see it that way. So he set off with a rag-tag army of mostly mercenaries to engage in an historic clash between two faiths and two empires. Talk about being ill-prepared! Colin McEvedy tells this story well.

The two armies met at Manzikert, by Lake Van. The Turks

354 · HOW THE WORLD WORKED

employed their usual tactics, their mounted bowmen retiring before each Byzantine advance, then wheeling around and pouring in volleys of arrows whenever the pursuit slackened.

Here, of course, we see an amazing parallel to Scythian tactics fifteen centuries earlier, with the usual result of frustrating and exhausting the pursuing army that is taking but not inflicting casualties.

The Byzantine army came unglued. Turkish soldiers of fortune could simply join Alp Arslan's forces. Apparently, other mercenaries, including a contingent of Normans, gave up and let the battle continue without them. McEvedy explains what happened next.

The remaining regiments struggled on, lost contact with each other and, sooner or later, found themselves surrounded by superior Turkish forces. By the time the Emperor was brought to the Sultan's tent that evening, the army he had led out from Constantinople had ceased to exist.

Manzikert was an epic defeat costing, as it did, all the Anatolian provinces of the Byzantine Empire. Only the Turk's inability to cross the Bosporus* saved those on European soil. Yet, the valiant Alp Arslan, whose name meant

---

* A very common spelling, indeed the one McEvedy uses, is "Bosphorus" which Webster's Geographical Dictionary explicitly declares inaccurate but commonly used.

Lion Hero, let Romanus IV Diogenes return home unharmed.

While Manzikert was huge, Byzantium had been losing territory in Asia Minor in a piecemeal fashion during the decades before the battle. The nomads and their herds simply obliterated the crops in the fields, and the whole of Asia Minor was being turned into a replica of the Ukrainian steppe. The Christian peasantry vanished, and with them an irreplaceable reserve of military manpower for the empire.

William McNeill points out the tremendous importance to Byzantine history of its bi-lobed configuration. Because the same enemy would be hard-pressed to strike simultaneously in the Balkans and in Anatolia, a crisis in one lobe could be met by resources culled from the other. Around 1100, the combined effects of a great battle, Manzikert, and decades of Turkish immigration abolished that option forever.

Another result of Manzikert was an imperial plea to the pope for help against the Infidel. After some time passed, the pope considered the request and decided to step it up a notch. In addition to returning Anatolia to the emperor, why not "liberate" Jerusalem and the Holy Lands while in the neighborhood? In 1095, Pope Urban preached a crusade. Then legions of itinerant priests took up the call. It would commence with a complete disaster.

Simple men, without arms or military training, were moved to action and there began what came to be called the People's Crusade. Despite urgent warnings from Pope Urban not to act in haste or without permission from their priests, these men took up the call. They descended on Constantinople and went on to face the Infidel armed with fervent excitement and not much else.

Their first battle was against the Seljuk Sultan of Rum, a breakaway subject of the Great Seljuk Empire. McEvedy tells the sad tale: "At the end of the day nearly all of the twenty-thousand poor souls were dead, dying or en route to the slave market. The Turks hardly lost a man."

That was not to last. Sturdier troops were on the way, led by some of the great knights of the day, including the son of William the Conqueror, as well as Bohemond, the eldest son of Robert Guiscard. Ironically, he had fought with his father in the Balkans during his bid to conquer Constantinople. Marching through Anatolia toward Jerusalem, these knights and their comrades killed many a Turk.

On July 15, 1099, the crusaders took Jerusalem. They massacred every Muslim and burned alive all the Jews in their main synagogue. In both cases, the carnage included non-combatants, the elderly, women, children and even babies. Not all, perhaps not even most, of the Crusaders were religious fanatics who would stop at nothing, but sadly, fanatics dominated both the spirit and conduct of he crusades.

Their wholesale slaughter certainly toughened the will ) resist among Muslims and Jews in subsequent encoun-rs. It also, and very importantly, ruptured the delicate bal-ce between Jews, Christians and Muslims that had been integral part of Byzantine survival by virtue of its geo-phic position at a major crossroads of three faiths. Arguably, this relentless intolerance was the reason for the ultimate failure of the whole crusading enterprise.*

## Venice and the Crusades

The Venetians were not at all keen on the whole idea of crusading. War was bad for business and, besides, they got on splendidly, and profitably, with Muslims and wanted to keep it that way. They had a secure arrangement with Egypt to sell her metals and timber in return for spices from the Orient. Venetians were also anxious to maintain good relations with the Seljuk Turks, because only through them could they connect with the caravan routes to Central Asia.

However, their commercial rivals, Genoa and Pisa, thought ferrying crusaders to the Levant might be a great way of boosting their access to the wealth of Constantinople and its surrounding empire. The Venetian oligarchy spotted the threat, and grudgingly joined the crusades. Nevertheless, they waited to set sail for the Levant until 1099, and then found a number of pressing tasks along the way. One involved trouncing the Pisan sailors and exacting their promise to stay out of the action, a promise they did not keep. Another was rounding up some holy relics, including one that they thought was the corpse of Saint Nick. It was not. But, for a time Venice added another attraction to its pilgrimage trade.

* For a cogent summary of the Crusades, McEvedy's *New Penguin Atlas of Medieval History* is quite helpful. The cast of characters includes Richard the Lion-hearted and Frederick Barbarossa.

Only when these chores were complete did they set off for Palestine. Arriving after the massacres, they found the victors in urgent need of naval power. Negotiations ensued. As Norwich puts it, "The Venetian's terms were hardly redolent of selfless Crusading zeal." Of their many demands, one was particularly pertinent. They wanted all of the Frankish state to be open to them as a free trade zone. This was to open up the western part of Western Europe to Venetian merchants, exempted from local taxes. They got this and much more.

In return, they were to help take Haifa, a predominantly Jewish town. Needless to say, the population resisted with all their might, considering what had happened to their co-religionists in Jerusalem less than a year before. In the end, they lost, and while a few escaped the majority of Jews and Muslims were killed. Just what role, if any, the Venetians played in the slaughter is not reflected in the scanty records of the day.

For a detailed account of Venice and the Crusades, Lord Norwich is great. For our purposes, a few general points can be made. Her principle motive for being involved at all was commercial rivalry with Genoa and Pisa. She could no longer count as exclusive her trading partners in the Levant, so she had to get in on the game.

Moreover, the terms of her various agreements to help the crusaders were always motivated by financial or commercial interests. When granted a section of a city, as she was in Acre, Venice insisted on her right to use her own weights and measures and to keep a magistrate of her own on the scene. All of which kept Venetian shipping extremely busy.

## A Wonderful Example of Economic Command

The Doge, Ordelafo, nationalized shipbuilding. Venetians had long thought of themselves as special and different and that made them a nation, with their own dialect and their distinctive way of life. In what was a clear example of a command economy, the government brought all the shipbuilding activities together on two small marshy islands called, in the Venetian dialect, *Zemelle* or twins. In this location, over the next fifty years

> there grew up that mighty complex of dockyards, foundries, magazines and workshops for carpenters, sailmakers, ropemakers and blacksmiths that Dante described in the *Inferno* and that gave a new word to the English language and many others – the Arsenal.

Norwich explains in a footnote that Arsenal is derived from the Arabic *Dar Sina'a* which means a House of Construction.

It would be quite some time until the Arsenal reached its full potential as a powerhouse of mass production. However, the concept of mass production was built into the original plan to centralize. This also provides for what are called "economies of scale." Building a lot of ships in one place lowers the cost of each individual ship. This allowed for the stockpiling of spare parts, which facilitated repairs. Also, with this concentration of production in one location, experts were brought together and their interaction might spark new ideas in design.

> It may be no coincidence that the foundation of the Arsenal roughly coincides with the development of rib and plank construction, by which a ship was assembled on a previously erected skeletal framework rather than being built steadily upwards from keel to gunwales; it is certainly true that the beginning of the twelfth century marks the moment when Venice begin to design certain vessels primarily for war and others for trade.

Norwich then argues that these distinctions should not be overblown. War ships always had room for loot as well as cargo, and their "war captains were never averse to trading on the side." What this frequently meant was that Venetian wars actually paid for themselves. At the same time, merchant ships were equipped with the ability to defend themselves from pirates and their commercial rivals.

> In feudal Europe, where the fighting nobility remained haughtily aloof from trade, such a system would be unthinkable, but in Venice there was no separate military caste; the nobles were merchants, the merchants noble, and the interests of both were identical.

So, when the Arsenal produced warships, the designers tried to include as much cargo space as possible without compromising the military mission. By the same token, the production of commercial shipping was done with an eye to defense.

This allows us to pause and revisit some of the earlier themes in the book. The Arsenal was a state-run command economy that was, unlike the Soviet state-run command economy, a huge success. Certainly a large factor in Venetian success was that everyone involved stood to benefit from strengthening Venetian shipping. The Soviet model was based on threats and fears, while the Venetian model rested on shared rewards.

From this point onward, Venice did not have to take an ad hoc approach to ship building. Instead, she could plan ahead and build ships as the state of public finances and the dangers on the horizon dictated. She could also amass spare parts to use as needed. By the thirteenth century, if not sooner, she could build and/or repair twenty-four galleys at a time.

### *Chrysobul* Revisited

The *chrysobul* promulgated by the Byzantine emperor in 1082 had actually given the Venetians a clear advantage over domestic producers and traders because they had tax obligations, which she did not. After thirty-six years in operation, it was obvious that imperial trade was suffocating. When John II succeeded his father to the Byzantine throne, he immediately annulled Venetian special privileges and announced that they would share an even playing field with Byzantine merchants and those of other Italian cities. Over many years, assuming the agreement was permanent, Venetians had made considerable capital investments in warehouses and the like. Genoa and Pisa were already causing them headaches, and this was the final blow. It would not be taken lying down. At the end of the day and, after some adventures, Venice won back her privileged status. John II had been forced to back down.

At this point, Venice had a free trade zone in the Frankish kingdom in the west and a free trade zone in the Byzantine Empire in the east. As a result of her participation in the siege of Tyre, she received a third of that city, with a Venetian governor enforcing Venetian laws, and a grand church dedicated to St. Mark. With this expansion, as Norwich observes:

> The Venetian overseas empire had begun; it was to endure nearly seven centuries, until the final downfall of the Republic – longer than any other in European history.

This was, beyond a doubt, a tribute to a stability that had its roots in a congruence of economic power, political power and naval power, all concentrated in the same oligarchy.

### Troubles

In Rome, there were two popes. Innocent II was the candidate of St. Bernard and soon became the general favorite. The other one, Anacletus, sought help from Roger II d'Hauteville, nephew of Robert Guiscard and the Count of Sicily. Roger promoted himself to king and demanded papal ratification in return for his support. Sicily was enjoying a tremendous boost in wealth and power, and neither the eastern nor the western emperor appreciated the change.

Sicily is almost at the exact center of the Mediterranean and is thus a sensible trading center for three continents. In Roger's day, it had thriving Greek and Arab populations co-mingled and living in peace. This made the port of Palermo particularly cosmopolitan and attractive. Besides becoming king, he had also enlarged his territory by appropriating the "property of his feckless and fortunately infertile cousins." That line comes from Norwich, but McEvedy can do just as well.

> He ruled from Palermo, where his court, with its black servants, its Saracen guards, its harem and its pleasure-domes became the scandal and envy of Christendom.

As it happened, Pope Innocent II fell into Roger's hands, and bought his own release by confirming his captor as the legitimate king of Sicily.

Manuel Comnenos inherited the Byzantine crown from his father, and began to question dad's conviction that Roger must be relentlessly opposed. Instead, might it not make more sense to become his ally? Fortunately for Venice these efforts failed. Manuel turned his attention to his own nuptials. In 1146, he married the sister-in-law of the Western Emperor Elect, Conrad. Shortly thereafter, St. Bernard, who could not resist meddling in politics and had a dismal track record, proclaimed the Second Crusade, which was, in brief, a complete disaster.

In the first few weeks of 1148, a Sicilian fleet sailed into Byzantine waters. It was commanded by George of Antioch, a man of low origins who rose to the most august title in Norman Sicily: Emir of Emirs. The job encompassed both the chief officer of state and the admiral of the fleet. He took the critical island of Corfu and then rounded the Peloponnese, "dropping further armed detachments at strategic points along the coast." From there, he raided and pillaged with impunity and became particularly rich from the spoils of the ancient cities of Thebes and Corinth.

Manuel desperately wanted Venetian support and had to grant valuable trade concessions to get it. At the same time, he was scrambling to get his own navy up to speed. The melding of the two was never a success. On one occasion, Venetian sailors could be seen mocking Manuel's dark complexion by dressing up an Ethiopian in imperial regalia and holding a mock coronation within plain view of their Greek "allies." Manuel never forgot or forgave the insult.

In 1171, under what everyone knew was a false pretext, he had all the Venetian citizens jailed, and their ships and property confiscated. A rumor that he might do this was scotched by his granting more guarantees to the Venetians, thus attracting more capital to Constantinople and beyond. When the hammer finally fell, he thus raked in an even larger prize.

Venice cried out for war, but there were two huge problems: manpower and finance. The number of Venetians in jail in the east reduced the number of fighters available, and quite a lot of capital had been seized. The war went badly. The Doge was duped into pausing for truce talks, which Manuel never took seriously. The talks were a waste of time and treasure, and with no deal, the Venetians were struck by plague. The Doge, Vitale Michiel II, returned home with his remaining troops in 1172. He was already under a cloud for his military and diplomatic missteps, but this cloud became a hailstorm when it was discovered that he had brought the plague back with him. He tried to flee but he was murdered in the streets. Naturally, there were no monuments built in his honor in Venice.

However, there was, for a long time, a reminder. Soon after the murder, the man who stabbed Vitale Michiel to death was convicted and executed, and his house was razed to the ground. It was further ordered that no stone edifice could ever be built on the site. That prohibition remained in force from 1172 until 1948, when a luxury hotel expanded onto the site.

Venice was not only enduring the plague. She had other troubles as well. Through the Greater Lombard League, she was at odds with Frederic Barbarossa. In Constantinople, Manuel Comnenos was an even stauncher enemy. The Venetian navy was at an ebb, as were her finances. Much of this could be, and was, blamed on Vitale Michiel. Nevertheless, a critical question remained: How was it that Vitale was not prevented from going so far off course? It was time to review the basic procedures of governance.

The constitutional reforms of Domenico Flabanico provided the Doge with two counselors empowered to question and limit his decision-making power. He was also obliged to solicit advice from other leading citizens – the *pregadi* – when necessary. Indeed, should he feel the need for an even wider array of views, he could ask an assembly of the whole people – the *arengo*. The problematic concept was "necessity." Does any political figure, bent on a particular course of action, think that additional advice is needed?

These reforms were now 150 years old. Time had sapped the authority of the two counselors. The views of the *pregadi* were seldom solicited, and an assembly of the whole people, the *arengo,* was both a logistical problem, as the population had increased dramatically, and a political disaster, as there was no way to control so large a crowd making rule by the "mob" a real danger.*

During a financial crisis the city had been divided into six sections – or *sestieri* – for the purposes of levying taxes. Under the new constitution, two representatives of each *sestieri* would serve for one year, during which time they would, by some process or another, nominate an assembly of 480 prominent citizens. This assembly, the *Comitia Majora* or Great Council, was empowered to appoint all the principle state officials, including those representing the *sestieri*.

In the first year of the new constitution, the people would be able to elect directly the two representatives for their *sestieri*. In all subsequent years, the Great Counsel would select

---

* From the point of view of the elites, an inevitable feature of a "mob" as distinct from a "crowd" is that they do not share the views or values of the elites. That is why "mobs cannot be trusted" to make sensible decisions about the great issues of the day.

the twelve representatives who would, in a completely circular and rigidly closed system, select the members of the next Great Council. The people were utterly out of the loop.

Where popular participation was mandatory, their effective power was curtailed in so far as possible. Their right to elect the Doge was their most cherished political resource and they did not part with it lightly. The first elite attempt to present the new election of a Doge as a *fait accompli* was met with rioting. The "compromise" thrown to the rioters was merely window dressing: the successful candidate must be formally presented to them in St. Mark's Square with the formula 'Here is your Doge, if it pleases you.' Thus the voice of the people was theoretically preserved; but it was a formality only, and the people knew it.

Another element in political reform was increasing the original and essentially powerless ducal counselors to six, and endowing them with reinvigorated authority. They were to be with the Doge constantly to monitor and limit his actions, which suggests some sort of veto power. The seven of them, with the Doge as *primus inter pares,** represented executive power. In time, they came to be called the *Signoria* or *consiglietto*. The leading citizens, the *pregadi*, turned into a Senate whose influence increased, especially in foreign affairs, to the point where they made decisions which would then be ratified or not by the Great Council.

The three constituent elements in Venetian government had been the Doge, his advisers and the people. What these

---

* This was the phrase, "first among equals," used by Augustus to describe his position.

constitutional reforms did was to strengthen the oligarchy against the Doge, and even more extensively against the people. There were double dangers here of a loss of ducal prestige and/or a loss of public cooperation. A cleverly Venetian solution was proposed to address both problems at once. After the selection of a new Doge, he was to be carried aloft on a special chair while he tossed largesse to the people. Evidently, it worked.

Venice tried, in vain, to reconcile with Manuel Comnenos and get their fellow citizens out of prison. This forced Venice to make an alliance with William II of Sicily. In 1175, they signed a twenty-year treaty that provided the Venetian merchant-nobles with "commercial terms far more favorable than any that they had previously enjoyed."

When, in 1177, it was time for Frederick Barbarossa to apologize to Pope Alexander, after the Lombard League had trounced him at Legnano, Venice's legendary beauty and her wealth, not to mention her status as a pilgrimage destination, made her a logical choice of venue. Wealth and beauty went hand in hand, because, for Venetians, a favorite choice for spending wealth, after commerce, was architecture.

Funding a beautiful church, specifically, had the dual gratifications of demonstrating piety and gaining status from conspicuous consumption.* The details of that historic

---

* Having a retinue was another form of conspicuous consumption. In this case, all the important visitors to Venice vied with one another over the relative size of each one's entourage. The Archbishop of Cologne brought no fewer than 400 including secretaries, chaplains, etc.

reconciliation are fascinating, but they are outside the scope of our story. That Venice was hosting the two most powerful men in the west, Emperor Frederick Barbarossa and Pope Alexander, put her, if not quite as their equal, at least in their league. Venice, alone among northern Italian cities, was recognized as a world power.

The Doge, Sebastiano Ziani, was not merely a superb diplomat and statesman, as well as an avid builder, but he also showed quite a flair for establishing sound legal and constitutional principles. He was also a masterful judge of the future ramifications of each of his reforms, all of which revolved around a central question: Does this reorganization, or that one, strengthen the oligarchic principles long dear to the Venetian elite? He always chose the ones that did.

Ziani was particularly concerned with the assignment of public offices to the very wealthiest and most powerful men. Right before he retired, he called a meeting with his chief magistrates enjoining them on the wisdom of this course. Such appointments clearly benefit the class as a whole, but sometimes members of a class do not see their collective best interest over their individual preferences. From the latter perspective, holding office was time consuming, burdensome and far less profitable than commerce. By 1185, turning down an appointment to public office carried with it a very heavy fine. The class as a whole insured the cooperation of its constituent members.

Ziani's final act in office was directed at factionalism within the oligarchy. If one clique gained ascendancy by a clever manipulation of the rules, others might be tempted to act outside the constitution. The current system had the Great Council choosing eleven of its members to elect the next Doge. A clique could rig enough of the eleven to insure its candidate was elected.

Ziani made the process more layered, with more checks and balances. He changed the number chosen by the Great Council from eleven to four. They, in turn, would select an election committee of forty members, each of whom must have received at least three of the four votes, and only one of whom could be from each family represented in the Council. The forty then elected the Doge. It was actually not the most complicated election strategy Venice would adopt to thwart the power of cliques. In 1178, it resulted in the election of an elderly but skilled diplomat. His skills would be needed.

In 1180, Manuel Comnenos died and his twelve-year-old son succeeded to the Byzantine throne with his Frankish mother as regent. She so thoroughly favored Franks over Greeks that intense hostility ensued. A Greek reprisal resulted in the massacre of nearly all westerners in Constantinople whether Frankish or not. Manuel's cousin, Andronicus, seized the city and attempted to impose martial law. He failed.

In time, he was replaced by an incompetent but docile Isaac II Angelus, who made a bizarre diplomatic arrangement with Venice. He agreed to compensate Venice for the property confiscated by Manuel Comnenos in 1171, and to ensure the safety of Venetian citizens and their property in the future. Finally, Venetians were commissioned to build between forty and one-hundred galleys at imperial expense, a considerable financial windfall and a monopoly on Byzantine shipbuilding. In the end this left the Empire of the East essentially defenseless against the nautical power of Venice.

On October 2, 1187, Jerusalem fell to the Muslim Saladin. When the news reached the pope, he died of shock. His replacement, Gregory VIII, preached the Third Crusade. Frederic Barbarossa heeded the call and drowned on the way. Richard the Lion Hearted also heeded the call, leaving his brother John to accept the nobles' terms in Magna Carta. Despite Richard's reputation for valor and chivalry, Lord Norwich is not a fan. He describes Richard's "massacre" of almost three thousand Muslim prisoners "in cold blood" as an "indelible stain on his reputation." Here is his summation: "The kindest thing that can be said about the Third Crusade is that it was a distinct improvement on the Second."

Venice's role was murky. She seems to have limited her martial activities to transporting men and material, and "we can be quietly confident that she received full payment for her services before withdrawing from the fray." Her merchants, who might well have been among the men transported, quickly reclaimed what had been briefly lost to them in the way of commercial opportunities. The Doge at the time was Orio Mastropiero, who made important changes to the judiciary and served the Republic well.

If he still strikes one as being somehow colourless, he is not entirely to blame; for it was his misfortune to fill the gap between the two greatest Doges of the medieval

Republic and the two most momentous chapters in its history. Of Sebastiano Ziani and the Peace of Venice the story has already been told; we must now turn to a darker and more shameful triumph: that grim adventure still ludicrously known as the Fourth Crusade, and its architect Enrico Dandolo.*

A new and utterly incompetent regime came to power in Constantinople, which presented an inviting target for western aggression. The Holy Land also looked vulnerable because, with Saladin dead, the forces of Islam had no unity. So it seemed a good time for a crusade.

Richard the Lion Hearted suggested that the most vulnerable spot for a crusading attack was Egypt, and the only possible source for the quantity of ships needed was Venice. While the Doge, Dandolo, was agreeing to provide the ships and setting a price for their hire, his agents were "in Cairo discussing a highly profitable trade agreement with the Sultan's Viceroy." It seems entirely likely that they also "gave a categorical assurance that Venice had no intention of being party to any attack on Egyptian territory."

When the crusaders arrived, they were much fewer than expected, and unable to pay the agreed upon price for their transport. Constantinople was weaker than it had ever been, having turned over its shipbuilding to Venice. To make matters worse, the current emperor had "allowed his principle

* Further details, both political and military, can be found in A *History of Venice* by Lord Norwich, who has been, and will continue to be, our reference for much of this chapter.

admiral (who was also his brother-in-law) to sell off the anchors, sails and rigging of his few remaining vessels."

The crusaders had a bill they could not pay. What little they knew about Constantinople included one salient point: It was wealthy beyond their wildest dreams, and "to any medieval army, whether or not it bore the Cross of Christ on its standard, a fabulously rich city meant only one thing – loot." Sadly, a series of imperial dunces had drained the Byzantine coffers, so they could not buy off their enemies. In 1204, after nine hundred years unscathed, Constantinople, that jewel of a city, was conquered and then thoroughly sacked. The only real difference between the Franks and the Venetians in this sacking had to do with artistic discernment. The Franks wrenched precious jewels and metals from their beautiful settings; Venetians kept the beauty whole and whisked it away before the Franks could notice and complain.

Under the terms of the peace treaty, Venice was entitled to three-eighths of the eastern empire. For the city of Constantinople, Dandolo chose the prime real estate, including "the whole district surrounding St. Sophia and the Patriarchate, reaching right down to the shore of the Golden Horn." For his three-eighths of the rest of the imperial territory, Dandolo chose for Venice, "those areas that would reinforce her mastery of the Mediterranean and give her an unbroken chain of ports ... from the lagoon to the Black Sea." Venice also got tariff-free trade in all the imperial dominions. At the same time, traders from Genoa and Pisa were denied any opportunity to compete.

> Thus it emerges beyond all doubt that it was the Venetians
> ... who were the real victors of the Fourth Crusade; and
> that their victory was due, almost entirely, to Enrico
> Dandolo .... [H]is diplomatic skill had shaped a treaty
> which gave Venice more than she had dared to hope and
> laid the foundations for her commercial empire.

Dandolo had been offered the imperial crown and very wisely turned it down. It would have created dreadful internal problems for the Republic, and could have brought down the Venetian constitution and even the Republic itself, whose very foundations hinged on collective governance by a body of equals.

He actively encouraged the Franks to impose feudalism on the Byzantine countryside, which alienated the peasants by increasing the burdens they carried and, as we have seen earlier, brought about the sort of political disunity that characterized the earlier stages of feudalism in the west. This was the same process we saw with the d'Hauteville conquests in southern Italy. At the same time, Dandolo kept Venice completely clear of the feudal order. Venice held her new possessions by right of conquest, and absolutely. She did not hold them as a vassal to the eastern emperor. "For a blind man not far short of ninety it was a remarkable achievement."

While Norwich credits Dandolo with his political acumen and his success in advancing Venetian interests, he also notes, with great sadness, that the sack of Constantinople brought nine centuries of greatness to an end.

Until that event, she had been

not just greatest and wealthiest metropolis of the world, but also the most cultivated both intellectually and artistically and the chief repository of Europe's classical heritage, both Greek and Roman. By its sack, Western Civilization suffered a loss greater even than by the sack of Rome by the barbarians in the fifth century or the burning of the library of Alexandria by the soldiers of the Prophet in the seventh – perhaps the most catastrophic single loss in all its history.

The economic and political damage was also beyond calculation. For more than fifty years, political hacks who milked the treasury were the appointees of the western powers. Even when better government was restored, it was a shadow of its former self. The feudalizing of the countryside had seen to that.* A powerful, well-governed and prosperous Byzantine Empire might have stemmed the Turkish tide before it was too late.

There was, as well, the potent psychological element in the sacking of Constantinople. Its walls had stood impregnable for centuries and that record itself was a deterrent to dreams of her conquest. In the end, as we know, the Ottoman Turks fought their way into the city, *Is tan polis*. These Turks were devout Muslims, so the Hagia Sophia, that magnificent church whose beauty persuaded a Russian delega-

---

* The peasants, regardless of their faith, so hated the feudal order that they welcomed the Turks as a liberating army.

tion to recommend Eastern Orthodoxy to their Czar, became a Mosque.

> There are few greater ironies in history than the fact that the fate of Eastern Christendom should be sealed ... by men who fought under the banner of the Cross. Those men were transported, inspired, encouraged and ultimately led by Enrico Dandolo in the name of the Venetian Republic; and, just as Venice derived the major advantage from the tragedy, so she and her magnificent old Doge must accept the major responsibility for the havoc they wrought upon the world.

Such is the judgment of Lord Norwich who, both as a man and as an historian, is notable for his great affection and admiration for the Republic.

It is a sad story, but then again, nine hundred years is a very good run. It is also sad to leave Venice at this low point in her conduct, but leave for now we must. There are more changes to the constitution, more profitable transactions and more wonderful stories, but Venice had, by 1204, established her basic character.

She was an independent Republic, with a noble, merchant oligarchy that steered the ship of state toward policies that would best benefit commerce. One of her principle commercial endeavors, shipbuilding, was decentralized and piecemeal until a Doge, in a strong example of a command economy, centralized it for more efficient mass production. Venice was a mercantile nation state. She would retain these characteristics until her conquest by the forces of Napoleon Bonaparte in 1797.

Mehmet II, the Turk who crushed and occupied Constantinople, came to be called Mehmet the Conqueror. He was not about to continue the sorts of favorable trade agreements with the west that had been the lifeblood of northern Italian commercial cities, and especially of Venice. Indeed, his terms for trade with Christendom were so harsh that his city, Istanbul, was no longer the entrepot* between east and west that its predecessor had been.

It has also been said that every cloud has a silver lining. When the Ottoman Turks blocked European consumers from their historic sources of silk, spices and other luxuries, their appetites did not dry up in the least. Henry of Portugal, called Henry the Navigator, sponsored expeditions to see if it might not be possible to circumnavigate Africa. When the ships, hugging the coast, were able to turn sharply east, hopes ran high. When they were forced to turn south again, disappointment reigned. In the end, of course, the Portuguese did reach the Orient by this route.

Meanwhile, the Spanish monarchs, Ferdinand and Isabella, decided to employ a navigator from Genoa, Cristoforo Colombo, to execute a bold and radical plan, based on the emerging theory that the world was actually round. If so, it should be possible to reach the Far East by sailing west. The theory was perfectly correct. The only wrinkle in this program was the existence of an extremely large obstacle blocking the way. We call it the Americas ... but that's a whole other story.

* In this case, an intermediate commercial center where goods are collected for transshipment elsewhere.

# Selected Bibliography

Anderson, Perry. *Passages from Antiquity to Feudalism.* London: Verso Editions, 1974.

Adkins, Lesley. *Empires of the Plain.* New York: St. Martin's Press, 2003.

Boatswain, Tim & Nicholson, Collin. *A Traveller's History of Greece.* Northampton, MA: Interlink Publishing Group, Inc., 2007.

Braudel, Fernand. *A History of Civilizations.* New York: Penguin Books, 1993.

Budge, E.A. Wallis. *The Dwellers on the Nile.* New York: Dover Publications, Inc., 1977.

Barrow, R.H. *The Romans.* Baltimore: Penguin Books, Inc., 1976.

Burn, A.R. *The Pelican History of Greece.* New York: Penguin Books, Inc., 1978.

Brondsted, Johannes. *The Vikings.* New York: Penguin Books, Inc., 1965.

Chadwick, John. *The Mycenaean World.* London: Cambridge University Press, 1976.

Cowell, F.R. *Life in Ancient Rome.* New York: Perigee Books, 1961.

Davidson, James. *Courtesans & Fishcakes*. New York: HarperCollins Publishers, Inc., 1997.

Einhard. *The Life of Charlemagne*. Ann Arbor: University of Michigan Press, 1960.

Finley, M.I. *The Ancient Economy*. Berkeley: University of California Press, 1974.

_____. *Aspects of Antiquity*. New York: Penguin Books, 1977.

_____. *Early Greece: The Bronze and Archaic Ages*. New York: W.W. Norton & Co., 1981.

_____. *Economy and Society of Ancient Greece*. New York: Penguin Books, 1983.

_____. *The World of Odysseus*. New York: Penguin Books, 1979.

Genovese, Eugene. *Roll, Jordan, Roll*. New York: Vintage Books, 1976.

Gies, Frances. *The Knight in History*. New York: Harper & Row Publishers, Inc., 1987.

Gies, Joseph and Frances. *Life in a Medieval City*. New York: Harper & Row Publishers, Inc., 1969.

_____. *Women in the Middle Ages*. Harper & Row Publishers, Inc., 1978.

Goodwin, Jason. *Lords of the Horizons*. New York: Picador, 2003.

Grant, Michael. *Gladiators*. New York: Barnes & Noble Inc., 1995.

_____. *The World of Rome*. New York: Penguin Books USA Inc., 1960.

Green, Peter. *Alexander of Macedon*. Berkeley: University

of California Press, 1991.

_____. *Ancient Greece: An Illustrated History*. London: Thames and Hudson, 1973.

Hamilton, Edith. *The Greek Way*. New York: W.W. Norton & Co., 1930.

_____. *The Roman Way*. New York: W.W. Norton & Co., 1932.

Heer, Friedrich. *The Medieval World*. New York: The New American Library, Inc., 1962.

Heilbroner, Robert L. and William Milberg. *The Making of Economic Society*. New Jersey: Prentice Hall, 2002.

Holland, Tom. *Persian Fire*. London: Little, Brown, 2005.

_____. *Rubicon: The Last Years of the Roman Republic*. New York: Random House, Inc., 2003.

Horace. *Satires and Epistles*. Translated by Niall Rudd. New York: Penguin Putnam Inc., 1957.

Lacey, Robert & Danziger, Danny. *The Year 1000*. Boston: Little, Brown and Co., 1999.

Livy. *The Early History of Rome*. Translated by Aubrey De Sélincourt. New York: Penguin Books, 1960.

Maurois, André. *A History of England*. London: The Bodley Head Ltd., 1956.

_____. *A History of France*. New York: New York Grove Press, Inc., 1960.

_____. *An Illustrated History of Germany*. London: The Bodley Head Ltd., 1966.

McEvedy, Colin. *The New Penguin Atlas of Ancient History*. London: Penguin Books Ltd., 2002.

_____. *The New Penguin Atlas of Medieval History*

London: Penguin Books Ltd., 1992.

McNeil, William H. *The Shape of European History*. New York: Oxford University Press, 1974.

Mentzel, Peter. *A Traveller's History of Venice*. Northampton, MA: Interlink Publishing Group, Inc., 2006.

Norwich, John Julius. *A History of Venice*. New York: Vintage Books, 1982.

Olmstead, A.T. *History of the Persian Empire*. Chicago: University of Chicago Press, 1948.

Oppenheim, A. Leo. *Ancient Mesopotamia: Portrait of a Dead Civilization*. Chicago: University of Chicago Press, 1977.

Ovid. *The Art of Love*. Translated by Rolfe Humphries. Bloomington: Indiana University Press, 1957.

Pallottino, Massimo. *The Etruscans*. New York: Penguin Books, 1975.

Plautus. *Three Comedies*. Translated by Erich Segal. New York: Harper and Row, Publishers, 1969.

Pollitt, J.J. *Art and Experience in Classical Greece*. Cambridge University Press: 1972.

Pomeroy, Sarah. *Goddesses, Wives, Whores and Slaves: Women in Classical Antiquity*. New York: Schocken Books, 1975.

Rostovtzeff, M. *Rome*. London: Oxford University Press, 1960.

Russell, Francis. *A Concise History of Germany*. New York: American Heritage Publishing Co., Inc.. 1973.

Segal, Erich. *Roman Laughter: The Comedy of Plautus*. Oxford: Oxford University Press, 1987.

*Song of Roland*. Translated by Dorothy L. Sayers. New York: Penguin Books, 1957.

Southern, R.W. *The Making of the Middle Ages*. New Haven: Yale University Press, 1953.

Steindorff, George and Seele, Keith. *When Egypt Ruled the East*. Chicago: University of Chicago Press, 1942.

Stephenson, Carl. *Mediaeval Feudalism*. Ithaca, NY: Cornell University Press, 1942.

Suetonius. *The Twelve Caesars*. Translated by Robert Graves. New York: Penguin Books, 1957.

Wallace-Hadrill, J.M. *The Barbarian West: The Early Middle Ages*. New York: Harper & Row, Publishers, 1962.

White, Jon Manchip. *Everyday Life in Ancient Egypt*. New York: G.P. Putnam's Sons, 1963.

Woolley, C. Leonard. *The Sumerians*. New York: W.W. Norton & Company, 1965.

# Index